T0331009

Thanatourism

Case Studies in Travel to the Dark Side

Pascal Mandelartz and Tony Johnston

(G) Goodfellow Publishers Ltd

Published by Goodfellow Publishers Limited,
26 Home Close, Wolvercote, Oxford OX2 8PS
http://www.goodfellowpublishers.com

British Library Cataloguing in Publication Data: a catalogue record for this
title is available from the British Library.

Library of Congress Catalog Card Number: on file.

ISBN: 978-1-910158-33-3

 Design and typesetting by P.K. McBride, www.macbride.org.uk

Printed by Baker & Taylor, www.baker-taylor.com

Contents

List of images

List of tables and figures

Introduction

This book explores the topic of thanatourism, or dark tourism, a form of tourism where tourists visit sites primarily associated with death and disaster. The editors and authors have long been researching thanatourism. Collectively we have visited hundreds of death sites, in more than two dozen countries, in personal and professional capacities, for over a decade. From meeting survivors at extermination camps, to interviewing DNA specialists at mass graves, to having a beer with Goths at gothic festivals, the authors have collectively encountered the widest spectrum of sites, people and issues affected by thanatourism. Collectively we have read hundreds of papers on the topic, attended dedicated conferences, presented our research, provided media features and taught the subject at various levels. We attempt to bring these rich affectations to life in this book, offering what we hope will be considered a useful and timely contribution to thanatourism teaching and scholarship.

The book is aimed primarily as a resource for teaching undergraduate level students who have some prior knowledge of dark tourism. The text is not intended to introduce dark tourism, nor attempt to redefine it. Rather the book offers a series of case studies which provide material for in-class discussion, support for term papers and assignments and observations on methodological challenges which may be beneficial to those writing dissertations on travel to the dark side. While we make no attempt to redefine dark tourism, the case studies offered within are broad and stretch the boundaries of the field.

Our approach for the book

Interest in writing the book stemmed from professional and personal interests. Professional, in that dark tourism is topical, a subject of its time and a relatively sensational theme in tourism studies which quickly captures students' imaginations. The authors involved have long enjoyed teaching the subject and reflect on that at various points within the book. Personal, in that death touches all of us and the authors have various personal affiliations to the sites under examination in the text. We do not hide from these subjectivities but take the rather unacademic position of embracing them and letting them influence the book throughout. We feel that this enhances the quality of discussion as opposed to detracting from it. The term 'thanatourism' is often interchangeably used with the term 'dark tourism', which in turn often has sinister and negative feelings and perceptions affiliated with it. We have deliberately chosen the term thanatourism as we feel that it not only describes the phenomenon more accurately, but also reflects a wider spectrum of perceptions, attitudes and feelings towards tourism associated with the atrocities of conflict, disaster, misfortune and death, as these sites, attractions and destinations often include an element of positivity, endowment and empathy. Academic conferences concerned with the topic are often the most light hearted as with a focus on occurrences which we would, in most cases, preferably avoid for ourselves can only be tackled when the research has a certain sense of humour.

Between us, we have visited in excess of one hundred dark sites, and little surprises us anymore about tourist behaviour at sites of death and disaster. We have witnessed emotive displays, for example, from tourists who cannot deal with or comprehend the tragedy they encounter at particularly notorious sites. Overwhelmed, they weep, shake, or otherwise visibly express reactions which demonstrate their engagement with the pain suffered by the victims. Equally however, we have witnessed tourists keen to be photographed, 'putting on' emotional displays for the camera in theatrical demonstrations worthy of Oscar nominations. Both groupings of course are equally worthy of study and help strip away the layers of these complex sites. We discuss such tourists at various points throughout the book.

While little surprises us anymore concerning such sites, we are regularly still appalled at what pleases the tourist eye. The most recent occurrence of this emotion came when I (Johnston) chanced across an online set of tourist photographs from Tibet, where Chinese tourists were captured in attendance at a sky burial. Long since bastardised from its original sanctity, the 'burial' was now modified to suit tourist desires. With their cameras flashing the tourists stripped all dignity away from the deceased as they snapped a pack of hungry vultures tearing apart the flesh of the cadaver. Such chilling images reinforce the need, we believe, to study this phenomena further.

The book takes cognisance of the discontent in the field. The argument "That is not dark tourism, it is heritage tourism" seems to be a regular theme, for one. So too does the notion that 'dark' is a misleading term, well past its sell-by date and usefulness in exploring this field. This book attempts to offer a broad perspective on thanatourism, where possible stretching the boundaries of what fits under the dark umbrella. While classic and notorious sites and events, such as the Holocaust and Auschwitz Birkenau are examined within, so too are lesser known phenomena. The book attempts to stretch the boundaries of dark tourism, teasing apart new perspectives on the theme. When calling for contributions and supplying author style guidelines, the editors were keen to stress that we wanted fresh perspectives on the topic to complement the need for further development on classic themes. To this end we invited a former journalist, now a current university press officer, to submit a chapter. We also invited early career academics to explore the topic, setting only the notional boundary that the chapter must feature tourism and death. Equally we asked an established and well published academic to write a personal piece, exploring a place which has significant personal meaning for him. We come from different backgrounds and our contributors have variously studied tourism, geography, business management and journalism. The result, we hope is that the book develops the classic themes, but also stretches the margins of what can be considered 'dark tourism'.

Chapter outlines

Chapter 1 focuses on traditional battlefield and war tourism sites and aims to stimulate undergraduates into considering secondary data sources in dark tourism research. The chapter presents a case study and proposed methodology for analysing dark tourism blog data, followed by analysis of a large volume of data related to consumption of the 1992-1995 Siege of Sarajevo. This is a chapter of its time – when Lennon and Foley coined the term dark tourism in 1996 it was likely that they were inspired by primary data observed in field. Today there is a wealth of secondary dark tourism data available which would have been unimaginable two decades earlier. There are thousands of travel blogs across the world's major blogging sites which contain rich and often emotive descriptions of personal encounters with death.

The book then moves to discuss tourism, not to sites associated with the death of people, but the death (and possible rebirth) of sites themselves. The chapter focuses on urban exploration, with Mandelartz examining how derelict sites and places can act as a precursor to mass tourism. The purpose of the chapter is to consider the role of place in dark tourism, prompting students to consider how the atmospheric qualities of a place contribute to its appeal. While urban exploration is not perhaps a dark form of travel, it is certainly a form of leisure activity which has resonance with many of the themes frequently discussed in dark tourism literature, as it is concerned with the aesthetic appeal of dark spaces and places but also creates a link to heritage. The travel to memorials has previously been included in the notion of thanatourism, and urban explorers often pay tribute to abandoned sites by documenting and valuing them.

Chapter 3 tackles some of the concerns faced by guardians of dark tourism sites. Networking, commercialisation and strategic approaches to delivering particular visitor experiences are explored, with reference to various well-discussed attractions, including Pompeii and ghost tours. Site management issues facing the managers of dark sites are discussed in practical terms, prompting students to consider how they might sensitively interact and network with other tourism and hospitality businesses should they be employed in such positions in future. The chapter additionally explores the importance of the 'story' at the dark tourism attraction.

Chapter 4 begins to stretch the definition of dark tourism and looks not at tourism impacts at specific sites of death, but rather at the travel habits of those who are interested in the Gothic subculture and representations of death. The chapter draws on primary data obtained at the Whitby Goth Weekend, a large bi-annual gathering of Gothic subculture lovers in the small market town of Whitby on the North East Coast of England. Whitby, one of the main locations in Stoker's *Dracula*, reaps great economic benefit from the festival and Mandelartz explores some of the reasons the town is frequented by those passionate about the Gothic subculture. The chapter also broadly establishes the characteristics of 'Goth Tourism', proposing that Goth travel habits could be mapped against four 'Hs'; Habitat, Heritage, History and Handicrafts.

Chapter 5, by Tim Heap, is a reflection on travel to a battlefield site, specifically to visit a tank from the First World War. The chapter challenges academic and contemporary definitions of dark tourism, adopting a personal and emotive tone throughout. Heap begins by noting that circular definitions of dark tourism over the past two decades have been to the detriment of the field and that several arguments and notions have become established, with little empirical evidence to give them credence. Heap proposes that the field needs to emerge 'out of darkness into light', to acknowledge the positive encounters between visitors and emotions at sites.

Chapter 6, by Geoff Shirt, returns to the oft-cited and notorious death camp of Auschwitz-Birkenau in Southern Poland. The camp, arguably the pinnacle, or benchmark, in dark tourism scholarship, provides many challenging questions which merit further attention. Shirt delves into some of the practicalities faced by the Auschwitz-Birkenau State Museum, which variously include ecological management, architectural preservation, site carrying capacity and contestation of history. The camp will likely be very familiar to students who have previously encountered dark tourism literature; it is arguably the pinnacle site in the research, given the scale and notoriety of the atrocity, the volume of visitors and the relative proximity of the event.

In Chapter 7, Marson provides an overview of the theoretical relationship between death and adventure tourism. The chapter argues that the nature of the commodification of adventure allows for death to be perceived in different ways. Marson broadens the debate surrounding dark tourism by incorporating niche tourism products such as adventure into the discussion, encouraging students to think about the relationship between 'darkness', death, tourism and adventure that also incorporates the thrill and excitement of extraordinary activities.

Chapter 8 returns to a more traditional, if lesser known, dark tourism site. John Phillips explores the village of Eyam, an English village in the Derbyshire Dales which suffered an outbreak of the Bubonic Plague in 1655. The villagers quarantined themselves and the village effectively survived the disease, albeit with huge numbers dying over the fourteen month period. In the chapter students are encouraged to think about how a historic event has become commodified and why controversy exists surrounding the commercialisation of an event in the distant past.

Chapter 9 remains with the theme of commercialisation and returns to the notorious Auschwitz-Birkenau to examine the online promotion of the camp by private tour operators. As with Chapter 2, a range of secondary data is presented, drawn from the websites of Polish tour companies who cater for tourists to Auschwitz. In the chapter we examine the language, images and approach adopted by these operators. The chapter particularly encourages students to think about the means and methods of commercialising the camp and what implications this might have for management; many of these concerns are also raised by Shirt in Chapter 6.

Chapter 10 concludes the book with an exploration of the complexities in teaching war history to school groups, with a particular focus on the battlegrounds of the First World War and Second World War. Heap draws on over a decade of experience of leading school groups to dark sites and his chapter will have great resonance with educators who are similarly dedicated to field based learning. Heap structures the chapter into three stages; 'the plan of attack', the 'operational phase' and the 'debrief', drawing on military terminology to organise his reflection on the visits.

Finally, a note on the cover image. This photograph was kindly provided by Khan Yang, a doctoral student in tourism at the University of Derby, Buxton. Khan was asked to supply an image, given his interest in many of the places discussed in the book and his keen interest in art and photography. However, rather than choose a traditional dark tourism image such as skulls, graves or a notorious site, Khan opted for an image of a scarecrow, made of hay. The photograph was deliberately chosen to be juxtaposed against the conventional images used by academia and the media to illustrate thanatourism. There are too many black and white artistic photographs of barb wire from Auschwitz-Birkenau for example, which are used to depict thanatourism. We wanted to move away from the conventional and into the abstract and hence the choice of the 'hayman'.

The image comes from a series of pictures that Khan took with his father during a visit to a small village in Yunnan, China in 2014. The village generally did not feature on any tourist itineraries, so a few young villagers created some haymen and randomly placed them across the village roads and between houses. This was surprisingly popular with tourists who would come to enjoy a family day out, and the haymen collection quickly became an object of desire for tourists' photos. Tourists posted their photos with scared faces online, and the village became incredibly popular for the summer season.

Reading the text

The book is aimed primarily at undergraduate students studying tourism and related subjects, but you may be reading this coming from another discipline. If so, we hope that your own perspective on thanatourism, whether it be geographical, sociological, literary, psychological, or from another school of thought altogether, casts fresh light on what we are attempting to explore here. Death by its very nature is multi-disciplinary. To help guide the reader we have placed a series of discussion points at the end of each chapter. These discussion points could be used to structure seminars, assessment questions and site visit considerations or simply to provoke further individual thoughts on some of the wider constructs affecting the theme of each chapter.

The book is accompanied by a series of PowerPoint files, available for download from the publisher's website. The PowerPoints contain images, learning outcomes, discussion points and summary details of the key points contained in each chapter. Chapter 5 is the only exception to this, as in this chapter Tim Heap, the author, argues for alternative methods for teaching tourism in general and a PowerPoint file would be contradictory in this instance.

We suggest you view the book as you would view a cadaver. Each chapter in the book represents a bone. Individually each chapter covers just one primary theme or site. Therefore each chapter is just a bone and is irrelevant on its own. What good is a bone? However, pieced together, a collection of bones may form a whole skeleton; or in this case, a skeleton of thanatourism knowledge which still needs further linkage. Without your contribution the book would remain just that, a skeleton of loosely connected bones, with some meaning certainly, but perhaps not reaching its full potential. We have thus included discussion points to allow flesh to be added to the skeleton. When the discussion points are considered by you the reader, the bones will have flesh added, to form a body of thought which will capture the subjectivities, richness and emotional nature of thanatourism research.

We hope you enjoy the book.

Tony Johnston & Pascal Mandelartz

1 Blogging the Dark Side of Travel:
Consuming the Siege of Sarajevo

Tony Johnston

Abstract

Between 1992 and 1995, Sarajevo, the capital city of Bosnia-Herzegovina, was subjected to the longest siege in recent European warfare. This chapter explores tourist consumption of the post-war landscapes of the siege, as recorded by travel bloggers between 2002 and 2013. Adopting an experiential perspective and drawing on blog entries for data, the chapter contributes to understanding the thanatourist experience. The chapter reveals travel blogs as a useful data source for thanatourism research; proposing that they represent a valuable resource for rich and reflective data in an emotionally charged environment.

Learning outcomes

1 To develop an understanding of how war is consumed by tourists.

2 To develop an appreciation of a potential secondary data source available for thanatourism research.

3 To understand the process used to rigorously analyse thanatourism blog data.

Introduction

Thanatourism, often termed dark tourism, has variously been defined as "travel to a location wholly, or partially, motivated by the desire for actual or symbolic encounters with death" (Seaton, 1996: 240), "the presentation and consumption (by visitors) of real and commodified death and disaster sites" (Foley & Lennon, 1996: 198) and recently by Stone (2011: 318) as "the social scientific study of tourism and tourists associated with sites of death, disaster or the seemingly macabre". Although it is not a new phenomenon, thanatourism is an increasingly pervasive feature of the contemporary tourism landscape, Stone (2006).

Since its inception as an academic term in 1996, the majority of thanatourism research has focused on site characteristics, with significantly less research exploring the tourist experience, Stone and Sharpley (2008: 592), a viewpoint affirmed by Seaton (2009a). In recent years research has started to address the supply-demand imbalance (see Bigley, Lee, Chon & Yoon *et al*, 2010; Biran, Poria & Oren, 2011; Dunkley, Morgan & Westwood, 2011; Hyde & Harman, 2011; Sharpley, 2012) by focusing on experience and motivation, approached primarily through interviews, large sample surveys and ethnography.

The overall aim of this research was to examine the thanatourism experience in Sarajevo through travel blog data. Despite recent attention turning towards the thanatourism experience, little research exists on tourist consumption of conflict in Sarajevo, the capital city of Bosnia-Herzegovina and one of the worst war damaged cities of the late 20th century. There is equally little work in thanatourism which utilizes travel blogs as a data source. This chapter addresses these gaps in the literature, suggesting that blogs are a potentially useful data source in understanding the thanatourism experience in Sarajevo. The research had two objectives:

1 To explore through online travel blogs, the tourist experience of conflict in Sarajevo;

2 To assess the usefulness of travel blogs as a data source for thanatourism experiential research.

Literature review

Thanatourism, describing tourism to sites of death, has been termed 'dark tourism' (Foley and Lennon, 1996), 'Holocaust tourism' (Ashworth, 2002), 'morbid tourism' (Blom, 2000), 'black spots' (Rojek, 1993) and the 'heritage of atrocity' (Ashworth, 2004). Although the terminology is often blurred and contested (Seaton, 2009a) thanatourism, in its broadest sense, has become one of the most popular areas of study in tourism research (Stone, 2012).

The majority of thanatourism research has emerged within tourism journals and tourism paradigms, but it has attracted significant interest across the disciplines, with contributions coming from geography, sociology, anthropology and law, among others. Conceptual work on thanatourism has come from a number of sources, notably in an edited collection from Sharpley and Stone (eds., 2009). This text situated thanatourism within a variety of frameworks, including within a broader sociology of death (Walter, 2009) and as a consequence of secularization and a quest for new moral spaces (Stone, 2009). Others have situated thanatourism under the umbrella of post-modernism (Lennon & Foley, 2000; Muzaini, Teo & Yeoh, 2007; Rojek, 1993), Orientalism (Seaton, 2009b) and sequestration (Stone, 2009).

Thanatourism research has utilized a number of lenses to interrogate the complex relationship between tourism and sites of death. The ethics of consuming raw landscapes for example, such as viewing a battle as it happens, has been studied by Seaton (1999), examining the aristocratic consumption of the Battle of Waterloo. Others have examined the physical features of thanatourism landscapes, with Iles (2008) noting the impact of tourism on the ecological fluidity of World War One sites. Others again have attempted to situate thanatourism in particular temporal paradigms, with Lennon and Foley (2000) situating it as a postmodern phenomenon, a notion disputed by Casbeard and Booth (2012), Johnston (2013) and Seaton (2009a) who point to historical thanatourism practices as rendering the postmodern approach unhistorical and incoherent.

Nonetheless, it is clear that temporal proximity affects the thanatourism experience. Several papers comment on the mediating impact of time on the consumption of death. Lennon and Foley (2000), for example, suggest that an intermittent period occurs before a tragic event is interpreted for tourist consumption. This intermittent period facilitates the evolution of 'scar' into 'attraction'. Miles (2002: 1176) observes the temporal question from a memorial perspective, noting that Holocaust memorials "must bridge the existential gap between the here-and-now of the tourist and the event (or events) of more than half a century prior. It must convert the memorial thing into a live memory" . The immediacy of the conflict in Sarajevo appears worthy of consideration in this context, given that twenty years have yet to pass since the end of the siege.

Despite the recent turn away from commodification towards consumption, (e.g. Iles, 2008, Biran, Biran, Poria & Oren, 2011, Stone & Sharpley, 2008), there remains much to be studied concerning the effects of consuming death as a tourist. We know little, for example, concerning how visiting sites of death configures a tourist's emotions, what tourists contemplate, why they feel the way they do about particular sites or how they respond to death tourism experiences post-visit. Such questions remain largely unstudied.

Stone and Sharpley (2008) write that we can draw upon a broader sociology of death to answer some of these questions, as thanatourism is just one example of a reflection of the relationship between death and society in contemporary times. Ultimately, thanatourism is a form of travel which represents an opportunity for an individual to face up to his or her inevitable demise. Stone and Sharpley go as far as to hint that thanatourism is a phenomenon which has replaced traditional church and societal instruction on death. They further suggest (2008: 583) that society's interaction with death has greatly changed, that death is now largely sequestered from public space and that "because contemporary society has deprived increasing numbers of people with an overarching, existentially meaningful, ritual structure" the prospect of death takes on a new level of fear for the general populace. The implication, therefore, is that the modern individual seeks out sites of death to better understand their own mortality.

The present chapter partly seeks to ascertain through exploration of travel blogs if this claim is true. Do tourists use sites of death and disaster to contemplate their own mortality and, if so, how does this contemplation occur?

Research setting

In 1992, Bosnia-Herzegovina declared independence from Yugoslavia. War quickly spread from the also newly declared neighbouring Croatia (ICJ, 2007), which ultimately became the biggest conflict in Europe since World War II. For the following four years Bosnia-Herzegovina was gripped by war, including ethnic cleansing, genocidal acts, forced mass migration, siege warfare, terrorism and urbicide.

A complex conflict, the Bosnian War existed primarily between the Bosnian-Serb population who wished to remain part of Yugoslavia and the Bosnian-Muslim population who wished to form an independent Bosnia-Herzegovina. In 1992, Croatia joined the conflict, supporting the Bosnian-Croat population against the Bosnian Serbs. The Bosnian Muslim government quickly came under siege in Sarajevo, with Bosnian Serb forces, who controlled around 70% of what would become Bosnia-Herzegovina, bombarding the city with shells. Throughout the 1992-1995 conflict, and until the signing of the 1995 Dayton Accord, which ultimately brought relative peace to the region, Sarajevo remained under siege, subject to relentless artillery fire. Up to 500 shells hit the city daily. By the end of the siege there were many thousands of civilian casualties and major landmarks were destroyed.

Today the legacy of the 1990s war is heavily commodified; tours to battlefield sites and siege lines exist, key war sites have been turned into tourist attractions and local craftsmen even turn old bullet and shell casings into souvenirs. Backpackers visit the city, keen to participate in war tours, take snapshots of the siege lines and purchase war memorabilia as souvenirs. The conflict is not yet twenty years old, yet already the sites associated with the siege in Sarajevo feature prominently on the tourist trail in the Bosnian capital, as will be demonstrated throughout this chapter.

There is little doubting the popularity of the siege sites, yet how visitation to these sites affects tourists has been largely unknown to date. Research on thanatourism in the Bosnian capital has thus far generally tended to explore the supply characteristics of thanatourism sites (Johnston 2010, Simic 2009) and tangentially the concept of 'phoenix tourism', (Causevic & Lynch, 2011), referring to the process and potential of memorialization of conflict in eliciting catharsis for reproducers and consumers of war tourism. Understanding how the consumption of the siege affects tourists is therefore a key focus of this chapter.

Image 1.1: Tourists visit a derelict hotel from the 1984 Winter Olympics. Image taken by author on Sarajevo war tour in 2011.

Methodology

To address the aim and objectives, the research drew on travel blog entries for data. Empirical thanatourism research has previously drawn upon interview data (e.g. Beech, 2000; Wilson, 2008), textual analysis (e.g. Seaton, 1999; Siegenthaler, 2002), participant observation (e.g. Iles, 2008, Miles, 2002), an oral history approach (e.g. Dunkley, Morgan & Westwood, 2011) and large surveys (e.g. Biran, Poria & Oren, 2011; Hyde & Harman, 2011). More recently Seaton (2012) and Sharpley (2012) have drawn upon guest book entries and blog entries respectively, but using qualitative approaches with relatively small samples. Another researcher, Winter (2011), utilized a quantitative approach to examine visitor book entries at World War One cemeteries, but her research was primarily focused on identifying visitor patterns and clusters and not on the tourist experiences of consuming death.

Despite various methodological concerns in thanatourism research there has yet to be significant engagement with travel blogs. This is surprising, given the fundamental nature of some of the concerns to date. Biran, Poria and Oren (2011: 838), for example, write that tourist fascination with death may not be fully revealed in an interview setting, due to the interviewees' belief that there may be particular societal perceptions of thanatourism.

Such an argument would appear to suggest a major methodological limitation with thanatourism research; as, if taken to its fullest, it may indicate that participants are not comfortable discussing death tourism with academic researchers. Blogs potentially provide a useful data source and overcome this purity concern. They have received surprisingly little attention to date, given the desire for richer empirical data (Seaton, 2009a) and their ease of access compared to other research methods. Travel blog communities have been in existence since the late 1990s (Akehurst, 2009) and are becoming increasingly popular as a data source for both industry and academia (Pan MacLaurin, Crotts, 2007; Zehrer, Crotts & Magnini, 2011).

Further to this, given the need for ethical sensitivity and a compassionate approach to understand the thanatourist experience (Seaton, 2009b), it seems appropriate to utilize blogs in an attempt to better understand the tourist experience at sites of death and disaster.

Data collection

To approach the quantitative dimension of the study, the author gathered the total population of Sarajevo blogs on two travel blog websites (n=530). The two most popular travel blog websites (Calcustat, 2013) were used to provide data for the research. The websites, *TravelBlog* and *TravelPod*, rank highly in terms of visitors to their sites, with estimates of over 400,000 visitors per day to TravelPod and circa 100,000 per day to TravelBlog (Calcustat, 2013). Both websites organize their blogs in a hierarchical fashion where site users can navigate through menus to a specific continent, country, region and city.

Under the 'Sarajevo' heading, TravelBlog contained 120 entries, posted between July 2002 and January 2013, while TravelPod contained 410 entries, posted between June 2003 and January 2013. The total 530 blogs were individually downloaded and placed in working files for analysis. From these blogs, several were discarded as they had been filed under the wrong region (*n*=9), were duplicates (*n*=2) or were non-English language entries (*n*=40). The author acknowledges that discounting non-English language entries is a minor study limitation, but given the array of languages comprising the 40 blogs, it was not feasible to include all in the study. Further research would be needed to assess if significant differences exist between English language and non-English language bloggers.

This collation resulted in 479 valid cases containing a total word count of 325,902 words and 5,391 images. The 530 blogs comprised the entire population of travel blogs posted on these websites since the sites' launch. Blogs ranged from zero to 4,868 words, with a mean of 678.84 words, and between zero and 193 images, mean of 12.38, (see Table 1.1). Blogs with zero words contained only images, but were retained for the purposes of the study due to their inclusion of war images. In total, 49 blogs contained less than ten words.

The data were subjected to quantitative analysis, conducted by two independent researchers utilizing methodologies adapted from those previously proposed by Pan *et al* (2007) and Choi, Lehto and Morrison, (2007). SPSS and qualitative data analysis software were used to assist with deconstructing, coding and analyzing the blog data. Initially, basic data were gathered from the blogs and entered in SPSS, including the title and date, the total number of views for the users' blogs, the number of images posted and the blog word count. Where appropriate, or where discrepancies arose, the mean was calculated and recorded.

Table 1.1: Descriptive statistics for Sarajevo travel blogs

Variable	N	Mean	Std Dev	Minimum	Maximum
Word count of blog	479	679	676	0	4868
Number of views for each blogger's account	479	7,769	19,877	5	214,193
How many images did the blogger post?	479	12	19	0	193

Data gathered from the blogs included lists of sites visited by bloggers, the most frequent topics discussed, the key themes raised, the number and types of photographs posted and any demographic data where available. The data were collected and entered into SPSS for analysis.

The second stage involved a qualitative approach, with a main objective of exploring the tourist gaze on war. Qualitative analysis was conducted by the two independent researchers to understand the bloggers' experience of war sites. Content analysis, based on Kassarjian's classic 1977 method to strengthen reliability and validity, was conducted by the two researchers. This involved creating lists of keywords and themes related to the siege and the tourist experience, based on a surface analysis of the blogs. Coding lists were created and qualitative and quantitative data were generated from these showing the volume of discussion on the conflict, the themes raised by bloggers who discussed the conflict and the range of conflict associated sites visited.

Quantitative data results

To give the study context, basic demographic data was initially collected where available. Unfortunately due to privacy settings and bloggers not consistently sharing information, exact demographic data were not available. However, comments from bloggers indicated origins primarily in the United States, the UK and Australia, with smaller numbers from Canada, Ireland and New Zealand. Blogs were frequently posted by solo travelers and couples, with occasional contributions from groups of friends and families.

The total views for the 479 bloggers' personal accounts numbered 3,721,232, a figure which illustrates the very public nature of online blogs. The number of views received by each blog ranged from single figures for very recently posted blogs to over 200,000 for one blog. The average number of views was 7,769. There was no immediately obvious reason why some blogs received significantly higher numbers of hits than others.

Although it is beyond the scope of this study, it is interesting to briefly consider why some blogs appeared more popular than others. A Pearson Correlation test to assess if the number of blog views was related to word count, or number of images, demonstrated no significant relationship (n=.041, n=.004). However, the same test against the year of the blog illustrated a slightly stronger relationship (n=.-206), suggesting, perhaps unsurprisingly, that older blogs, which have likely been online longer, have received more views.

Table 1.2: The correlations between number of views, year of blog, word count and image count

		Number of views per blog	Year of blog	Word count	Image count
Number of views for each blog	Pearson Correlation	1	-.206**	.041	.004
	Sig. (2-tailed)		.000	.373	.923
	N	479	479	479	479

**. Correlation is significant at the 0.01 level (2-tailed)

Many bloggers opened their blogs by discussing the war in general; either highlighting their perceived good knowledge of it, or commenting that they felt their knowledge of the war was inadequate and they did not know what to expect in Sarajevo. Of the 479 blogs, the mean result from the researchers indicated a majority 71.4% (n=342) discussed the war in some fashion, with 65.14% of bloggers (n=312) visiting a war site while in Sarajevo. Although visits to war sites may have been serendipitous in nature – especially given the extensive damage to the city centre in Sarajevo – it became immediately clear that the 1990s conflict formed the dominant topic of discussion in blogs.

In terms of sites visited, the blogs illustrated that the most popular war locations in Sarajevo included the Tunnel Museum (a museum to a one kilometer relief tunnel used by civilians and military during the siege), Markale Market (a fruit and bread market which was twice heavily shelled during the war), Sniper Alley (a major road in Sarajevo where Serbian snipers targeted civilians and military) and the war damaged 1984 Winter Olympic infrastructure, which was hosted by Sarajevo. A sample of these sites are displayed in Image 1.2.

Image 1.2: Left: A city cemetery with graves from the 1992-1995 conflict, Right: The Tunnel Museum. Images taken by author.

Other sites commonly observed by bloggers included landmine clearing and warning signs, The Holiday Inn Hotel (an iconic yellow hotel used by journalists during the siege), war damaged residential buildings (see Image 1.3) and Sarajevo Roses. Sarajevo Roses are memorialized shell marks, which utilize red cement to fill in and preserve the damage from the shells. These occur in several locations throughout Sarajevo where shells caused loss of life during the siege.

A slight minority of bloggers (46.35%, n=222) posted photographs depicting damage caused by the conflict. These included photographs of cemeteries, the shelled Markale Market, the Tunnel Museum, residential, civic and commercial buildings with bullets and shell marks, Sarajevo Roses and war memorabilia and souvenirs sold by city centre craftsmen. Further SPSS analysis illustrated that 66.99% (n=209) of bloggers who visited war sites posted images associated with the conflict.

Image 1.3: A war damaged building in Sarajevo which typifies the images of damaged buildings posted by bloggers. Image courtesy of Mike Bauermeister.

Images of damaged buildings, bullet holes and shell scars were posted and referred to in war discussions by bloggers, yet some blogs had no description or clear link between the text and the posted images. These bloggers may simply have been interested in the spaces around them or been unaware of the cause of damage. Nonetheless, the cross tabulation suggests that those who visit war sites in Sarajevo are likely to photograph them.

Overall, quantitative analysis indicated that the 1992-1995 siege was the dominant experience for bloggers. The most commonly visited site was the Tunnel Museum, with 33.19% of bloggers (n=159) recording a visit to the museum. The next most commonly visited site were the city's war cemeteries, which are almost unavoidable to walk past, given their city centre locations. 22.1% (n=106) of bloggers recorded visits to the city's war cemeteries.

While official statistics for the number of visits to the tunnel are not available, the high number of visits to the museum recorded by bloggers appear to be broadly representative of tourist trends in Sarajevo in this period. In 2009, for example, Sarajevo received 180,000 visitors and The Tunnel Museum was recorded as the city's top attraction by the capital's tourist board (Balkan Insight, 2010).

Further content analysis of the blogs revealed that the war was also the most frequently discussed topic. Table 1.3 illustrates the word count frequency from the 479 blogs, with each instance of the word, used in context, recorded as an entry. The left columns illustrate the mean frequency of the discussion of the conflict made by the bloggers as recorded by the two researchers. Activities on the right illustrate other common pursuits undertaken by tourists to Sarajevo who blogged about their experiences. This figure is not an exhaustive list of activities and is presented simply to illustrate the overall flavour of the blogs.

1990s war related themes & frequency mentioned		Other activities & frequency mentioned	
War	1084	Food, coffee, restaurant, diner	753
Siege	340	Pub, bar or beer	369
Bullet, shells/ missiles	284	Walking	207
Sniper	150	Mosques	187
Sarajevo Roses	117	Franz Ferdinand	155
Damage/ destruction	113	Olympic(s)	140
Ethnic cleansing	48	Film Festival	62
Srebrenica	46	Shopping	38

Table 1.3: Sarajevo 2003-2013 blogger activity content analysis word counts

Qualitative data results

Although not the primary focus of the chapter, data from the blogs illustrated that tourists exhibited a range of motivations to visit Sarajevo, including to learn about the conflict, to experience the food, drink and nightlife, to visit friends and family, as part of a European wide itinerary, as a hub on inter-rail travel and for the annual film festival. Consumption of the 1992-1995 siege emerged as just one motivation to visit the city, but bloggers also desired Oriental encounters, with frequent mentions of Sarajevo's position as an 'East meets West' city. Others simply visited Sarajevo as part of a wider itinerary in the Balkans, with no clear indication of their motivations.

Situating the siege: Temporal proximity

Evidence from the blogs illustrated that tourists use a variety of spatial and temporal references to better understand the siege. Frequently, bloggers recounted where *they* were, what *they* were doing and how *they* heard about the siege in the 1990s. Several bloggers attempted to reconnect themselves temporally to the events of the early 1990s in ex-Yugoslavia, recalling their own lives between 1992 and 1995. For example, one blogger posted that:

> Between the ages of 14-17 I was finishing the last years of my school-
> ing, starting my first job, played squash and tennis in my free time,
> met up with mates and doing the usual stuff most of us did during
> the years of 1992 to 1995. During this time, the news reported on a
> country called Bosnia, and specifically a city called Sarajevo.
>
> Blog 93, March 2007

Comments such as "Footage of the massacre made it into news reports around the world. I remember watching them." (Blog 81, August 2007), or "I recognised many vistas from the news back in the 90s" (Blog 50, July 2009), were a regular feature, with bloggers contrasting the 'mundaneness' of their own personal lives at the time to the lives of Sarajevo civilians during the siege. Such examples where Sarajevo's pain was juxtaposed against their childhood bliss was one of the most immediately visible themes visible throughout the blogs.

Bloggers frequently discussed the brutality of the siege framed within discussion of it happening in their lifetime, 'as recently as the 1990s', or positioned as being 50 years after World War 2. For example, one blogger, upon meeting a United Nations DNA specialist working on mass graves, commented:

> His job was made all the more difficult by the fact that Serbs often
> destroyed the bodies and left limbs, etc. in different locations. One
> man had been found in 14 different graves. I was again silenced by
> the thought that this happened within my lifetime, and that similar
> things are probably still happening in the Middle East.
>
> Blog 403, August 2007

Finally, in relation to temporal mediations, frequent comparisons were made by bloggers to the Iraq war, with one blogger questioning if "Baghdad [is] now like Sarajevo during the siege? Will I be in Baghdad in 10 years' time thinking how could this have happened to this city and its people?" (Blog 97, January 2007). Others predicted that the consumption of other conflicts would be possible in future, noting that the proximity afforded by tourism brought home the impact of war.

> Who of us knows the differences between the factions in Iraq and
> why it is happening. We hear of people being killed and hurt all the
> time, but as it happens daily it just doesn't seem real. Well it is and
> when you visit Iraq in 10-20 years which I'm sure we will be able to,
> then it will hit you like a ton of bricks like it has me in Bosnia.
>
> Blog 93, March 2007

Situating the siege: Spatial proximity

As with the temporal immediacy to the siege, the physical proximity of the war sites formed a key component of the tourist experience for many. Standing at the infamous siege locations afforded bloggers the opportunity to see the damage of war with their own eyes, as opposed to through a camera lens. For many bloggers, the war sites were spectacular landscapes, brought to life by dramatic features and clear symbols of death; including land mine clearance sites, cemeteries, Sarajevo Roses and notable media images. This emerged particularly through the bloggers' photography, which was dominated by images of cemeteries, shell and sniper damaged buildings and notable siege sites, such as the Holiday Inn and Markale Market.

Image 1.4: Tourists peer through holes in the 1984 Winter Olympic bobsled luge, Mount Trebevic, Sarajevo. This image is provided by of Mike Bauermeister, who took part in a war tour in Sarajevo in May 2011.

Cemeteries were the most frequently photographed landscape. 22.1% (*n*=106) of bloggers discussed the city's war graves, with many bloggers commenting on the dates of the graves, particularly noting their proximity to main shopping and commercial areas. Being able to see and touch such war scars formed a key part of the tourist experience, (see Image 1.4); in particular the opportunity to touch the war damaged 1984 Winter Olympic infrastructure. Guided visits exist to all four of the Winter Olympic mountains in Sarajevo; Igman, Trebevic, Bjelasnica and Jahorina. Many bloggers participated in such tours, offered by Sarajevo's tour companies, hostels and tour guides.

Two of the four mountains bear very visible and dramatic war scars, with evidence of United Nations presence and battle marks, including bullet holes, shell damage and land mine signage. On the mountains, tourists can touch bullet holes, climb into the sporting infrastructure and take photographs in front of landmine signs, United Nations logos and shelled hotel buildings. The ability to touch this raw history emerged as an important experience for many bloggers, several of whom mentioned climbing into the war damaged bobsled track (see Image 1.4 for an example of this), their sighting of landmine clearance teams and the ability to converse with war victims and survivors as important aspects of their experience.

Consuming the siege

In addition to understanding the siege through temporal and spatial lenses, data from the blogs suggested that the siege had varying impacts on the emotions of the tourists. Impacts ranged from contemplation of death, to discussion of geopolitics, to re-evaluation of the blogger's perspectives on world affairs. One blogger, for example, experienced something close to pure thanatopsis while in central Sarajevo, as he/ she imagined being sniped at from the surrounding mountains.

> In vain I tried to picture every bullet piercing the walls of Sarajevo's buildings. I would look to the dominating hills that surround the city. I would imagine a sniper who just last decade was looking at that exact position where I was standing through the eyes of a gun. I imagined him pulling the trigger, and bang! Right behind me was the evidence.
>
> Blog 97, January 2007

Other bloggers noted how learning about the siege impacted on their own personal politics.

> Well, I have my thoughts on this, and I have now seen what the Bosnian Serb/Serbian army did to the Muslims here. Now I can understand what my relatives went through during WW2. I can now understand why they think I should not go to Germany
>
> Blog 516, July 2005

Several bloggers commented on personal guilt for not knowing more about the conflict. Anger and sadness frequently emerged as emotional responses, triggered by bloggers' encounters with the people and places of Sarajevo. While this anger and sadness was frequently personal, evidence further suggested that the actions of western media and institutions heavily mediated how many understood the siege.

For many, the lack of quick western intervention was a significant mediating factor; evidenced by regular comments on the United Nations' responses in particular; examples including; "starvation after the pathetic attempts of the UN", (Blog 89, June 2007) and "when someone was able to escape the siege, the UN would send them back into the city. 11,000 people died in Sarajevo." (Blog 497, June 2006) and "when asked about the UN we were told that they were 'professional apologisers'." (Blog 394, Sept 2007).

Bloggers often exhibited curiosity about the background of their tour guides, relating their own childhoods to that of the guide. Several bloggers noted that their guides readily discussed their own life at the time of the siege, with some even commenting that it formed an integral part of their tourist experience. Death was openly discussed with some guides, who frequently recounted their loss of loved ones during the siege. The selected quote from the blog below is generally representative of interest in the livelihood of guides during the siege.

> Our own history tour operator who was 12 to 16 yrs [sic] old through
> the siege told us about how he regularly bicycled across the city
> carrying 50L of water… He regaled us with stories about how he
> lived in a bomb shelter underground for these 4 years along with 80
> other families… I was asking how they could focus on school and
> get on with normal life when it was so dangerous on street level. He
> assured me that after a while it just became their normal life.
>
> Blog 394, Sept 2007

Other bloggers commented on the personal experience of being guided by those who were deeply affected by the conflict, including victims and survivors. The opportunity to meet and converse with locals mediated the experience for many bloggers, with one writing that "During the war, this old lady helped the troops carry the supplies. The old lady still lives there, and we got to see her! It was a really cool experience." (Blog 31, December 2009). Discussion of children additionally featured regularly, again juxtaposed against violence, with one blogger writing upon observing images of children in a museum:

> Most poignant of all are the pictures of the children. The corruption
> here was widespread, but it is the childhood innocence that is the
> most costly victim of the war. The children handling guns, the
> make-shift schools (often a target of the bombers) in stair-wells or

cellars and the wish-lists and diaries of the children who only knew
of a life of conflict and fear.

Blog 206, July 2011

Finally, bloggers also commented on the iconic images associated with the
war, frequently mentioning damaged buildings and Sarajevo Roses. Bloggers
noted their desire to find a rose before they left the city (Blog 302, August 2007),
the poignancy of the red floral pattern (Blog 230, February 2011), the way the
roses are now dusty and blend into the city (Blog 120, July 2002) and the dis-
sonance caused by the preservation of this heritage; "later in the day I saw a
local spit on one of them, either showing his disregard for the Bosnian killed
there, or the Serb who fired the shell", (Blog 442, Feb 2007). Other bloggers (Blog
422, June 2007) commented that the roses were "pretty hard to find anymore (I
haven't found any, in fact)", found 'fairly frequently' (Blog 385, December 2007)
and a 'bit strange' to sit across from while having a coffee (Blog 510, Sept 2005).

Discussion

Causevic and Lynch (2011) suggest that the presentation and consumption of
difficult heritage could eventually act as a pre-cursor to more normal forms
of economic tourism development in a post-conflict setting, i.e., thanatourism
may ultimately pave the way for the presentation and commodification of
non-war heritage as wounds evolve from scars into memorials. They further
suggest (2011: 794) that tour guides in Bosnia Herzegovina strive to achieve
social catharsis for tourists, writing that exposure to conflict sites can result in
an emotional experience for participants. Such experiences, they write, should
not be reduced to the "oversimplification and conceptual reductionism" of dark
tourism paradigms.

However, while the blog research found that while war memorialization
inspires a contemplation of morality, or emotions concurrent to Causevic and
Lynch's phoenix tourism theory, morality contemplation was not a singular
experience. Bloggers frequently contemplated their own *mortality*, noting how
this contemplation may affect their outlook on life in future. Consumption of the
siege emerged as the dominant tourist experience for those who blogged about
Sarajevo. The impact of this experience was deep and personally meaningful for
many bloggers.

Comments from those who found the experience meaningful suggested that
their visit to Sarajevo was self-transforming; likely the type of tourist experience Cohen (1979) would posit as 'existential'. Indeed, pure thanatopsis, or the
contemplation of death, was evident in many blogs; provoked by the experience
afforded by the spatial and temporal proximity to death, mediated through
bloggers' personal experiences and the interpretation provided by guides and
symbols. While bloggers often channeled any contemplation of death into

relatively positive outcomes, as they considered peace, harmony, post-conflict cooperation and multi-culturalism, discussion was equally frequently 'morbid' (Blog 436, April 2007) or focused on 'terror' (Blog 472, July 2006).

Secondly, blogs are revealed here as a rich source of data for thanatourism research. Despite the burgeoning and multi-disciplinary interest in thanatourism, little remains known about the thanatourism experience, arguably as a result of the focus on the supply side of the phenomenon. We know little, for example, concerning what tourists actually think about when contemplating death, and the blog data provided clues to such questions, with many demonstrating detailed reflection on thanatopsis in their writing. Blogger 97, for example, imagined being sniped at, describing what he/ she would do in the face of death. This is a thought which appears to raise some vulnerability in the blogger, who attempts to comprehend the enormity of the war.

This finding is interesting both from thanatological and methodological viewpoints; little is known about what the contemplation of death provokes at tourist sites and less perhaps on how to document and explore these ontologies. Blogs – and indeed other social media – may prove to be an invaluable data source in future thanatourism research. The growing number of travel blogs presents opportunities for researchers to explore large volumes of thanatourism experience data without the need for field visits, more traditional research methods, such as interviews, or access issues obtaining what could potentially be sensitive and emotive data.

There are methodological challenges with using travel blogs as a data source; the vast majority of tourists do not blog about their experience. The sample is arguably therefore not representative of the wider tourist market. It is noted that an element of conspicuous consumption may exist in travel blogs, a conspicuousness which may deviate from wider societal consumption habits. Entries may, for example, have been dramatized for popular consumption, written for an external audience or intended to elicit particular responses.

In addition, the travel blogs selected for this chapter are only representative of tourist bloggers on two well-known sites, who blog about visiting Sarajevo, in the English language. Non-English language entries ($n=40$) were discarded for the study. Further research would be needed to assess if significant differences exist between English language and non-English language bloggers.

Finally, the wealth of information published in blogs, from basic demographic data, to potential insights into the tourist gaze as captured through bloggers' photography, to the blog text itself, which is often rich and detailed, offers researchers an opportunity to quickly obtain thanatourism experience data without the need for primary fieldwork. The public availability and easy accessibility of this data provides researchers with great opportunity to further develop understanding of how visits to sites of death affects tourists.

Conclusion

> Once we enter the museum, we begin to absorb the sombre mood of the city. As tourists, there is almost a guilt factor. We are fascinated by the history and it is almost exciting to spot the vestiges of the recent conflict taking place here. Yet it seems odd to be taking photos of evidence of such misery and suffering as has clearly taken place here.
>
> Blog 206, July 2011

It is clear that great educational tourism potential exists at the Sarajevo Siege sites; the close spatial and temporal proximity of war tourism in Sarajevo provokes many questions concerning humanity and morality. When this proximity is framed within conflict and genocide education discourse and interpreted by survivors, a potentially powerful message can emerge. A need to understand barbarity was evident in blogs, with a sense of discovery, on both personal and spatial levels emerging in many. Bloggers expressed disbelief that they could so readily visit the siege lines, stand at the edge of mine fields and meet with survivors. This proximity elicited a number of cathartic coping strategies for many, as bloggers attempted to escape the emotional impact of their war tour encounters by writing poetry, discussing rebuilding, peace and hope and putting their own personal problems into perspective. However, exploring such discourses within a thanatourism framework remains relevant and highly appropriate for a number of reason; as evidenced throughout the chapter, internalization of conflict, abstraction from place and contemplation of mortality featured prominently for many bloggers.

Using blogs to understand emotive experiences therefore yields great advantages over other methods; travel blogs allows greater time and space for the subject to reflect on his/ her experience. While other research methods, such as interviews, perhaps benefit from capturing the impacts of the immediacy of place on tourists, findings from this chapter further suggest that understanding the thanatourist experience should be equally concerned with post-visit experience and reflection. The chapter therefore proposes that travel blogs are a valuable source of data which can be rich in detail, provide thick descriptions and suffer less from power relationships and bias between interviewer and subject.

As death is a complex and sensitive subject, blog entries may provide an ethically sound and less intrusive data source than primary data collection. Recent use of travel blog research by Sharpley (2012), guestbook comments (Seaton, 2012), ethnographic methods by Iles (2008) and Dunkley, Morgan and Westwood's (2011) compassionate oral history approach suggests that there is arguably a desire for less conventional approaches to collecting qualitative empirical thanatourism data. Although blog research is not without its methodological challenges as noted by Pan *et al* (2007) and throughout this present chapter, it may be useful in thanatourism research to overcome what Biran, Poria and Oren (2011: 838) identify as a possible subject reluctance to admit to a difficult emotional experience.

Discussion questions

1 Why do tourists blog about visits to war sites/attractions associated with death and disaster? Is it a form of conspicuous consumption or do they have more responsible motives?

2 What impact might the publication of travel blogs have on the sites themselves and the host community?

3 What other sources might provide novel secondary data related to tourist consumption of death and disaster?

References

Akehurst, G. (2009). User generated content: the use of blogs for tourism organizations and tourism consumers. *Service Business*, **3**(1), 51-61.

Ashworth, G. (2002). Holocaust tourism: The experience of Krakow-Kazimierz. *International Research in Geographical and Environmental Education*, **11**, 363–367.

Ashworth, G. (2004). Tourism and the heritage of atrocity: Managing the heritage of South African Apartheid for entertainment. In T. Singh. (Ed.), *New Horizons in Tourism, Strange Experiences and Stranger Practices* (pp. 95–108). London: Cabi Publishing.

Balkan Insight (2010). *Sarajevo Experiencing a Tourism Boom*. http://www.balkaninsight.com/en/article/sarajevo-experiencing-a-tourism-boom. Accessed 10th April 2014.

Beech, J. (2000). The enigma of Holocaust Sites as tourist attractions: The case of Buchenwald. *Managing Leisure*, **5**, 29-41.

Bigley, J.D., Lee, C.K., Chon, J., Yoon, Y. (2010). Motivations for war-related tourism: A case of DMZ visitors in Korea. *Tourism Geographies*, **12**(3), 371-394.

Biran, A, Poria Y, Oren G. (2011). Sought experiences at (dark) heritage sites. *Annals of Tourism Research*, **38**(3), 820-841.

Blom, T. (2000). Morbid tourism - A postmodern market niche with an example from Althorp. *Norsk Geografisk Tidsskrift - Norwegian Journal of Geography*, **54**, 29-36.

Bruner, E.M. (1989). Of cannibals, tourists and ethnographers. *Cultural Anthropology*, **4**(4), 438–445.

Calcustat, (2013). *Searches for 'travelblog.org' and 'travelpod.com'*. http://www.calcustat.com. Accessed 10th April 2014.

Casbeard, R. & Booth, C. (2012). Post-modernity and the exceptionalism of the present in dark tourism. *Journal of Unconventional Parks, Tourism & Recreation Research,* **4**(1) 2-8.

Causevic, S. & Lynch, P. (2011). Phoenix tourism: Post-conflict tourism role. *Annals of Tourism Research,* **38**(3), 780-800.

Choi, S., Lehto, X.Y., & Morrison, A.M. (2007). Destination image representation on the web: Content analysis of Macau travel related websites. *Tourism Management,* **28**, 118–129.

Cohen, E. (1979). A phenomenology of tourist experiences. *Sociology,* **13**(2), 179–201.

Dunkley, R., Morgan. N., Westwood, S. (2011). Visiting the trenches: Exploring meanings and motivations in battlefield tourism. *Tourism Management,* **32**, 860-868.

Foley, M. & Lennon, J. (1996). J.F.K. and Dark Tourism: A Fascination with Assassination. *International Journal of Heritage Studies,* **2**, 198-211.

Hyde, K. & Harman, S. (2011). Motives for a secular pilgrimage to the Gallipoli battlefields. *Tourism Management,* **32**(6), 1343-1351.

Iles, J (2008). Encounters in the fields - tourism to the battlefields of the Western Front. *Journal of Tourism and Cultural Change,* **6**(2), 138-154.

I.C.J. (International Court of Justice) (2007). *Application of the convention on the prevention and punishment of the crime of genocide (Bosnia and Herzegovina v. Serbia and Montenegro)*, Judgment, I.C.J. Reports 2007.

Johnston, T. (2010). Thanatourism and the commodification of space in post-war Croatia and Bosnia. In R. Sharpley and P.R. Stone. (Eds.), *The Tourist Experience Contemporary Perspectives* (pp. 43-56), London: Routledge.

Johnston, T. (2013) Mark Twain and The Innocents Abroad: Illuminating the gaze on death. *International Journal of Culture, Tourism and Hospitality Research,* **7**(3(, 199 – 213.

Kassarjian, H.H. (1977). Content analysis in consumer research. *Journal of Consumer Research,* **4**(1), 8-18.

Lennon, J. & Foley, M. (2000). *Dark tourism: [The attraction of death and disaster]*. London: Continuum.

Miles, W.F.S. (2002). Auschwitz: Museum interpretation and darker tourism. *Annals of Tourism Research,* 29 (4), 1175-1178.

Muzaini, H., Teo, P. & Yeoh, B. (2007). Intimations of postmodernity in dark tourism: The fate of history at Fort Siloso, Singapore. *Journal of Tourism and Cultural Change,* **5**(1), 28-45.

Pan, B., MacLaurin, T., & Crotts, J.C. (2007). Travel Blogs and their Implications for Destination Marketing. *Journal of Travel* Research, *46*(1), 35-45.

Rojek, C. (1993). *Ways of Escape: Modern Transformations in Leisure and Travel.* London, England: Macmillan.

Seaton, A. (1996). From Thanatopsis to Thanatourism: Guided by the Dark. *International Journal of Heritage Studies,* **2**, 234-244.

Seaton, A. (1999). War and thanatourism: Waterloo 1815-1914. *Annals of Tourism Research,* **26**, 234-244.

Seaton, A. (2009a). Thanatourism and its discontents: An appraisal of a decade's work with some future issues and directions. In T. Jamal and M. Robinson (Eds.), *The Handbook of Tourism Studies* (pp. 521-542). London: Sage.

Seaton, A. (2009b). Purposeful otherness: Approaches to the management of thanatourism. In R. Sharpley & P.R. Stone, (Eds.), *The Darker Side of Travel: The Theory and Practice of Dark Tourism* (pp. 75-108). Bristol: Channel View.

Seaton, A. (2012). Gothic holidays in a macabre home: the Thanatourist at Lansdown Tower. Paper presented at the *Association of American Geographers Annual Meeting,* February, New York.

Sharpley, R. (2012). Towards and understanding 'genocide tourism', an analysis of visitors' accounts of their experience of recent genocide sites. In R. Sharpley and P.R. Stone (Eds.), *Contemporary Tourist Experience: Concepts and Consequences* (pp. 95-109), Oxon: Routledge.

Sharpley, R.A. & Stone, P.R. (eds.) (2009). *The Darker Side of Travel: The Theory and Practice of Dark Tourism.* Bristol: Channel View.

Siegenthaler, P. (2002). Hiroshima and Nagasaki in Japanese Guidebooks. *Annals of Tourism Research,* 29(4), 1111-1137.

Simic, O. (2009). Dark Tourism: Remembering, visiting and placing the dead: Law, authority and genocide in Srebrenica. *Law, Text, Culture,* **13**(1), 273-310.

Simko, D. (2006). Sarajevo: Isolation in a country falling apart. In R. Schneider-Sliwa (Ed.), *Cities in Transition, Globalization, Political Change and Urban Development* (pp. 95-123). Netherlands: Springer.

Skinner, J. (Ed.) (2012). *Writing the Dark Side of Travel.* Oxford, England: Berghahn Books.

Stone, P. R. (2006). A dark tourism spectrum: Towards a typology of death and macabre related tourist sites, attractions and exhibitions. *Tourism: An Interdisciplinary International Journal,* **52**, 145-160.

Stone, P.R. (2009). Dark Tourism: Morality and New Moral Spaces. In R. Sharpley & P. R. Stone, (Eds.), *The Darker Side of Travel: The Theory and Practice of Dark Tourism* (pp. 56-74). Bristol: Channel View.

Stone, P.R. (2011). Dark tourism: towards a new post-disciplinary research agenda. *International Journal of Tourism Anthropology,* **1**(3/4), 318–332.

Stone, P. R. and Sharpley, R. (2008). Consuming Dark Tourism: A Thanatological Perspective. *Annals of Tourism Research,* **35**, 574-595.

Urry, J. & Larsen, J. (2011, 3ʳᵈ Ed.) *The Tourist Gaze 3.* London: Sage.

Walter, T. (2009). Dark Tourism: Mediating Between the Dead and the Living. In R. Sharpley & P. R. Stone, (Eds.), *The Darker Side of Travel: The Theory and Practice of Dark Tourism* (pp. 39–55). Bristol: Channel View.

Wilson, J. (2008). *Prison: Cultural Memory and Dark Tourism.* New York: Peter Lang.

Winter, C. (2011). First World War cemeteries: Insights from visitor books. *Tourism Geographies,* **13**(3), 462-479.

Zehrer, A., Crotts, J. C., & Magnini, V. P. (2011). The perceived usefulness of blog postings: An extension of the expectancy-disconfirmation paradigm. *Tourism Management,* **32**(1), 106–113.

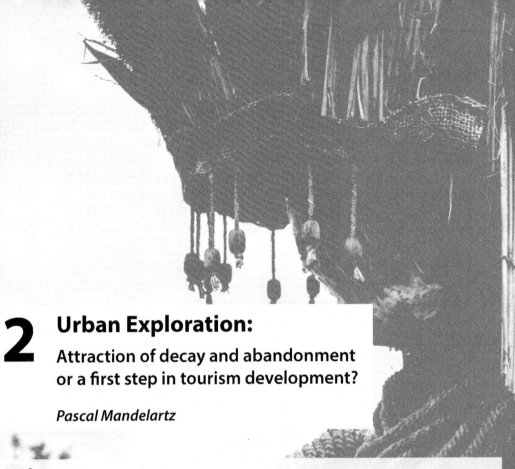

2 Urban Exploration:

Attraction of decay and abandonment or a first step in tourism development?

Pascal Mandelartz

Abstract

Derelict industrial sites, abandoned underground stations and hospitals, off-limits factories; places and spaces people usually avoid, but there is a prospering subculture on the rise, consisting of people who are attracted by these decaying landmarks, called urban exploration. This chapter sheds light into the bunkers, catacombs and underground railway systems by reviewing 'Urbex' under the lens of tourism studies and discussing the activity in relation to fundamental tourism theory as well as perceptions by members of the subculture, thereby providing insights into the subculture's attitudes and what it is that lures people to these places. It is suggested that when given the time and scope to develop, many urban exploration sites have the potential to become mass tourism attractions. The chapter proposes a spectrum of uncommodified and commodified urban exploration sites. It is suggested that Urban Explorers therefore also take the role of explorers within Butler's tourism area life cycle.

Learning outcomes

1 To understand the attraction of urban exploration.

2 To view urban exploration in relation to tourism theory.

3 To gain insights into the multitude of motivational factors.

4 To explore a spectrum of urban exploration sites within a tourism development context.

Introduction

Type 'urban exploration' into a search engine and you will gain insights into a vast spectrum of communities whose members like to spend their leisure or professional time seeking man-made abandoned structures and buildings, "the unadorned backsides of the city, the alleys, culverts, service areas, and other microspaces, along with wastelands, railway sidings, spaces behind billboards, and unofficial rubbish tips" (Edensor 2005:833). Urban exploration as an interest has approximately 42,700 likes on Facebook (as of January 2015). Urban exploration has grown to become a widespread and more recognised leisure practice (High and Lewis 2007).

Only the term urban exploration is coeval but the activity itself has a rather rich and long history. The Urbex fanzine *Infiltration* has outlined an urban exploration timeline (infiltration.org, 2015) of which some points are worth noting within the context of this chapter (Figure 2.1).

1793	Philibert Aspairt dies whilst exploring the Parisian catacombs by candlelight. His body is found 11 years later.
1955	Debord publishes his *Introduction to a Critique of Urban Geography* and develops a practice called *dérive*, which consists of travelling through urban environments and noting psychogeographical variations. In the decade that follows, members of the left-leaning Situationist International movement argue that society consists largely of passive spectators and consumers of packaged experiences, and suggest that individuals can shake up this state of affairs by engaging in creative play.
1990	Outdoorsman Alan S. North writes *The Urban Adventure Handbook*, a guide in which he encourages people to climb buildings and explore the city as an accessible alternative to climbing mountains and exploring wilderness. Although not widely read, the handbook inspires a few people to begin using the term 'urban adventure' in their writings. In Russia, the Diggers of the Underground Planet officially register with the Moscow government as the 'Center of Underground Research'.
1996	Wes Modes puts up a website called *Adventuring*, archiving his writings about freighthopping and buildering. The site brings the term 'urban adventure' from North's book to the web. (See http://modes.io/urbanadventure/ and http://www.thespoon.com/trainhop/) Ninjalicious alias Jeff Chapman, publishes the first issue of the paper zine *Infiltration*. In the editorial of the first issue, he coins the term 'urban exploration' and introduces the idea of exploring off-limits areas of all types as a hobby.
1997	Berliner Unterwelten, or the Berlin Underground Association, is founded in Germany. In Scotland, the Milk Grate Gang forms with the purpose of exploring the Glaswegian underworld, and places its adventures online at *Subterranean Glasgow*.

1998	Explorer and photographer Stanley Greenberg publishes *Invisible New York: The Hidden Infrastructure of the City*.
	Julia Solis establishes a *Dark Passage* website (http://www.solis.darkpassage.com/). German explorers Dietmar Arnold and Frieder Salm, of Berliner Underwelten, publish *Dunkle Welten*, a German-language guide to the worlds beneath Berlin.
1999	Ninjalicious establishes the *Infilnews* mailing list and sends out the first edition of a semi-annual e-mail newsletter covering events of interest to urban explorers.
	Julia Solis and her explorer friends stage an event called 'Dark Passage' in the subway tunnels beneath New York City.
2000	Eku Wand and Dietmar Arnold, of Berliner Unterwelten, release *Berlin im Untergrund: Potsdamer Platz*, an interactive multimedia CD offering tours of subterranean Berlin. The newspaper *Hamburger Abendblatt* comments that 'Berlin in the Underground' is so exciting that, when visiting Berlin the next time, the main attraction will be the S-Bahnhof railway station and not the Sony Centre. (29.1.2002) (see http://www.eku.de)
2001	Julia Solis stumbles upon an unmoderated DMOZ category (DMOZ is a multilingual open-content directory of World Wide Web links. The site and community who maintain it are also known as the Open Directory Project (ODP)). It is owned by AOL but constructed and maintained by a community of volunteer editors) called 'urban speleology', which she adopts and adapts to urban exploration.
2002	Julia Solis and her collaborators in New York City form Ars Subterranea, a society populated by artists, architects, historians and urban explorers.
2005	Explorers from the world over unite again for a weekend of exploration and seminars in Montreal, Quebec, organized by urban exploration Montreal. The event is named Office Products Expo 95.
	Ninjalicious publishes *Access All Areas*: a user's guide to the art of urban exploration, a more than 240-page book full of UE knowledge, advice and theory.

Figure 2.1: Urban exploration timeline

Today, urban exploration communities are spreading around the globe, with the majority located in agglomerations of the western world. Urbex has certain characteristics that are similar to that of other subcultures such as skateboarding, graffiti and underground raves, but also shares certain attributes with Punk or even the quirky Tiki subculture, who often identify themselves as urban archaeologists, piecing together human activity of the past, through the recovery and analysis of the material culture and environmental data that has been left behind by contemporary human populations. This includes architecture, artefacts, ecofacts and cultural landscapes, and is also concerned with interaction and process.

Aronsson and Gradén (2013) talk about negotiating the past, Guttormson and Hedeager (2015) add that contemporary societies negotiate by exclusion and inclusion in regards of what is defined as worth remembering. It is about people's communication when using heritage and the past for their own ends in contemporary societies. As they define what is worth remembering, it might be suggested that this could be a trigger for the development of a tourist attraction and there are various motivational factors to be considered, of which urban archaeology is only one aspect that might attract people to abandoned spaces.

What defines urban exploration is interpreted differently by different people. The majority of scholars differentiate urban exploration from tourism. Garrett (2012) states that, "exploration is not something you do, it's who you are", but if it is who you are, does that not mean that it is inherently connected to the touristic choices being made? We are talking about a phenomenon that includes travelogues, photography of sites, guidebooks, maps, websites, newsletters, events, forums and equipment. Although, to be fair, there has to be a spectrum on the intensity and time that urban exploration occupies in someone's life, and Garrett has truly embedded the urban exploration philosophy, as can be seen on his website (Garret, 2012).

The rise in popularity of this activity has grasped the attention of scholars within geography and tourism studies, which as Mott and Roberts (2013: 2) state "is not surprising, considering the discipline's long standing interest in exploration, space, landscapes, cities and the meanings of place". These scholars have documented and examined various aspects of the activity. Garret (2011: 1050) describes how "places with beautiful, amusing, disturbing and dark histories are all given space for recognition" thereby creating a link to dark tourism.

Dark tourism sites are of interest to some in the Urbex world, though Urbexers would typically seek out the abandoned and off-limits sites and explicitly avoid any organised tourist attraction where memory is officially scripted. However, operators around the globe such as London Street Art Tours (www.londongraffititours.com, accessed on 08.06.2015), Detroiturbex (www. detroiturbex.com) or Berliner Unterwelten (www.berliner-unterwelten.de) have introduced the masses to urban exploration, thereby creating a tourist bubble that possibly strips the activity of many aspects sought after by urban explorers in the first place. Could it be that they are not just urban explorers, but explorers as outlined within Butler's (2006) tourism area life cycle? And what attracts visitors to decaying buildings and structures?

Theoretical underpinnings of urban exploration

The historic events outlined in Figure 2.1 suggest a certain curiosity about the unknown and often forbidden that has lured in people from various backgrounds and age groups. For some Urbex has become a hobby, sometimes linked to passion for history, heritage, architecture and photography. It is about collecting new and extraordinary experiences, documenting and capturing them, in a similar way to tourists capturing keepsakes and tangibles from their journeys and attractions. On the other hand the interest can come out of a professional curiosity, for example, in terms of art and research.

Image 2.1: Rubble, Decay, Potential, by Dirk Schäpers

The decay creates a momentum and uniqueness as an opportunity for the arts with its 'surreal' and 'post-apocalyptic' appeal and as Pinder (2005: 387) describes "transgresses boundaries between art and everyday space, to explore the street and public realm through artistic practice". This notion includes the fascination with the TOADS (Temporary, Obsolete, Abandoned and Derelict Spaces) which hold a distinctive visual aesthetic, and in terms of photography incorporates the technical challenges of capturing complex and often dark scenes on camera (Mott and Robertson, 2013). Within that context, quite a few scholars have picked up on what is called 'ruin porn',(e.g. Greco, 2012; Mullins, 2012; Strangleman, 2013) as a narrative to describe ruins photography that sees artistic value in modern urban decay.

Image 2.2: Nature reclaiming a building, by Dirk Schäpers

There is also a pop-cultural effect that has its origins in subcultures like the hip-hop/graffiti scene and various links to underground raves to unauthorised and authorised parties taking place in disused and decaying buildings and structures. 'Going underground' is cultural capital and creates status when wanting to be separate to the mainstream, but where there's a trend, others will follow. With the subcultures comes also an element of rebelliousness. Being allowed to undertake activities in environments that would normally be prohibited can provide a certain sense of freedom and provides enrapture.

Bennett (2010: 422) discernibly portrays the urban explorer as a *flâneur* observing "the noise and chaos and frisson of the metropolis with a mix of fear and intoxication", what he describes as a 'tantalising fear', "evocatively portrayed in Edgar Allan Poe's 1840 (2003) short story *The Man of the Crowd*, a subtle evocation of the urban Gothic – the gentleman observer following a stranger amidst the crowd down back alleys and through half-open doors" (see Chapter 4 for further insights into the Gothic traveller). Or does the fear evoke a thrill similar to the one described in Chapter 7 of this book by Marson? In this chapter Marson explores where death as uncertainty (real risk component) features as a motivating and inhibiting factor for adventure participation.

Abandoned structures illustrate the fragility of human creation; unprotected from forces of nature they provide evidence that nature re-conquers what is unguarded. Fraser (2012) has previously acknowledged a connection between urban exploration as adventure tourism. Furthermore there is an interesting link to the term 'urban speleology' from caving and cave explorations which Julia Solis (Solis, 2015) has adopted by creating a DMOZ category for urban exploration as it creates a relationship with the wilderness that has also been acknowledged by Bunting (2014).

Kaplan and Talbot (1983: 163) have investigated the psychological benefits of the 'wilderness experience' stating that "a person's experiences in wilderness surroundings can cause panic and fear, or they can inspire a deep sense of tranquillity and peace rarely matched in other surroundings. From a cultural point of view, wilderness is a particularly significant category of nature." They ask: "Does wilderness offer sanctuary or danger? Should wilderness areas be preserved or ploughed over? Does an individual experience in the wilderness offer an enriched perspective on life, or does it merely tempt a person to disregard the just claims of society?"

Wilderness in the case of urban exploration does not just simply act as a metaphor but raises insightful questions concerning the nature of urban exploration. Has the urban jungle become our substitute for the wilderness, as wilderness has become inaccessible and in many places is non-existent? After all, it has been suggested that we are living within the Anthropocene (Crutzen, 2006), an epoch in which human activities are exerting increasing impacts on the environment on all scales and are in many ways outcompeting natural processes.

Furthermore, we as mankind have already explored everything. Unless going into outer space or the deep sea, nothing truly remains unexplored. It reminds the author of the seekers of authenticity who travel to find the authentic but instead are presented with a hyperreal world where there is staged authenticity.

Urban explorers are seeking an authentic wilderness experience but they take an *avant-garde* role similar to that of the first explorers of the Amazon River or Mount Everest wanting to experience what no one before has experienced, thereby triggering the tourism area life cycle and demolishing the characteristics of the destinations they enjoyed. Berliner Unterwelten, the society that guides tours through Berlin's underground, tunnels and bunkers has recorded around 300,000 visitors in 2014 (Berliner Unterwelten, 2015). People post their urban exploration experiences on Trip Advisor and Facebook and Derelictlondon. com, for example, offers guided tours through the abandoned sites of the city of London.

But how are these sites formed? And have many iconic attractions started out as sites of urban exploration and archaeology? Is the Coliseum, for example, not an attraction that had been abandoned and demolished, ready to decay until Pope Benedict XIV ordered its preservation in the mid-18th century? What about the Berlin Wall, an urban structure that has been torn down in most parts, but where leftovers are still scattered around the city, forming a route of memorials, museums and other places of interests along its way? Also the less well sustained structures of an urban landscape form part of its character. In Berlin the tearing down of a 22 meter stretch of what is called the Eastside Gallery (a part of the Berlin Wall with artist paintings) caused an outrage and demonstrations amongst the local population underlining the emotional attachment to the physical surrounding.

Some urban exploration sites therefore follow in the steps in Butler's (2006) tourism area life cycle (see Figure 2.1). Urban exploration sites are first (re-) discovered by members of the (urban exploration) community. Through word-of-mouth news will spread and peradventure find its way to the internet and online forums. Perhaps the place becomes more popular with photographers. Tour operators and event managers might begin to recognise the attraction of a site and the development of an infrastructure begins. What turns out to be an oxymoron is that the decay that has attracted the urban explorers in the first place has to be put on hold to create a tourism product that can be sustained over time. The justification for the decay line inserted into the model is the judgement that visitors to ruins pick up and re-arrange objects. The first step to refurbishment.

The abandoned might be filled with life once again. However there is no necessity inherent to this. Abandoned structures might decay and will not spark further interest, whereas others have the potential to become famous landmarks. Heritage can thereby be an important factor in whether further development goes ahead as there is a cultural interest to maintain these sites for commemorative and historical purposes. The state of refurbishment and maintenance depend on the nature of the site, hence the split of the decay line within the model. A site many only be maintained to a certain level to leave room for the urban exploration aesthetic and ambience, therefore the line is straight. If the site is developed further, decay decreases, if interest in the site decreases, decay continues.

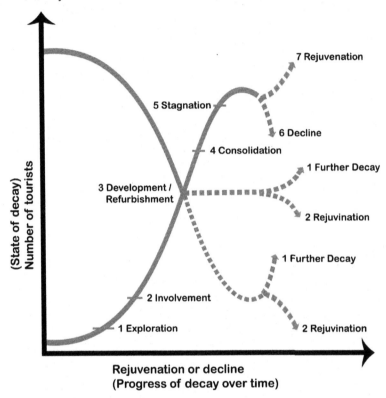

Figure 2.2: Tourism area life cycle in relation to the progress of decay

Urban exploration suffers exactly like other subcultures from commodification, lifting it into the mainstream, which was supposed to counteract it in the first place. A certain resemblance to the backpacker community might be proposed, as per O'Reilly's observation (2006: 998). He states that backpacking "once considered a marginal activity undertaken by society's drop-outs,... has gradually entered the tourism mainstream". Can the participation of members of the subculture in urban exploration activities suitable for the masses be doubted, or do we have to widen the aforementioned urban exploration spectrum from the die-hard Urbexer who seeks to truly explore the 'unknown' to the weekend tourist in New York, Berlin, Melbourne or London who might regard it as *en-vogue* or simply participate as it is part of the tourist offering of a destination?

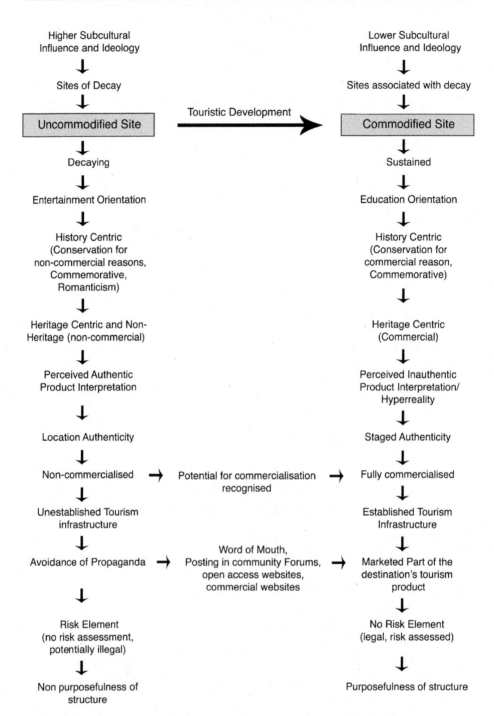

Figure 2.3: Proposed tourism development spectrum of urban exploration sites

In order to visualise a possible spectrum Stone's (2006) dark tourism spectrum has inspired the creation for a model on urban exploration sites illustrating perceived site features of urban exploration tourism developments within an uncommodified and commodified framework (see Figure 2.3). The model has been taken out of its dark tourism narrative but is useful as it offers site characteristics that can be translated into urban exploration sites and furthermore illustrates the possibilities of urban exploration site development over time. The diagram outlines possible steps in the development of a site from the first explorers who visit an uncommodified structure, to the spreading of word of mouth, to online forums to the introduction of a tourism infrastructure. The model acts as a conceptual framework that will require further debate and justification through research. Nonetheless, if taking some existing urban exploration sites such as Berliner Unterwelten as an example to verify the model, there seems to be evidence for the proposed suggestions.

Where the various segments on the Urbexer spectrum from die hard to mass tourism mingle will require further debate and investigation, but what they have in common are the "epistemic strategies commonly found in urban exploration" as outlined by Bennett (2010: 428) in his case study on Bunkerology:

- *The joy of knowledge.* The accumulation of knowledge of a place or thing as a means of self-fulfilment and status. The roots of this strategy lie in empiricism (specifically taxonomy and positivism).

- *Memorialisation and/or conservation of heritage.* Through study, visitation, and reporting. The roots of this strategy lie in a heterogeneous blend of Romanticism, nostalgia, and community activism/resistance.

- *Communing with the spirit of the place.* Communing with the essence/ spirit/`ghosts' of a place through deep (and open) experience of it, and/ or through encounters with artefacts (material culture). The roots of this strategy lie in phenomenology.

To gain further understanding of the urban exploration subculture and its motivational factors, semi-structured interviews were conducted with members of the subculture from the UK and Germany who regularly participate in urban exploration activities. Questions asked included: How do you define urban exploration? What attracts you to urban decaying structures? Do you see Urbex as part of a subculture? Do you visit some sites more often than others? How do you decide on places to visit? Do you stay within the local region or do you travel for Urbex? When travelling, is Urbex a component of your plans?

Their comments are used here to build a relationship between the theoretical debate and perceptions of members of the subculture. Examples from their responses allow the reader to cross-examine interpretations (Figure 2.4). The categories have emerged *a priori* from the theoretical debate as Art/Photography/

Ruin Porn, Fascination with the TOADS, Avant-garde, Experiencing wilderness, Commodification, The joy of knowledge, Memorialisation and/or conservation of heritage and Communing with the spirit of the place.

The importance of art and photography and the capturing of sites on photos as keepsakes was inherent in the primary data. The fascination with the TOADS was a major push factor that can be identified. Some respondents commented on the distinction to the main stream and on Avant-Garde elements pointing to a perceived differentiation of the activity from main stream activities. Comments such as "a few years back there were still areas of Zeche Zollverein (Unesco Heritage site in Essen, Germany) that had not been developed touristically"(Interview 5) underline an understanding, or demonstrate at least a realisation that commodification might pick-up eventually and impact on the appearance of sites. The joy of knowledge within the responses was linked to experiencing heritage without it being presented and curated. They want to experience 'unspoilt' and 'raw' evidence of heritage sites that can also be linked to the communing with the spirit of the place and possibly portrays authenticity.

Theoretical concept	Interview response
Art/ Photography/ Ruin Porn	It is about collecting impressions and shoot great photos.
	The site should be extraordinary and should definitely offer the opportunity for some great photos.
Fascination with the TOADS	To me urban exploration is simply the perambulation of abandoned buildings.
	Using a derelict/abandoned man-made structure to explore, whether this is walking around or climbing up.
	They are often dark, old and somewhat daunting in sight. They look intimidating and extremely unnatural. I often find them repulsive and interesting at the same time. The thing that interests me the most is the risk element and the possibility of finding cool things.
	Intact sites do not have the same 'feel' behind them. The fact that they are decaying buildings adds a more sinister character to the building and changes your mentality of being in a building to being somewhere you should not be.
Avant-garde	Seeing places nobody else sees anymore.
	Although the concept of trespassing also adds an element of risk to the activity because it clearly states that you should not be there and breaking rules, no matter how minor adds adrenaline to an activity. That is why people never 'explore' an in-use office building.

Experiencing wilderness	Derelict, how nature eventually claims it, and sometimes accessing places is a challenge which is always fun.
	I find it thrilling, I like adrenaline and it's not harmful to anyone and as long I keep everything the way I found it, I'm not causing problems.
	In Portugal the hotel next to where I was staying had an abandoned hotel and I decided to look in it, because it was there I would never go out of my way to explore because I am much more interested in natural exploration and climbing.
	It is a by-product of natural exploration/climbing.
	The re-possession of nature over buildings is beautiful and interesting.
	I am in intact buildings on a daily basis. This is extraordinary as it is about history and adventure.
Commodification	How do you decide on places to visit?
	Whichever places haven't already started building on.
	Intact sites are everywhere. You have to find a decaying site.
	A few years back there were still areas of Zeche Zollverein (Unesco Heritage site in Essen, Germany) that had not been developed touristically.
	For me, it's the lure of the old and forgotten.
The joy of knowledge	I revisited these places for two reasons; I was visiting with someone new and to expand my search for ground I may have missed. I would happily visit a site numerously as they never cease to be interesting.
Memorialisation and/or conservation of heritage	As being from the Ruhr region (the former industrial heartland of Germany) I am mainly interested in the former coal and steel factories. I'd rather climb through an old coking plant than going to a museum.
	Thrill and history.
	I'm passionate about history and urban exploration offers insight of past times and generations. That for me is an important component.
	I don't tend to consider aesthetic attractive a factor. What attracts me to it is the history.
	You feel the buzz of the history surrounding you. It's quite poetic.
Communing with the spirit of the place	I like places especially where there had been people living or working. The left behind newspaper or mouldy coffee mug in a pile of dust and rubble make a nice picture. It's the hunt for treasures.
	Some of my favourite places to explore are old hospitals or asylums, when you step inside these places you can feel the soul of the place.

Subculture	Yes in their online presence.
	Group meet ups/discussions. Sharing hobbies.
	From my experience I would say no. Only because I view Urbex as something that I use only if it is there I would not go out of my way to explore buildings and I have not met many people that call themselves 'Urban Explorers'.
	There are various forums and websites where people organise themselves and there are certain rules like not publishing directions and addresses with pictures but I doubt that this is enough to define a subculture but I am lacking the sociological background to be sure.
	A secretive one, but a subculture nonetheless. These forums are usually shrouded in anonymity, as Urb Ex is mainly an illegal act. I have yet to see a site or forum that organises group trips or tours of sites so it certainly isn't a sociable subculture, as far as I'm aware.
Other motivational Factors	Breaking and entering.
	The possibility of collapse adds the sense of physical danger. Most of these sites you are not allowed to go into so the possibility of getting caught adds to physiological danger. The possibility of finding something of value that has been left behind.
	Although I do have a penchant for the creepy, so the place with the most disturbing history will definitely appeal to me more so then other sites.
	It's more fun if it's illegal. What can I say, I'm a thrill seeker.

Figure 2.4: Example of data analysis 7

The communing with the spirit of the place is drawing attention to the (possible) tourism development of a site. Sites will have to introduce an infrastructure if tourists are to be guided to and through a site, this means establishing sites ready for tourists, involving risk assessments, facilities and tidying up the place. Within this process lies the danger of re-enacting the site and 'authenticity' should it exist is replaced by staged authenticity and a hyperreality is created, which can already be witnessed in attractions such as Berliner Unterwelten.

The wilderness experiences which could be subconscious but might be a motivational factor nevertheless could be lost within sites that have been commodified or are in the process of commodification. The good news for die-hard Urbexers is that there will be continuous supply of new 'undiscovered' structures emerging within the constant process of renewal and refurbishment of contemporary society. New structures will emerge as others diminish. Demolition is slow, costly and unpopular (Power, 2010).

Image 2.3: The still life of a building, by Dirk Schäpers

Conclusion

Urban explorers are explorers in the sense of the definition as persons visiting and investigating places and spaces that are unknown to the wider public. There are manifold reasons and motivational factors that attract people to decaying abandoned structures. As buildings deteriorate and become re-possessed by nature, they attract those that want to unearth evidence in an archaeological manner or those looking for motives that tell stories, a communing with the spirit that can only take place where artefacts have not been arranged and directed. It is the sense of a still life. The motives and stories often find their way to urban exploration forums and platforms where they are shared with the community. Although there seemingly is an avant-garde spirit and etiquette amongst Urbexers in the sense of not taking artefacts away and re-arranging items within a structure, the sharing of content ultimately leads to followers and people jumping on the bandwagon.

It is suggested that this may spark off tourism development, especially where there are inherent links to history and heritage. Heritage can thereby be an important factor in determining whether further development goes ahead depending on the cultural interest to maintain these sites for commemorative and historical purposes or where other economic benefits that might be gained from the site play a role. Urbexers, on the other hand, seek first-hand experiences rather than being presented a staged reality, but the popularity of certain places can over time initiate tourism development.

The creation of an area developmental life cycle and spectrum aided in the visualisation of urban exploration sites, indicating their progress over time and also highlighting the dilemma of decrease in level of decay as well as the commodification of heritage. Further debate and research is required to validate the proposed models and investigate the various developmental stages in further depth.

Howbeit, there is a vast array of attractions and sites that can be used to exemplify the suggested models with some of these formerly 'unrecognised by the public' spaces having developed into iconic tourist attractions. Examples include the area around Tower Bridge in London, that had an unpleasant reputation as a retreat for prostitutes and pickpockets before it got refurbished and turned into an exhibition space. Ghost towns in the United States, for example, become re-discovered, attract explores, build infrastructure and stage events for the tourist market (Brown Hunt, 2014).

Dimitri Hegemann, a pioneer in Berlin's techno club culture is planning on bringing his concept of re-utilising rundown buildings and factories as night-clubs to Detroit, furthering the idea to include hospitality facilities within the decaying motor city buildings. "Detroit may not be appreciated by everyone, but it has one thing that soulless, bland cities don't have: a unique, authentic, creative culture. That quality is more important than money. Economy follows culture, not vice versa. You can't buy culture." (Creager, 2015)

Within the Ruhr valley of Germany, former industrial sites left to decay for decades have been re-invented and claimed back by society as UNESCO Heritage sites, such as the Zeche Zollverein in Essen. The value of a derelict steel factory in Duisburg has also been recognised. Latz (2000) acknowledged the importance of the site's condition, allowing the polluted soils to remain in place and be remediated through phytoremediation, as well as finding new uses for many of the abandoned structures. Marot (2003), in relation to architecture and memory states that territories must be deepened to provide places where memory can be fostered for cultural needs.

Unfortunately for the Urbexers that means making places accessible for the public and hence, implementing a certain infrastructure. The Duisburg as well as the Detroit example depict the symbiosis of heritage, decay, art, architecture, adventure and leisure space in a constant negotiation of re-development and maintaining the site for commemoration, the result being the creation of a hyper reality and staged authenticity that dismantles the place from the characteristics sought after by Urban explorers in the beginning. Duisburg has introduced an events calendar for activities throughout the year: exhibitions, climbing walls, playgrounds for children, even a diving centre. It represents the spoilt rather than the unspoilt, the guarded rather than the unguarded, managed and risk assessed. It is the difference between entering a WWII bunker that has remained untouched since the war and is re-discovered for the first time, and entering the bunkers presented by Berliner Unterwelten nowadays, where bunk beds and helmets and first aid gear has been rearranged to fit the tourist gaze.

As with so many subcultural aspects, once they become mainstream, they lose some of their attraction to the subculture. What was supposed to be a compensation for the mundane and a form of escapism has been swallowed up by it. A built pleasure park cannot replicate the thrill and adventure of the urban jungle. Disapproved by some Urbexers, but encouraged by others, travel-directory.org (2015) lists an abundance of links for travellers interested in the activity.

Fortunately for the Urbex community, the slow process of refurbishment and demolition of sites is providing a landscape with plenty of Urban exploration opportunities still to be discovered or that are at least currently undiscovered by the general public and industry.

Discussion questions

1　Is urban exploration the appropriate term for the activity?

2　Which spaces and places does the urban community consider for their activity?

   3 Which activities can be linked to urban exploration?

   4 What motivates people to explore urban places?

   5 Identify urban exploration Sites in your local area.

References

Arnold, D., & Salm, F. (2007). *Dunkle Welten: Bunker, Tunnel und Gewölbe unter Berlin*. Berlin: Ch. Links Verlag.

Aronsson, P. & Gradén, L. (2013). *Performing Nordic Heritage: Everyday Practices and Institutional Culture*. Farnham: Ashgate.

Bennett, L. (2011). Bunkerology a case study in the theory and practice of urban exploration. *Environment and Planning D: Society and Space*, **29**, 421-434.

Berliner-Unterwelten (2015). Berliner Unterwelten, Available at http://www.berliner-unterwelten.de. Accessed on 20th June 2015.

Brown Hunt, K. (2014). America's coolest Ghost towns. *Travel and Leisure*. Available at http://www.travelandleisure.com/slideshows/americas-coolest-ghost-towns. Accessed 20th June 2015.

Bunting, B. S. (2014). An alternative wilderness: How urban exploration brings wildness to the city. *Interdisciplinary Studies in Literature and Environment*, **93**, 1-21.

Butler, R. (Ed.) (2006). *The Tourism Area Life Cycle* (Vol. 1). Bristol: Channel View.

Creager, E. (2015). Berlin borrows from Detroit to renew vibrancy. Available http://www.freep.com/story/travel/michigan/2015/05/30/detroit-like-berlin/28086927/. Accessed 20th June 2015.

Crutzen, P. J. (2006). *The 'Anthropocene'*, Berlin Heidelberg: Springer.

Debord, G. (1955). Introduction to a critique of urban geography. In K. Knabb (Ed.), *Situationist International Anthology*. Berkley Bureau of Public Secrets. Pp. 50-54

Detroit Urbex (2015). Detroit urban exploration, Available at http://www.detroiturbex.com, Accessed 8th May 2015.

Edensor, T. (2005). *Industrial Ruins: Space, Aesthetics and Materiality*. Oxford: Berg Publishers.

Fraser, E. (2012). Urban exploration as adventure tourism. In H. Andrews and L. Roberts (Eds.), *Liminal Landscapes: Travel, Experience and Spaces In-Between* (136-150). New York, NY: Routledge.

Garrett, B. (2011). Assaying history: creating temporal junctions through urban exploration. *Environment and Planning-Part D*, **29**(6), 1048 – 1067.

Garret, B. (2012). Convergence, Transmission & Storage. Available at http://www.placehacking.co.uk/2012/11/15/finalpost/, Accessed 10th June 2015.

Greco J (2012) The psychology of ruin porn. Atlantic Cities. Available at http://www.theatlanticcities.com/design/2012/01/psychology-ruin-porn/886/. Accessed 29th June 2015

Greenberg, S., & Garver, T. (1998). *Invisible New York: The hidden infrastructure of the city*. JHU Press.

Guttormsen, T. S., & Hedeager, L. (2015). Introduction: interactions of archaeology and the public. *World Archaeology*, **47**(2), 189-193.

Hamburger Abendblatt (2002). *Die Hauptstadt von Unten*. Zeitungsarchiv.

High, S. & Lewis, D. (2007). *Corporate Wasteland: The Landscape and Memory of Deindustrialization*. Ithaca: Cornell University Press.

Infiltration (2015). Infiltration, Available at www.infiltration.org. Accessed 1st June 2015.

Kaplan, S., & Talbot, J. F. (1983). *Psychological Benefits of a Wilderness Experience. In Behavior and The Natural Environment*. USA: Springer.

Latz, P. (2003). The Idea of Making Time Visible. *Topos* 33, 94 - 99.

London Graffiti Tours (2015). London Graffiti Tours. Available at http://www.londongraffititours.com. Accessed 1st June 2015.

Marot, S. (2003). *Sub-Urbanism and the Art of Memory*. London: Architectectural Association.

Mott, C., & Roberts, S. M. (2014). Not everyone has (the) balls: Urban exploration and the persistence of masculinist geography. *Antipode*, 46(1), 229-245.

Mullins, P. (2012) The Politics and Archaeology of 'Ruin Porn', *Archaeology and Material Culture* blog, 19 August. Available http://paulmullins.wordpress.com/2012/08/19/the-politics-and-archaeology-of-ruinporn/. Accessed 20th June 2015.

Ninjalicious. (2005). *Access All Areas: A User's Guide to the Art of urban exploration*. Toronto: Coach House Books.

North, A. S. (1990). *The Urban Adventure Handbook*. Berkeley: Ten Speed Press.

O'Reilly, C. C. (2006). From drifter to gap year tourist: Mainstreaming backpacker travel. *Annals of Tourism Research*, **33**(4), 998-1017.

Pinder, D. (2005). Arts of urban exploration. *Cultural Geographies*, **12**(4), 383-411.

Poe, E. A. (2003). `The man of the crowd', in *The Fall of the House of Usher and Other Writings*, Penguin: London.

Power, A. (2010). Housing and sustainability: demolition or refurbishment?. *Proceedings of the ICE-Urban Design and Planning*, **163**(4), 205-216.

Solis, J. (2015). Dark Passage. Available http://www.solis.darkpassage.com/. Accessed 29th June 2015.

Stone, P. (2006). A dark tourism spectrum: Towards a typology of death and macabre related tourist sites, attractions and exhibitions. *Tourism: An Interdisciplinary International Journal*, **54**(2), 145-160.

Strangleman, T. (2013). 'Smokestack Nostalgia', 'Ruin Porn' or Working-Class Obituary: The Role and Meaning of Deindustrial Representation. *International Labor and Working-Class History*, **84**, 23-37.

travel-directory.org (2015). Urban Speleology. Available http://www.travel-directory.org/Activities/Outdoors/Speleology/Urban_Speleology/. Accessed 29th June 2015.

3 Site Management and Consuming Death:
The attraction of death, disaster and the macabre

Peter Wiltshier

Abstract

There are many examples of good practice in tourism site management (DuCros, 2008; Olsen, 2006; Poria et al, 2006; Shackley, 2006, 2003) which may have relevance to the management of sites primarily associated with death and disaster. This chapter explores what is meant by good practice to site managers and to visitors. It considers ways in which public and private sector stakeholders could develop future strategic approaches to delivering consistent experiences to visitors at the best possible price. There are implications for training, funding skills, partnership and network development.

Learning outcomes

1 Review the centrality and relevance of staff recruitment and retention at tourist attractions;

2 Reflect on the consistency of storytelling at dark tourist sites;

3 Understand why volunteers are effectively managed to provide critical roles at dark tourism sites;

4 Consider a stakeholder perspective on managing thanatourism that embeds longevity, replicability and sustainability;

5 Develop concepts of networks and partnership in the supply chain.

Introduction

We can never underestimate the human need for social interaction and involvement with the leisure and recreation sector in an informal, yet ongoing, ritual of vacation and experience activities with our built and natural environment. We need only examine recent data on the desire to travel and recreate, to identify that tourism is a global industry in span and evolution and accompanies many forms of human endeavour to develop, engage and reflect on our achievements.

In a complex and highly technology-enhanced demand environment, it has become more important that suppliers understand the identity and association that visitors seek from thanatourism attractions. Visitors are not universally technology savvy; it could be argued that many older tourists have some resistance to using technology. After all, until recently these visitors seldom used technology as part of their own education and usually depend heavily for their data and recommendations from word-of-mouth. However, younger visitors and those who have accepted the challenge of mastery of the world wide web will seek their own information to check identity and relevance to the attraction. Therefore a double-headed approach to information and communications of offers is still most relevant to ensure that messages are reaching the target and wider audiences. A web master will create an interactive booking site for you. A dedicated team of web marketeers will supplement the traditional marketing and sales team that you will already have identified as essential to your future success (Weaver, 2013; Shaw et al, 2011).

According to recent data from Visit Britain, over 1.5 million people were directly employed in tourism in 2013. Growth in jobs in both the direct and indirect businesses reached 5% of national gross domestic product. In terms of gross value added the figure is £127 billion or 9% of the country's total economy (Deloitte, 2013). Dark tourism attractions have no need to despair over the trajectory identified and the complex inter-linked sets of organisations that drive and deliver tourism. It is against this background that management action needs exploration and certain components of a successful attraction business need reinforcing.

> Tourists do not only encounter cultural heritage as just 'the past',
> but rather the past of a particular people or community in a living
> context. Tourists engage with the cultural heritage of a destination
> not only through monumental forms but in more intangible ways as
> the past enshrined in contemporary behaviours and practices.'
>
> Robinson & Picard, (2006: 19)

This chapter argues that the key to success in managing dark tourism attractions is to engage the staff in storytelling. Whether the staff member has a distinct front-line role perhaps as a guide, or works in retail, catering, or in operations behind the scenes, all staff need to understand the relevant narrative for each and every visitor. Storytelling skills should be embedded in staff recruitment procedures and retention and reward practices to ensure continuity of the narrative, to ensure consistency of the story telling and to ensure that the unique selling position of the site is not compromised by variation from key selling messages.

How to identify the attraction

In many ways it is the consumer who determines the power that your dark tourism attraction has to compel visitors to detour, to engage with, to view and to participate in and to recommend to future visitors. We need only consider the pulling power of electronic media to track visitors' perspectives, activities and reflections, to understand how significant e-media have become in the past five years. The reality is that all visitors, young and educated, older and less technology-savvy, are launching into the era of knowledge-sharing through technology. Past ways of attracting visitors through an established distribution system (the *place* and *promotion* of the marketing mix) have proven useful to a point in reaching visitors for your attraction. The problem is that the established distribution system relied quite heavily on visitors using tourism information centres at destinations, collecting paper brochures and using travel agents and tour operators for details. Of course we can reflect on the reality that today's visitors sit at their laptop, tablet or smart phone and make decisions about their visit using the technology. Maybe only reflecting on their original choices and knowledge (selection of choices) using personal contact or a hard copy document after they have identified the choices. So we need to establish the reality of the potential demand for the attraction through e-media and the following steps might prove useful to deliver returns.

Ways in which you can supplement the attraction

Having decided that your dark tourism attraction has the required visibility to the selected market and also has potential with as yet undecided market segments, you may turn your attention to diversification and deepening the demand from the potentials. Seasonality has an important impact on the delivery of your attraction to potential visitors. If you are subject to the highest demand during good weather then your focus might change to unlock the potential of those visitors who have unfulfilled needs for shoulder and low season demand during the autumn or winter. To unlock this potential you may need to turn to the local destination management organisation (DMO) and tourist information centres (TIC) to identify and accept partnership with existing attractions that have a higher than normal demand in the shoulder and low season. Let's now look at examples of this partnership in action.

Refreshments and attractions

Recent enquiries into successful ventures in tourism reflect on the critical role that offers of locally produced food and beverages play in connecting the visitor to the destination. E-media and social media websites are commonly visited before taking a trip. Visitors will consider a range of accommodation, dining and transport options at the time of considering the choices for the trip as well as at the time of booking. Inevitably visitors compare customer feedback through on-line reviews. Two key issues: does the attraction offer a range of recent feedback reviews; and do these reviewers also provide feedback on those ancillary services considered essential in the contemporary offer.

- Norwich Cathedral provides an excellent refectory, which is a purpose-built restaurant and function venue adjacent to the Cathedral. Visitors are aware that consumption of the heritage is inextricably linked to an offer for food. Reviewers rating the Cathedral are actively encouraged to review the food as well.

- The intriguing story of destruction and desolation post-eruption at Pompeii adjacent to the volcano Vesuvius in Campania Province close to Naples are typically surrounded by convenient restaurants and trattoria for visitors to consume locally produced food and drink in relative comfort and moderate cost. In fact many of the visitors establish the opportunity to consume local produce before setting off on the day tour (typical tours of Pompeii last four hours).

- The story of Hungary's oppressive recent past is well told in the Terror House museum on Andrassy Street in Budapest. The social media web reviews are full of places to eat and drink adjacent to the venue. There are valid reasons for attractions to miss out on visitors who will travel to the site and spend several hours on site but resist the chance to experience any extended visit if there are no viable refreshment venues adjacent. A sense of partnership in the vertical supply chain is now essential for the informed and discerning visitor.

- The United Kingdom's National Trust have understood the need for refreshments on site to contribute to the visitor experience and ensure their guests leave the attraction with a complete and well-rounded experience that incorporates various services that appeal to a wide range of current and potential visitors. Locally produced food and drink items are therefore important to help visitors to enjoy and immerse themselves in an experience. It is not surprising therefore that membership of the National Trust has doubled to four million in the past decade.

Heritage tourism and retailing

The Cathedral of Derby, All Saints, has some major heritage attractions that link the building to specific related sites around the City and County. One of these is the tomb of Bess of Hardwick, a contemporary of Queen Elizabeth 1st and an extraordinarily wealthy woman and latterly Countess of Shrewsbury and forbear of the Dukes of Devonshire through her marriage to Thomas Cavendish. The connection between Bess and the Guildhall Catacombs are presently being developed as a curiosity in the City's heritage and physically interpreted by Richard Felix, tour guide and ghost hunter. Central to Richard's offer is the unlikely combination of religious heritage and a retail experience in Derby's Irongate independent shopping street and the Derby Market place located immediately above the Catacombs. The key to successful management of the experience is the link created by Richard Felix in connecting the gruesome Catacombs with their black history of felons and miscreants to a site of religious worship and pilgrimage at the Cathedral and the Cavendish family heritage in the City and County.

There have been other notable projects linking heritage tourism and retailing,for example, York Minster and Harrogate in the north of the country, and the Natural History Museum and Victoria & Albert Museum and South Kensington retail experience in the south.

The key in linking partners in the heritage sector to major retailers is the exchange of ideas and concepts of understanding customer expectations and perceptions through pre- and post-visit surveys. The latest player is the National Trust, with an estimated four million members being electronically tagged for their time and date of visit and purchase of food and drink and retail souvenirs and branded products now underway. Dark tourism attractions survey their visitors by random sampling post-visit and identify what other attractions or products and services the visitor will also include in their visit to the site. Inevitably some form of periodic review of benefits and barriers is needed. Visitors' use of their disposable income is impacted by multiple factors which reflect changed economic, social, environmental and political factors that are beyond the control of the attraction or destination. Electronic point of sale, electronic admission and vehicle counts in car parks and access roads can help predict and forecast demand but some in-depth survey instruments gauging consumer expectations and perceptions on a random sample of visitors is an essential tool for measuring management interventions and reviewing strategies.

Natural environment and attractions

Demand for accessible leisure and recreation spaces has increased rapidly in an era of heightened awareness of the benefits of regular exercise and of the natural environment. This demand and awareness is linked to increased aspirations in most developed nations for self-actualisation and perceived as an inalienable right by us all. Today's visitors will continue to seek to build their own identity in the context of the site visited. In terms of dark tourism and heritage this extends to stretching boundaries and opening imaginations as visitors seek to relate to the past in the context of its present existence.

Commentators perceive this increased demand in the contemporary more-developed locations has a parallel growth in the expectation of physical engagement with space and places. This growth mirrors human desire to be active, not passive, and underpins a growing dialogue on co-creation and the ability of visitors to identify and agree on heritage that can be explored more fully with active participation of visitors and hosts at specific sites. So, a burgeoning demand for services and products that are co-created by hosts and visitors underpins the need for greater collaboration between site guardians at both dark tourism sites and natural heritage sites. We will examine specific examples of co-creation and integrated product offers in the case studies, Calke Abbey, Pitt Rivers Museum and Pompeii that follow.

Partners in consumption

There is a wide body of evidence from both attractions and from contemporary peer-reviewed academic research that partnerships are central to the ongoing health and future of the sector (for examples see Mariani et al 2014; Rusko et al, 2013; Kylanen & Mariani, 2012; Wang & Krakover, 2008).

Funding, originally derived from European Union grants, is still available to some regions where skills are in short supply (skills for identified development industries and services can include hospitality, catering, events and tourism) or where regional development is a critical issue for the destination where the attraction is located. In Derbyshire and Nottinghamshire (local economic partnership or LEP), arguably important destinations for UK and international visitors to the UK – for example the Peak District National Park and the legacy of legends like Robin Hood and Sherwood Forest – offer examples of where local government acts as a conduit to new start-up businesses. This LEP is currently evaluating ways to make natural and built heritage accessible to visitors and more productive to the local communities. The partnership that is created may be sustained by grant funding for several years; enough time to allow the organisations providing a visitor service to seek private sector funding for projects in the limelight with EU, ESF or ERDF grants.

Transportation partnerships

In Derby the existence and confidence of the transportation sector is important as a driver of the visitor sector. Rolls Royce, Bombardier, Toyota, JCB and others have important roles in two areas: initially attracting business tourism visitors to the sites and secondly, developing programmes to attract and entertain partner programmes and as hosts of delegates on meeting and incentive tourism activity.

There are two ways of attracting partnerships with these companies. Initially providing a venue for meetings and conferences. Additional opportunities through partner programmes for guests and partners of delegates include visits to related natural and built heritage attractions within the vicinity. Partner attractions provide accommodation and venues for entertainment and diverse activities that are perceived to be draw cards for the destination as well as the transport sector. Examples include Alton Towers, Chatsworth Estate, Haddon Hall, Wollaton Hall, day spas retreats and team-building venues such as Go Ape, East Lodge at Rowsley. Calke Abbey, one of the case studies, amply demonstrates how a bewildering and somewhat dilapidated eighteenth century aristocrat's residence can now be used as a venue for fund raising events such as summer outdoors film shows in addition to weddings and corporate events. The partnership at Calke Abbey between the National Trust and key corporate players such as JCB and Rolls Royce is not unique. What the partnership does demonstrate is that the stakeholders in all organisations understand how they can bring individual strengths in hosting guests at unique venues.

Training people

In this chapter we identified the need for effective communicators (marketeers and sales staff) as well as technicians who will enable you to use the potential of the web and open your site to new partners and collaborators in meeting visitors' needs. You will need to consider recruitment, retention and reward for the communicators and technicians. To ensure that you reach the proposed market you will need to give the recruits sufficient opportunity to work on your own product and liaise with partners in your supply chain. Traditionally the recruits will not consider that they are destined to work with hotels, food and beverage outlets, function venues, arts and crafts venues, performance sites and souvenir retailers. It becomes your role to engender within your recruits the concept of 'one industry' (see related examples from Barron et al, 2014; Deslandes & Goldsmith, 2015; Kokkranikal et al, 2011). You must ensure that vertical, horizontal and diagonal supply chain recruiters' needs are considered alongside your own. If these issues are not raised, you face the likelihood of competent and enthusiastic staff being poached away from your own business.

Volunteers

A gap emerges in the work place in the twenty-first century. Traditionally, younger recruits came from a background of temporary work in the service sector – a low wage sector typically not wishing to invest in recruits whose length of stay within an organisation would not exceed the limited time invested in training by the employer. Cafes, restaurants, bars, retailers and some events organisations have seldom, if ever, relied on volunteers.

Therefore, as the population ages and a disproportionate number of workers retire early, enjoy better overall health and standards of living, there is a new sector in which volunteers can develop their own esteem, build a new identity and become more adept and competent at job roles that traditionally were allotted to the elderly retiree or the green-behind-the-ears recruit from school or college (Holmes et al, 2013; Holmes & Smith, 2012).

Placements

In addition to non-traditional volunteering opportunities for the early retiree with a healthy outlook on life and an enthusiasm for a new identity we also note the importance of the paid intern on placement. If you elect to recruit from your local college or university, then advertise a paid placement to cover the busy season when colleges and students traditionally take a break over summer. Not only will you secure bright and enthusiastic new support staff for the times you need it, but also you will be able to maximise the return on supervision and training that accords with your values. Consider placements as short-term apprentices. These placements can also offer you a business advantage; they have skills, they have the flair and personality that you seek but they also provide a reserve of potential employees for the future when your business is ready to grow (Choudhury & McIntosh, 2013). Dark tourism attractions can also seek opinions and perspectives from placement students that will deepen the consumers' engagement with the attraction. We should not underestimate the diversity of views that volunteers and placement students bring to the refreshed exhibits and unfolding stories of our dark tourism heritage.

Recruitment

Visitor attractions depend on the spread of excitement, enthusiasm and entertainment that is promised in the marketing materials. To achieve the high levels of continuous performance required of dark tourism venues necessitates an investment in recruiting to the message and collateral provided rather than recruiting to a job description, and profiling potential employees that can use their initiative, innovate and enthuse without prompting. Recruiters must explore the boundaries of team working and role playing in the performance anticipated in the attraction. The other core behaviour and aptitude is empathy (Ladkin, 2011; Hjalager & Andersen, 2001). The high levels of emotional intelligence required are sometimes hard to inculcate in training programmes or within education. However it should be an imperative that any recruit has enjoyed prior experience of working with a highly dynamic and motivated team. The experience is important; the team work essential.

Reward

One of the ongoing rumours circulating in the market place is that star performance in visitor attractions work is not rewarded appropriately. Partly this is because tourism, hospitality and related performance in events and reconstructions is the domain of the young. Observations of rewards for high performance equate to early burn out, where recruits are often students earning pocket money or female employees who are paid below award levels. Both students and women are traditionally seeking employment that is short-term and therefore feature high levels of turnover and staff churn. Career development does not equate to short-term employment and high turnover of staff. Universities and colleges need to develop skills in recruits that feature a good understanding or practices of employees, supervisor and managers. Without embedding the skills in new recruits the cycle of short-termism and high churn will continue (Hausknecht et al, 2009; Hwang & Lockwood, 2006; Jolliffe & Farnsworth, 2003). Rewards can be expressed in terms of social hours, seasonal opportunities to take annual leave, performance bonus, team building excursions and opportunities to develop leadership skills (as is quite standard with most businesses).

The good news is that disposable income, whilst impacted by global recession and banking crises in 2008, is ring-fenced for most families in the United Kingdom and the outcome is that holidays are maintained as they were prior to the recession. Visitors are taking more holidays of a shorter duration; there are more people interested in taking vacations closer to home to reduce transport costs and avoid the vagaries of international travel. That means traditional visitor attractions can anticipate a market share equal or in excess of that split with international travel since 2007. Visitors are more demanding of performance, and reliability (repeated experiences and greater additional value for money) are keys to success.

What this effectively means for the new recruit is a burgeoning visitor industry at home and an emphasis on improved skills, and contemporary risks are minimised as consumer demand for high quality experiences is increasing. Jobs secured within the sector are paralleling exceptional consumer opinion (e-media) and increased profitability as visitor numbers increase, revenues improve with that increased demand and reputation is reinforced through multiple lines of communications.

Retention

Having developed high levels of performance, reliability and the results of investment in skills, attractions can focus on ways to avoid losing staff to competitors, staff electing to move into other services and self-managed businesses, or taking retirement or leave to move jobs and change roles in the sector. The cost of losing competent staff is high and outweighs the cost of recruiting new people. Attractions have the ability to manage careers with the support of professional networks such as Association of Leading Visitor Attractions in the United Kingdom (ALVA). The support of networks and partnerships established through marketing, through the supply chain and through the public sector should represent an opportunity for managers to steer existing high performing staff into careers that are rewarding, and recognised within the organisation and the sector (Deery, 2008). Benchmarking rewards and developing skills should be an annual review activity for all. Examples of annual reviews and benchmarking outcomes include Visit England's annual visitor survey –'Visits to Visitor Attractions'. This survey conducted annually reveals which heritage visitor attractions, including many ghost tours and sites of dark tourism, have improved on their visitor numbers. It also details admission fees which allows for price benchmarking.

Supporting diversification of skills within the attraction is also a driver of higher levels of retention. Allowing operational staff to contribute to special events and marketing to a more diverse audience is key to valuing and developing skills. Encouraging skills development in finance, people management, research and development will help reinforce messages of longevity and growing skills that the attraction needs for the future health and strategy is perceived as better than importing skills and new staff as expansion occurs. Growing people within the organisation breeds loyalty from staff (Ladkin, 2014; Robinson et al, 2013; Solnet et al, 2013).

The smart way forward: Triple Bottom Line realities

Central to the themes around managing people in any heritage environment is understanding the experience anticipated and, in almost all cases, demanded of the visitor. Visitors have specific demands of most sites that are marked by unique features – a visitor wants elements of the scarce and inimitable. Therefore the manager of an attraction must focus most attention on delivering what is special and innovative in itself and continuously seek ways to add value to ensure repeat performance is possible and that visitors feel a return visit may be signified by special features which can only be added by the site's manager. We should perhaps also acknowledge that what is being delivered and demanded in the experience is largely intangible. Sustainability demands that goods and services are delivered responsibly and locally sourced items contribute to the delivery. Finally, the site manage must respond to visitors' mobility and need for actualisation. The manager must deliver on inspiration for the individual and innovation for the site. Bourdieu would have us understand that the visitor is reflexive and sets the scene for themself by situating within the attraction, and to some extent would appreciate the opportunity to differentiate the offer and themself from others whilst at the site, and again, on reflection (Edensor, 2001). Special activities therefore to deliver on unique features are important differentiators and allow individual reflexivity and shared performance. Rituals that capture the selling position of the heritage attraction will permit shared and separate identities to be created, re-formed and reflected at various stages during and following consumption. These shared identities and reflections are important elements in sustaining credibility at the site and reinforcing shared values for visitors and importantly for staff on site.

The examples of Calke Abbey and the Pitt Rivers Museum strongly reflect the credibility of the individual values and beliefs of visitors and the shared experiences of staff and visitors at all stages during the experience. The visitor carries away an intangible experience of wonder, intrigue and a complete story; the staff devise further experiences and seek further stories to deliver against a stage which has compelling histories to recount. These are tools by which the staff and manager can provide experiences.

Sustainability and responsibility can reflect a commitment to building attachment to the site. Managers must seek to deliver experiences that commit staff and visitors to a shared history, or as Lewicka terms it, *roots* (Lewicka, 2005). The importance of authenticity and commitment to sustainability can be driven by attachment and creating an environment where the visitor is bonded to aspects of the experience through unfolding stories and issues that are refreshed and ever popular to visitors. As Johnson asserts, attachments and affiliation can be mediated through the array of objects, stories and the relating of narratives that link these to the visitor (Johnson, 1999). As mentioned at the outset it is the quality and consistency of storytelling that determines the reaction of visitors and the personal recommendation from reviews that visitors create. Without the ability of key personnel, in effect, all staff employed at the site, to relate the central story of the site with elements that register with a variety of visitors, there can be no consistent identity, brand and longevity. As has also been discussed it is the contribution made in co-creation by visitors and staff that determines relevance and eventually satisfaction to all engaged in the supply chain.

New forms of capital and heritage creation are delivered through the narratives and the compulsion to participate, immerse and audition for created on site. The interaction between heritage objects, sites and stories creates new capital shared between visitors and hosts. It is the quality and enduring value created which delivers sustainability and increased demand for social interaction. This interaction and the package of performance and objects is at the heart of new values and social capital underpinning the sustainability of the community and its offer, and the viability of the dark tourism attraction, longevity of the site and durability of the planning for future exchanges and trust between all stakeholders (Falk & Kilpatrick, 2000).

1: Pitt Rivers Museum, part of the Oxford Museum

Image 3.1: Interior of the Pitt Rivers Museum Oxford (source author)

Victorians were phenomenal and earnest world travellers. The founder of the collection at Oxford, now known as the Pitt Rivers Museum, was just such a traveller and authoritative archivist in the late nineteenth century. In the contemporary era of highly mobile, technologically interfaced travellers the concept of an authority on artefacts, collected somewhat haphazardly from a variety of sources, is engaging. The elements of the collection that provoke peoples' reaction comprise humble clothing and daily used items for meals and hygiene through to vicious tools of combat and domination. It is the collection, and the ephemera that create interest to current visitors. A traditional display in glass cases with dark mahogany cabinets through perceived dusty and ancient exhibits dramatically enhances the adventure, mystery and intrigue surrounding these eclectic attractions. Old stories can be re-told through the Victorian setting.

2: Calke Abbey, Derbyshire

Image 3.2: Old staff quarters, Calke Abbey, Derbyshire (source author)

In 2006, one commentator contested that "heritage held out the promise of a con-nection to the past, one that provided the promise of an almost familial relationship. As such, the past became projected as that which was held in common, a shared legacy that seemingly could bind a nation together even as its contemporary 'society' was publicly derided as a chimera. Heritage would then serve as a unifying concept" (Trimm, 2005: 5). This perspective is valid in a politicized context as the 1979 Tory government focus returned to national pride and highlighted specific icons of herit-age such as Calke Abbey, which is a reference point for Trimm. In fact, the UK National Trust was established with just such a mission, to conserve and present such iconic cultural heritage for all for the future (Daniels & Cowell, 2011; Sully & Malkogeorgu; ND, Brewster, 1997).

In the vicinity of one much visited English National Park is the enchanting yet dilapi-dated aristocratic residence of the Harpur-Crewe family of South Derbyshire. In the 1990s the National Trust took over maintenance and operations of the property and decided within weeks of taking over that Calke Abbey needed conservation in the state in which it was inherited by the Trust. Effectively that meant that no further work would be carried out to enhance the appearance of Calke Abbey and the property would be minimally maintained to demonstrate the ravages of time and nature's steady encroachment on the estate. This has had a positive effect for visitors to the site. Instead of viewing burnished gold, silver and tapestries the visitor can see the depredations of nature including rusting, water damage, decay and mould as essential components of the property in situ. Visitor numbers are rising (170,000 in 2013) and this unusual heritage site is attracting repeaters on the basis of its ability to deteriorate and have that managed and interpreted for all.

3: Pompeii

Image 3.3: Ash coated former resident of Pompeii (source author)

Our final case study is the ancient site of Pompeii, a wealthy market town close to Naples, of the Roman era and destroyed by the violent eruption of Mt Vesuvius in AD 79. Pompeii's interpretation and management is not dissimilar from Calke Abbey.

The site is prodigiously large and imposing and approached by two visitor entrances: one from the autostrada and one from the railway station. Visitors are immediately captivated by two issues: the first is the scale of the development; the second relates to the variety and demography of a Roman town. The very belief that human life and endeavour are unassailable and trappings and infrastructure are relatively impregnable, are immediate shocks and surprise. It might be fair to assume that visitors to Naples and its province Campania are almost always visitors to Pompeii and the tourist honeypots of Sorrento, Capri and Ischia. A contrast for visitors here is the managed experience of disaster interpretation commingling with the sunny shores of the Mediterranean and lemon groves and sailing vessels making their way around these shores. The juxtaposition of disaster and hedonic is interesting and not at all incompatible for visitors' expectations and perceptions.

Discussion

 1 How to deal with the competition: there is a thought that co-opetition is a smart way to keep your 'enemy' closer than your friends. In reality how do you manage expectations of consumers and suppliers when your 'enemy' has taken the vanguard position?

 2 How to refresh a sad attraction at no cost – often an attraction takes a hit when the crowd surges in and overwhelms what you want to offer visitors.

 3 How can partnerships and collaboration help marketing at dark tourism attractions? Even more important is the way in which networks bring in new resources, people and cash to keep your project alive, ahead of the crowd and a star repeat performance attraction.

References

Ashworth, G. J. (2010). Consuming heritage places: revisiting established assumptions. *Tourism Recreation Research*, **35**(3), 281-290.

Brewster, L. (1997). The Harpur Crewe collection of natural history at Calke Abbey, Derbyshire. *Journal of the History of Collections*, **9**(1), 131-138.

Choudhury, N., & McIntosh, A. (2013). Retaining students as employees: Owner operated small hospitality businesses in a university town in New Zealand. *International Journal of Hospitality Management*, **32**, 261-269.

Daniels, S., & Cowell, B. (2011). Living Landscapes. In J.Bate (ed.), *The Public Value of the Humanities*, London: Bloomsbury, pp. 105 -117.

Deery, M. (2008). Talent management, work-life balance and retention strategies. *International Journal of Contemporary Hospitality Management*, **20**(7), 792-806.

Deloitte MCS Ltd (2013) *Tourism Economy; Contributing to UK Growth*, Deloitte MCS ,UK.

Deslandes, D. D., & Goldsmith, R. E. (2015, January). Destination branding: A new concept for tourism marketing. In *Proceedings of the 2002 Academy of Marketing Science (AMS) Annual Conference* (pp. 130-137). Springer International Publishing.

Edensor, T. (2001). Performing tourism, staging tourism (Re) producing tourist space and practice. *Tourist studies*, **1**(1), 59-81.

Falk, I., & Kilpatrick, S. (2000). What is social capital? A study of interaction in a rural community. *Sociologia ruralis*, **40**(1), 87-110.

Hjalager, A. M., & Andersen, S. (2001). Tourism employment: contingent work or professional career? *Employee Relations*, **23**(2), 115-129.

Hausknecht, J. P., Rodda, J., & Howard, M. J. (2009). Targeted employee retention: Performance-based and job-related differences in reported reasons for staying. *Human Resource Management*, **48**(2), 269-288.

Holmes, K., Lockstone-Binney, L., & Deery, M. (2013). Constraints across the volunteer life cycle: Implications for Australian tourism organisations.

Holmes, K., & Smith, K. (2012). *Managing Volunteers in Tourism*. London: Routledge.

Hwang, L. J. J., & Lockwood, A. (2006). Understanding the challenges of implementing best practices in hospitality and tourism SMEs. *Benchmarking: An International Journal*, **13**(3), 337-354.

Johnson, N. C. (1999). Framing the past: time, space and the politics of heritage tourism in Ireland. *Political Geography*, **18**(2), 187-207.

Jolliffe, L., & Farnsworth, R. (2003). Seasonality in tourism employment: human resource challenges. *International Journal of Contemporary Hospitality Management*, **15**(6), 312-316.

Kokkranikal, J., Wilson, J., Cronje, P., (2011). Human empowerment, management and tourism. In L. Moutinho (Ed.), *Strategic Management in Tourism (2nd ed.), Wallingford: CAB International*, pp. 158-181.

Kylänen, M., & Rusko, R. (2011). Unintentional co-opetition in the service industries: The case of Pyhä-Luosto tourism destination in the Finnish Lapland. *European Management Journal*, **29**(3), 193-205.

Ladkin, A. (2014). Labour mobility and labour market structures in tourism. In A.A. Lew, C. M. Hall and A.M. Williams (Eds.), *The Wiley Blackwell Companion to Tourism*, pp. 132-142.

Ladkin, A. (2011). Exploring tourism labour. *Annals of Tourism Research*, **38**(3), 1135-1155.

Lewicka, M. (2005). Ways to make people active: The role of place attachment, cultural capital, and neighbourhood ties. *Journal of Environmental Psychology*, **25**(4), 381-395.

Mariani, M. M., & Kylänen, M. (2014). The relevance of public–private partnerships in co-opetition: empirical evidence from the tourism sector. *International Journal of Business Environment*, **6**(1), 106-125.

Robinson, P., Lück, M., & Smith, S. (2013). Tourism as employer. *Tourism*, 55-82.

Robinson, M. and Picard, D. (2006) *Tourism, Culture and Sustainable Development*, Division of Cultural Policies and Intercultural Dialogue, UNESCO.

Rusko, R., Merenheimo, P., & Haanpää, M. (2013). Co-opetition, Resource-Based View and Legend: Cases of Christmas Tourism and City of

Rovaniemi. *International Journal of Marketing Studies,* **5**(6), 37 – 51.

Shaw, G., Bailey, A., & Williams, A. (2011). Aspects of service-dominant logic and its implications for tourism management: Examples from the hotel industry. *Tourism Management,* **32**(2), 207-214.

Solnet, D. J., Baum, T., Kralj, A., Robinson, R. N., Ritchie, B. W., & Olsen, M. (2013). The Asia-Pacific tourism workforce of the future: Using Delphi techniques to identify possible scenarios. *Journal of Travel Research,* 693-704.

Sully, D., & Malkogeorgou, P. (ND) The preservation of Calke Abbey: Romantic ideas and contemporary values. *Public Archaeology.*

Trimm, R. S. (2005). Nation, heritage, and hospitality in Britain after Thatcher. *CLCWeb: Comparative Literature and Culture,* **7**(2), 8.

Wang, Y., & Krakover, S. (2008). Destination marketing: competition, cooperation or co-opetition? *International Journal of Contemporary Hospitality Management,* **20**(2), 126-141.

Weaver, D. B. (2013). Asymmetrical dialectics of sustainable tourism: Toward enlightened mass tourism. *Journal of Travel Research,* **53**, 131-140.

4 Goth Tourism:

Sun, sea, sex and dark leisure? Insights into the tourist identity of the Gothic culture

Pascal Mandelartz

Abstract

This chapter sheds light on 'Goth tourism' through a postmodern lens, as it is sceptical of concrete definitions of the term Gothic and what it means to be part of the Gothic subculture. These often claim to be valid for all groups, sub-subcultures, traditions, and interpretations. Instead this chapter focuses on the travel preferences of individuals who identify themselves as being Goth. Having used the 4Ss theory (Sun, Sea, Sex and Sangria) as a starting point to characterise Gothic Tourism, the 4 Hs theory (Habitat, Heritage, History, Handicrafts), seemingly described the traits of Gothic Tourism more coherently. Each aspect of the 4Hs theory is elaborated in comparison to the findings from research conducted during two Gothic Festivals in Whitby, thereby enabling insights into perceptions, attitudes and travelling decisions made by members of the subculture, allowing for a localised characterisation of the term Gothic Tourism.

Learning outcomes

1 To view the Gothic subculture through a touristic and postmodern lens.

2 To outline similarities between the interpretations of Gothic subculture and indigenous cultures in regards to tourism.

3 To appreciate the importance of niche segments within the tourism market.

4 To establish the characteristics of Goth Tourism.

Introduction

Architecture, tribalism, literature, aesthetics, music, fashion and art, various meanings have been attached to the term 'Gothic'. Some people have created a lifestyle and subculture of what in their interpretation is associated with the term. "From counter-culture to subculture, to the ubiquity of every black-clad wannabe vampire hanging around the centre of Wes tern cities, Goth has transcended a musical style to become a part of everyday leisure and popular culture"(Spracklen and Spracklen, 2012: 351). There is plenty of literature on Gothic identity and culture (see Hodkinson, 2002; Lee, 2012; Spracklen and Spracklen, 2012). Notwithstanding, there seems to be a gap of literature concerning Gothic tourism.

Only few authors have taken on the topic. These studies are place-specific (McEvoy, 2010; McDonald, 2011) or introducing the term (Hughes, 2003; Trower, 2012). This research investigates the subcultures' interpretation of tourism and identifies characteristics of the Gothic traveller. It attempts to answer where members of the subculture travel, what attracts them to a destination, which role the subculture plays in the decision-making process of where to travel, and to gain an appreciation of destinations' push and pull factors considered by Goths by applying the concepts of 4Ss tourism and 4Hs tourism to interpret primary data.

Background/postmodernity

The aim of this research does not lie with the participation in the debate on what is part of the subculture and what is not, but focusses on attitudes and perceptions of travel intentions of members or those who consider themselves members of the Gothic subculture. Nonetheless, there are aspects within the debate that are of value to this study. Spracklen and Spracklen (2012) in their study identify the differences in interpretation of the Goth identity using the concepts of dark leisure (Rojek, 2000) and communicative and instrumental rationalities (Habermas, 1984, 1987).

Dark leisure is associated with intentionality and agency. Individuals in postmodernity have the freedom to choose to reject mainstream leisure forms in favour of ones that disturb. Postmodernism within this research is understood, as per Eagleton (1985), as the process of wakening from the totalitarian ideas of modernity into the laid-back pluralism of the postmodern, that heterogeneous range of lifestyles and language games which has renounced the nostalgic urge to totalise and legitimate itself. What is valuable for postmodernist theory is more the formal fact of plurality of these cultures than their intrinsic content

(Eagleton, 2013). Said (1993: xxv) furthermore suggests that "all cultures are involved in one another; none is single and pure, all are hybrid, heterogeneous, extraordinarily differentiated, and unmonolithic".

Dark leisure is the kind of leisure activity that rejects the mainstream, transgresses norms and values and allows the people undertaking that leisure to identify themselves as liminal, deviant, alternative, rebellious non-conformists (Rojek, 2000; Williams, 2009). Communicative rationality is the application of free reason and democratic discourse to the construction of the public sphere, the way in which we discuss and make choices about the things we do in life (such as the sports we play and the books we read, or the parties we vote for), ideally free from constraint: a rationality that constructs what Habermas (1984) calls the lifeworld. Tourism is also a part of most people's lifeworld and the Gothic subcultural aspects could be an influential factor in the decision-making process. Howbeit, it raises the question of whether it is utilitarian to the body of knowledge to further elaborate on such a postmodern niche market.

Ontologically speaking the answer is yes. What Dracula and vampires have done for Yorkshire's tourism, and Whitby's tourism in particular is incalculable in terms of marketing and promotion of the destination as well as providing part of an identity. In terms of numbers, tourist chiefs have approximated that Goths contribute £1.1m per annum to the local economy (BBC, 2012). The Whitby Goth Weekend attracts around 10,000 people each year (*The Guardian*, 2015) and Gothness is not just a Yorkshire phenomenon. 18,000-20,000 people attend the Wave Gotik Treffen in Leipzig, Germany each year. Additonally, there are Ghost Walks, Renaissance fairs, Viking and Pagan markets, Gothic Romance events, film premieres, literary readings, artist signing events, brunches celebrating absinthe, fetish events, and many late-night clubs which are regularly frequented by members of the subculture. Tourist attractions like the Dennis Severs House also have a huge following in this particular subculture.

So how can we go about conducting research on this particular market segment? One focus would be to look for common themes amongst those who identify themselves as part of the subculture. The subculture is seemingly acting as an umbrella term for a wide array of meaning and interpretation, which the author believes to be created through the notion of postmodernity. This is mirrored, for example, in the highly fragmented and diverse range of musical genres and styles, which Fey (2000) has summed up as folk, metal, punk, Gregorian chants, baroque minuets and old world musical instruments as well as in the fashion aesthetics, ranging from bondage trousers to space-age inspired outfits to Victorian and Edwardian costumes.

The question is what influences trends like these within the subculture and will such diversity be represented when it comes to tourist choice? A possible impact might come from the use of the internet. We cannot deny the influence of the media, social media and the growth in information and availability of trends and fashion. Although for some this may constitute a form of entrapment for others it may represent freedom of choice, access to information and greater flexibility (Goulding, 2003), thereby impacting on perceptions and response mechanisms.

There surely exists a wide spectrum of differing groups within the Goth subculture, but what is interesting in terms of tourism studies and an oxymoron in terms of postmodernity is their commonality, the underlying foundation of their motivations to travel to Gothic destinations and events. When investigating such a diverse range of individuals, which nonetheless have communality, in keeping with the postmodern spirit, it would make more sense to examine each specific context and to look for localised theories which give rich, critical and meaningful insights into contemporary consumer experiences.

Theoretical debate

People seem to be prisoners of the instant and caught in the increasingly complete elimination of meaning which leaves them with a kaleidoscopic culture. Spracklen and Spracklen (2012) provide an example for this suggestion from the investigated subculture: "when we arrive in Whitby, there is a preponderance of people in Victorian fancy dress, but there is little in this playful costuming that could be identified as essentially Goth: no fetish wear, extravagant hair or makeup. It is, in fact, as if someone has misunderstood the definition of Goth subculture as something to do with Victorian Gothic (which is not necessarily true, Dracula notwithstanding), and has given out the order to dress accordingly" (Spracklen and Spracklen: 354). The dilemma is that each individual is holding their own definition of what it means to be Goth. Without a general definition, who is to decide what part of the subculture is and what is not? To those in Victorian fancy dress it is probably their idea of being a Goth. Cultures as well as subcultures are constantly evolving, being reinvented, interpreted and possibly commodified.

What does this kaleidoscopic nature and perspective bring to the travel intentions of those who consider themselves 'Goth'? Within contemporary postmodern society Goth does not have to be the meta-narrative of people within the subculture but rather one aspect amongst many as people are multiform. There can be no 'ultimate' truth (Firat and Venkatesh, 1995). Constructionist theory holds that humans are social constructs and that their social spaces of all sorts are constructs upheld by humans acting according to their images of reality. Possibly, we are therefore attempting to construct a new 'reality' that is Gothic tourism.

Spracklen (2009) raises the question of how authenticity can ever be understood when everything is a construction of some kind. It is argued that performance of the tourist role or the performativity of subcultural identities such as Goth presupposes an understanding by agents of the roles and scripts that are permissible on the public stage and the work involved to pass (Goffmann, 1971). Performativity, then, relates to questions of the authentic: how do agents demonstrate their authenticity? How do they pass – as 'real' tourists or Goths? In this study it is argued that it is the individual's interpretation of a certain role. How to behave as a tourist or how to dress and behave as a Goth are certainly not set in stone. In fact they are just labels to begin with, in the case of Goths probably even given by outsiders. Sticking to these overarching definitions is therefore dismissed within this research as the belief in a meta-narrative rather than postmodern pluralism.

The same might be true for the term Goth or Gothic tourism, which, as far as the literature is concerned, is about visiting dark, fiendish and gloomy locations. It is about the aesthetics and architecture and themes that can be related to the term Gothic. The spectrum includes the likes of Dracula, torture museums, ghosts and the Dennis Severs house in London. But is this just another modernist stigma of trying to pigeonhole people into classifications and segments and are these people in reality interested in Sun, Sea, Sand and Sex as suggested when marketing to the mass market? Unfortunately there seems to be a gap of knowledge when it comes to defining Gothic tourism, which is hardly surprising considering the debate as to defining a Goth or more ridiculously levels of Gothness, where the Victorian fancy dress is a little bit Gothic, and the fetish and hair is a little bit more Gothic, and what does a person have to do to be truly a fully-fledged Goth? In the context of this research, it raises the question whether Gothic tourism is concerned with travel to destinations with a Gothic vibe or whether Gothic tourism is describing the travel and tourism undertaken by members of the subculture? This study focusses on the people and their travelling intentions and the role the subculture plays in the decision-making process.

Goth Tourism: Sun, sea, sex and dark leisure: insights into the tourist identity of the Gothic culture. The title was selected to represent possible motivational factors for the Goth community to travel to a certain destination, assuming that in the postmodern culture there would be elements from mass tourism represented within the subculture nonetheless. Whilst trying to identify the origins of the 4 Ss theory (sun, sea/sand, sex, sangria), which are labels acting as metaphors for all tourism, tourism has to be located geographically (sea/sand), have a relationship with landscape (sea/sand), visiting patterns determined by climate (sun), involve exploration, entertainment and activities (sex) and requires food and drink (sangria) the author came across the 4 Hs theory. Just as the four Ss are used to describe the tourism phenomenon, the 4 Hs (habitat, heritage, history and handicrafts) describe the indigenous tourism phenomenon (Smith, Butler and Hinch, 1996). These features of indigenous tourism seemingly match those present at Gothic tourism attractions and events. They allegedly offer useful insights not only into how Goth tourism may be defined but also into subcultural motivators. This brought forward many more commonalities of indigenous people and the Gothic tribe.

There is no single definition of indigenous culture but there are several characteristics that are used to describe this anthropologic segment, i.e.:

- The voluntary perception of cultural distinctiveness

- An experience of subjugation, marginalisation and dispossession

- Self- identification.

The United Nations Development Program (2004) furthermore includes:

1 Self-identification and identification by others as being part of a distinct indigenous cultural group, and the display of desire to preserve that cultural identity;

2 Linguistic identity different from that of the dominant society;

3 Social, cultural, economic, and political traditions and institutions distinct from the dominant culture;

4 Economic systems oriented more toward traditional systems of production than mainstream systems;

5 Unique ties and attractions to traditional habitats and ancestral territories and natural resources in these habitats and territories.

Butler and Hinch (2007) raise awareness of the limitations of this definition as culture is dynamic and that there is an ever-changing contemporary dimension to these groups that does not invalidate the indigenous status although it may complicate it. This might also include the Gothic tribe.

Indigenous tourism refers to tourism activities in which indigenous people are directly involved either through control and/ or by having their culture serve as the essence of the attraction. The factor of control is a key in any discussion of development. Whoever has control or exercises power generally determines such critical factors as the scale, pace, nature, and indeed, the outcomes of development.

As per the seemingly astonishing similarities of indigenous and Gothic tourism, it was found to be useful to apply the 4Ss as well as the 4Hs as benchmarks in defining Gothic tourism. The blurred boundaries of the authentic, the commodification of a culture by outsiders, the hyper-reality and staged authenticity created by the tourism industry in places like Whitby are traits all seemingly shared by the two forms of tourism. A difference is that compared to indigenous tribes, the Gothic tribe never had a geographical territory they could call their own. But like indigenous people seeking spaces and places where they can live their cultural norms and values, so do members of the Gothic tribe. An example comes from Hodkinson (2002) stating that at Whitby Goths could dress as playfully as they liked, and feel safe from abuse and lascivious gazes from outsiders.

So how can we start characterising Gothic tourism? The author considers Goth tourism to be a postmodern phenomenon and postmodern theories have offered insightful explanations of cultural phenomena, but "the foremost priority should be the effective and situated study of consumers and consumption" (Miles, 1999: 146). For this research the author therefore conducted his study at Whitby Goth Weekends in November 2013 and April 2014. The concepts of 4Ss tourism and 4Hs tourism will therefore act as benchmarks to structure the data analysis and discussion further elaborated within the following section.

Methodology

In theory a postmodern approach could offer tremendous opportunity for representing consumer experiences in a rich and vivid manner, drawing upon a wide array of techniques to illustrate the phenomenon. Within this research this included walk-along interviews, observational notes and photography. This also leaves the researcher with more freedom within the research process to adapt to, and adopt changing situations.

The primary research was conducted at Whitby Goth Weekends in November 2013 and April 2014. The Whitby Goth Weekend is a music festival for members of the Goth subculture but also attracts various other related subcultures and market segments interested. It takes place twice a year in Whitby, North Yorkshire, England. It includes various fringe events such as gigs, ghost walks, club nights, markets, a custom car show and a charity football match. The event brings quite a substantial economic benefit to the town of Whitby as the Goths contribute £1.1m per annum (BBC, 2012).

The researcher chose street methodology as a means of investigating the subculture and their behaviour. The method attached to street phenomenology are go-along or walk-along interviews which is a combination of participant observation and interviews, where the researchers accompany individual informants on their activities and through asking questions, listening and observing actively exploring their subjects' experiences and practices as they move through and interact with their physical and social environment.

This form of research has many advantages. Walk-along interviews are a systematic and outcome-orientated version of 'hanging out' with key informants. This practice, rooted in ethnography, is often highly recommended in virtually all fieldwork manuals and textbooks as a key strategy. The paradigm is beneficial for this research as the subjects are within their subcultural environment and were easily identifiable but also because they are 'on the move' and engaged in activities.

20 such interviews were conducted with festival participants that could easily be identified by their costumes and fashion sense. Field notes were taken as well to support the observation. The sample was randomly selected amongst those who attended the festival and considered themselves part of the subculture. Within the following discussion, it would be beneficial to present the findings from the primary research in relation to apposite theory and concepts from the literature, thereby facilitating an engaging debate.

Discussion

The discussion section is structured around the themes which emerged from the theoretical discussion and the primary research. This includes 4Ss, 4Hs, identity, Goth related travel, other travel interests and postmodernity. Findings will be evaluated, providing examples from the primary research. These have purposefully been presented as 'raw' data allowing the reader to interpret the examples in relation to the theoretical concepts themselves, thereby providing touristic insights into the subculture.

Sun (climate)

One hypothesis that stems from the 4 Ss theory is climate as a pull factor to a destination.

Poon (1993), describes this form of tourism as inexpert, standard, mass tourism in search of hot weather and a suntan within the framework of a rigidly packaged holiday. At the Whitby Goth Weekend climate does not seem to be the main criteria to visit the destination or indeed the reason for the Gothic subculture to hold their biggest gathering within the UK in this coastal town. Admittedly, Whitby is not renowned for its warm suntan climate. Nonetheless there is some evidence that suggests that Whitby's climate does have a certain appeal to the Gothic subculture.

From observational notes:

'At dusk, we are following the crowds, a mixture of Victorian, Vampire costumes and other extravagant fancy dresses towards the illuminated Whitby Abbey. We walk the 199 steps past the decaying gravestones of St Mary's Church graveyard, whilst overviewing the coastline. As we are approaching the Abbey a thunderstorm is brewing, causing the waves to crash even heavier against the coastline whilst thunder is grumbling and the night sky is brightened from lightning. This causes quite the excitement amongst the visitors. It seems to be one of those moments where the imagination of a place is matched by reality. The momentum almost portrays a feeling of staged authenticity and hyper-reality as if planned and outlined within a film script. As if in analogy to my thoughts some people are starting to make howling sounds to add to the atmosphere.'

Robin Jarvis, the author of *The Whitby Witches*, a trilogy of young adult novels, recalls "The first time I visited Whitby, I stepped off the train and knew I was somewhere very special. It was a grey, drizzling day but that only added to the haunting beauty and lonely atmosphere of the place." As sun is only regarded as a metaphor for climate, one might suggest that climate does play a role as a destination attraction factor, especially when matching the aesthetics of the subculture. This is also true for the geographical location.

Sea/ sand (geographical location)

Connected to the above is the geographical location, as it is important for tourism providers and destinations to match the expected image which has been constructed. These tourist images often become self-perpetuating and self-reinforcing. Whitby seems to reflect the Gothic image of a place best in terms of climate, geography, architecture and aesthetics. Another destination mentioned quite often in the interviews was York.

There was a general consensus amongst those interviewed about their interest in the aesthetics, architecture and history of the destinations they have visited and would like to visit in the future. One could almost suggest a certain geekiness in their responses as they passionately talk about Cathedrals visited and the beauty of their architecture (see Figure 4.1), but this is only one activity amongst many.

Image 4.1: Photos of Whitby/ illuminated Abbey

Sex (activity)

The activity when visiting Whitby Goth Weekend for members of the sub-culture is seemingly a given. The activities are centered around the main festival, where the main attraction are the music acts performing as well as WGW fringe events, which have over the years have almost become as important as the main event. Sex does, however, play an important role, especially in connection to fashion and in some cases lifestyle. This also becomes obvious when visiting the market stalls and seeing the clothes on offer. Other activities include visits to Whitby Abbey, and for many posing and having their photographs taken.

Image 4.2: Photo of person posing

One might suggest a certain similarity to other forms of tourism, including indigenous tourism, where the tourist gazes upon the host often resulting in a commodification of that culture as also outlined in the film *Framing the Other* by Kok and Timmers (2011), in which Western tourists come to see the unusually adorned natives from the Mursi tribe in Ethiopia; posing for camera-toting visitors where they embellish their 'costumes' and finery in such a manner that less of their original 'authentic' culture remains. The difference here is that many members of the subculture seemingly seek the attention. Lee and Gretzel (2013) speak about the 'mutual gaze', in which tourists and hosts gaze upon each other and those gazes are influences by the media, reinforcing stereotypes where the relationship is shallow and superficial but where fixed images can change through real and close interactions. In Whitby however it is not about hosts and guests, as many locals are part of the subculture, it is the dominant culture having an interest in the exoticness of the subculture and the subculture in that case is happy to get the attention. People can portray their subculturally infused images and the ordinary can gaze upon the extraordinary. As the examples suggest this also attracts a big crowd of photographers seeking unique images, some of them possibly with questionable intentions.

Sangria (food and beverage)

F&B does play a role as visitors are gathering in the restaurants and pubs around Whitby as meeting places. The webpage for WGW also announces that "The Spa Pavilion also has a bar and a kitchen open during the day for the sale of alcohol, soft drinks, tea, coffee and food" (Whitby Goth Weekend, 2015). Although drinking with peers is a component of the festival it can be doubted that it plays any major role within the decision making process of where to travel as a member of the subculture, but certainly is a component of the experience.

Habitat

The United Nations Development Programme (2004) in regards to characterising indigenous cultures talks about unique ties and attractions to traditional habitats and ancestral territories and natural resources in these habitats and territories. Examples from the interviews underline this being the case for many Goths as they are showing a keen interest into the architecture and aesthetics of a place (see Figure 4.1).

Image 4.3: Cologne Cathedral

Heritage

For the purpose of this chapter, heritage tourism is defined as per Timothy (2011, p4) as 'travellers seeing or experiencing built heritage, living culture or contemporary arts...visits are motivated by a desire to enhance one's own cultural self, to learn something new, to spend time with friends and family, to satisfy one's curiosity or simply to use excess time, it encompasses a multitude of motives, resources and experiences and is different for every individual.' As being Goth is regarded as a subculture in its own right, the culture also becomes a part of people's identity. Linked to this identity is a sense of belonging and acceptance from 'your' group. This may be linked to sexual identity as well as cultural festivities as outlined in the interviews (see Figure 4.1).

History

Connected to the heritage is the history of a place. In the case of Whitby there is the Abbey but also the pop-cultural artefact of the novel *Dracula*. Sugawa-Shimada (2015a, 2015b) in her research about the Japanese Rekijo subculture talks about a pop-culture-mediated pilgrimage to sites that are related to historical events, resulting in changes to the consumption of pop-cultural products. She questions whether this attraction stems from a nostalgic appreciation and reconceptualization of 'Japanese-ness'. As this chapter has created a link between pop-culture and indigenous characteristics the nostalgic appreciation and reconceptualisation of British heritage or even a common European heritage might be questioned in the same way. The image (Image 4.4) relates to 'Mr & Mrs Hazel', the Victorian undertakers.

Image 4.4: Photograph of Victorian Goths, image courtesy of Si's Photography, Whitby 2013

The performance historians have appeared at Whitby a number of times in relation to Halloween and the Goth Festival. They perform a show/presentation in which 'Mr Hazel' recounts the nature of the death-cult in Victorian England and it concludes with the children (and some adults) being dressed as characters in a funeral procession - the vicar, mourners etc. who, after processing, arrive back at an authentic 'Gothic' coffin for a 'funeral service', after which tourists are offered the opportunity to see 'Great Aunt Eliza' for the last time - she is in the coffin. The lid is lifted and there is a 'corpse', in a shroud, in the coffin and everyone then has their photos taken. Indeed a morbid sounding activity, but related to history and heritage and presented in a popular cultural manner. The 'undertaker' re-enacted by John White states that the funeral is a very popular activity for visitors at the Goth weekend. (see www.selectsociety.co.uk)

Handicrafts

Image 4.5: Photos of Market stalls, Whitby (source author)

Many members of the subculture engage in handicrafts and selling products on market stalls, as well as at pagan or medieval markets. This is best depicted in photos of the market stalls at Whitby, including the Bizarre Bazaar. The official website reads:

> We're pleased to announce an additional new official trading venue for the Whitby Goth Weekend's Bizarre Bazaar Alternative Market. In addition to the Spa Pavilion and Whitby Leisure Centre, WGW will also be hosting Trade Stalls in The Brunswick Centre.

> The venue will mostly feature traders that are new to the Goth Weekend, but will obviously be of the same high standard that you have come to expect from the Goth Weekend's official trade stalls.

> Located halfway down the hill on Brunswick Street between the Little Angel Pub and the Bus Station, this beautiful 200 year old Grade 2 listed former church still retains many of its original features.

> Just around the corner from the legendary Elsinore where the event has its roots and a few short steps from Whitby's perennial Goth shop Pandemonium, it couldn't be a more fitting place for WGW. We

envisage this as being a perfect venue for those selling gifts, jewellery, accessories and hand made goods. So, if you'd like to be part of a whole new chapter of WGW then please come along and visit us in the Brunswick Centre.

Whitby Goth Weekend, 2015

Some visitors also mention their enthusiasm for markets and handicrafts.

Overarching 4Hs/ indigenous identity

There are several characteristics used to describe the indigenous culture which have a resemblance to the Gothic subculture.

- The voluntary perception of cultural distinctiveness

- An experience of subjugation, marginalisation and dispossession

- Self- identification

- Self-identification and identification by others as being part of a distinct indigenous cultural group, and the display of desire to preserve that cultural identity;

- Linguistic identity different from that of the dominant society;

- Social, cultural, economic, and political traditions and institutions distinct from the dominant culture;

- Economic systems oriented more toward traditional systems of production than mainstream systems;

- Unique ties and attractions to traditional habitats and ancestral territories and natural resources in these habitats and territories.

Extracts from the interviews, which can be directly linked to these characteristics, demonstrate the analogy between the two terms (see Figure 4.1).

Interviewees are identified by their research reference numbers and preferred travel destinations

Travel characteristics	Indigenous identity	Notable comment
1 The goth festival in Leipzig, Germany, Croatia		
Subcultural, Habitat, History, Heritage	Self-identification and identification by others as being part of a distinct indigenous cultural group, and the display of desire to preserve that cultural identity. Economic systems oriented more toward traditional systems of production than mainstream systems	A lot of non-goths attend these festivals. I could never do an all-inclusive package where you just all day lay on the beach. Music is a big part of it. Interviewer: What sort of gothic sites do you like? 'Cathedrals.' 'I study architecture … and I am looking for something a little bit esoteric.' It is the way to go and if you are young you can make your own clothes. It's not like it's made by "George". I have had a firework thrown at me.
3 Regional. Doesn't travel abroad often, visits Whitby annually.		
Subcultural	An experience of subjugation, marginalisation and dispossession	We haven't actually travelled overseas as customs was too much of a hassle. Boots off, hats off. I remember the last trip we had abroad and the guy was quite angry at what I was wearing and I said if I was a terrorist would I actually want to stand out? Would I actually look this different? And he could not say anything. 'We have been coming for the last 19 years so we have seen it basically from the beginning. We like the clothing and it is an extension of what we have at home and you can go slightly madder than you would when shopping at home as where we come from people are a little "chavtastic".
5 Regional. Camden, Manchester, Sweden, International		
Subcultural, Habitat, History, Heritage	Social, cultural, economic, and political traditions and institutions distinct from the dominant culture An experience of subjugation, marginalisation and dispossession	I would identify Camden Town as being more welcoming than others. They all have their one area, and Manchester has some areas that are friendlier. The gays, bi-sexual and transgender all come to festivals like this as it's about finding acceptance and sometimes these go hand in hand I am really into architecture. I am trying to plan a trip to the Netherlands as it's quite famous for its gothic architecture. Yes I had some friends who struggled to find work as they had tattoos and piercings. I had one friend recently who was fired due to his sexuality so he is taking them to Court. It is a difficult area when it comes to employment. In an ideal world, every company owner would say "well, you do what you want it's fine"

7 Frequent traveller, International		
Subcultural, Habitat, Heritage	Social, cultural, economic, and political traditions and institutions distinct from the dominant culture	Gothic does have special attraction as we got married up here as it meant we could be gothic with our wedding. Yes we do a lot of city visits and we go and look at the architecture then. We go and look at a lot of gothic churches for the architecture.
8 Alternative festivals, Regional, International, Prague		
Subcultural, 4S		It is good in Prague. You can have beer breakfasts.
9 Alternative festivals, Transylvania		
Subcultural	The voluntary perception of cultural distinctiveness Economic systems oriented more toward traditional systems of production than mainstream systems	'There are gothic cruises. You can go on a Gothic cruise liner. Yes you can Google it. They have a huge shopping areas and all sorts of things organised – like crèches for children. I think money stops people now when you come to Whitby on the Friday there is a 'bring and buy' and I got my coat last year at a ridiculous price as someone did not want it anymore. And I got a pair of £175 boots for £45. There is a train that takes you to Transylvania.
10 Alternative festivals, Regional		
Subcultural		It is all sub-culture related yeah.
12 Frequent traveller, International		
History, Heritage, 4S		Whitby and York are my favourite destinations but I've just been to Cuba as well.
14 Regional. Wales		
Subcultural, History, Heritage, Habitat		I stick within the UK, if I do go abroad, it has to be somewhere with some history. Here at Whitby, Lincoln, York, anywhere with castles and I love Wales. Interviewer: How much of your travel is sub-culture related? 'About half of it. I do visit a lot of places with family so that is not like this.'
17 Regional, Whitby, York		
Heritage, Habitat		Whitby and York as well.
18 Regional, International, Frequent traveller, York		
Heritage, Habitat		Around this area, York. I like Leicester and here and Eastern Europe as well. I have been to Germany quite a lot. I like travelling in the UK as well, we like Whitby. I have been to Scotland.'

20 Regional. London, Cornwall, Lake District, York	
Heritage, Habitat	We like Yorkshire and the Lake District and we go down to London for a little bit, been to Cornwall.

Figure 4.1: Travel patterns of Whitby Goth Weekend attendees

Goth subculture related travel aspects

Apart from certain traits shared with indigenous tourism there are many other aspects which stood out from the interviews. First and foremost subcultural events that are related to the Gothic scene attract the Gothic tourist. Without wanting to state the blatantly obvious, it is important to mention the vast array of sub-categories of these events which are often music and fashion related. To name but a few, there is the relation to Punk, New Wave, Metal and Rock music genres.

The fashion includes a wide spectrum of androgynous, Victorian, Steam Punk and postmodern combinations of all of the above. Many identify themselves more within their subgenre but regard Gothic as part of it or as the main influence. Steam Punk, for example, merges Victorian imagery with quirky technology. The links between the Steam Punk and Goth culture are the Victorian writers who inspired the genre, including Mary Shelley and Edgar Allen Poe. The communalities are often difficult to understand from an outsider's perspective and perhaps even for an insider. Again, there seems to be a fragmented reality. First generation Goths may have a different definition of the term than Steam Punk Santa or the guy dressed up as Beetlejuice or a cross-dresser attending the event. Each person will most likely offer you their personal experience of what they perceive to be Gothic and their individual interpretation of the term. What is important within the context of this chapter is how this relates to the Goth as a tourist. Attracting the Gothic tourist may require catering for a wide array of sub-genres within the scene which is a given in Whitby as well as in Leipzig in Germany, two of the main venues for the genre.

Another characteristic that can be highlighted from the primary data is the keen interest in culture, especially regarding poetry, history and Gothic architecture, which seem to be two important pull factors for the Gothic tourist. This supports the notion of Dunja Brill who intensively studied the subculture (2007, 2008) stating that Goths are refined and sensitive, keen on poetry and books, not big on drugs or anti-social behaviour and are also likely to stay Goths into their adult life. There seems to be a possibly underestimated sophistication in the travel desires of the Gothic tourist.

Being against anti-social behaviour was another factor frequently mentioned in the interviews. Those interviewed emphasised on the importance of a tolerant environment whilst travelling, an environment where you can 'be yourself'. Contrasting itself to mainstream society often has caused prejudice, intolerance, non-acceptance and sometimes even violence against the members of the sub-culture, meaning that a lot of them feel that they can only safely dress up in their fashion within certain places and spaces. When travelling, this often means to 'dress-down' to not be offensive, which is also happening in many other tourism contexts when one culture clashes with another.

Overall it can be said that the travelling desires of Goths are incredibly diverse as the subculture is only a single component of the individual's identity. This could mean that one Goth is averse to mass tourism, whereas another person does not mind at all.

Image 4.6: Steam Punk Santa, photograph courtesy of Marta Johnston, Whitby, 2013.

Postmodernity

The previous sections have offered plenty of indication for a kaleidoscopic and fragmented identity of the Goth tourist in which 'Goth' is individually interpreted and re-interpreted. It is a common denominator under whose umbrella a vast amount of sub-genres and sub-subcultures are mingling. Nonetheless, conjoined themes and interests do emerge which do allow constructing insights into Goth tourism. The following are examples that underpin the postmodern nature of the Goth tourist identity.

	Postmodern narrative	Notable comment
1	Subcultural Identity, Fashion	*Interviewer:* What does Goth mean to you guys? It is a lifestyle. *Interviewer:* Would you identify yourself as a Goth? Yeah.
2	Fashion, Kaleidoscopic	Most Goths are weekend Goths. *Interviewer:* What does the gothic sub-culture mean to you? Fuck all.
3	Subcultural Identity, Fashion, Costuming	We like it all – we do a lot of the Victorian, the Literacy and the Steam Punk so we can dress up and put on what we wish. We are very, very alternative all the time and at Whitby you can go and nobody bothers but at home you have to be slightly more circumspect. But we do push the boundaries.
4	Subcultural Identity, Fashion, Photography, Voyeurism, Costuming	You were getting dirty old men round all the young girls and they were dressed up like Little Miss Muffet. There was one girl and basically she was dressed up and a really pretty girl. She is a steam punk and there is all these dirty old man creeping round her and taking pictures and it's just weird. This is my first time here and she was just posing. There are a few women here who must like dressing and love the attention. I found it creepy as you have got all these guys dressed up in this weird stuff and a few guys dressed up as women as well. There was a girl dressed up in all this lacy stuff and all the old men were crowding round her taking pictures and I'm like oh fucking hell. To dress up and it's very newsworthy and you get some good pictures taken as obviously people here dress like this
5	Subcultural Identity, Kaleidoscopic	I would struggle to define myself as I don't think that anybody is a particular theme but I love the gothic culture and all of the subculture of being Goth. My philosophy is: 'if you have got it - flaunt it' and if that's what you want to look like, well you look like it. You have every right to identify yourself as who you want to be.
6	Fashion, Kaleidoscopic, Voyeurism	I am just generally interested in all things fashion rather than being a Goth. *Interviewer:* Are you here for the Goth week? Of course. I just come as I love fashion and I love to see what people wear.
7	Subcultural Identity	It is about self-expression and coming out and enjoying yourself in an atmosphere that is relaxed and dressing in a way that you would not normally dress. *Interviewer:* Is the expression dome mostly via dress? For me it is but I know a lot of the people come for the music. I know if you look on the notes on the Facebook page for Whitby there is even a split on there between the Victorian gothics and the modern gothics and the modern gothics just come for the music festival side. And later on in the evening the Victorian gothics come.

8	Kaleidoscopic	*Interviewer:* What type of music are you into then?
		Anything you can think of, it is diverse and not settled to one sort. Yeah it's pretty broad to be honest.
9	Costuming	Age wise it goes across all ages and there are lots of different genres, including Johnny Depp Pirates of the Caribbean, Screaming Faces.
		There is an elderly man here and we know him as Beverley from Birmingham as he has a Cinderella dress. A great big Cinderella dress and he is here every single year. A person we met last night is an MD and he dressed as a female with all the makeup, the rings and the net – everything. His wife is very pretty she makes all her own clothes and she said that her daughter doesn't know and they do it all behind closed doors. Keith wears his clothes all the time socially.
15	Kaleidoscopic, Subcultural	No I got dragged into the Goth one and got hooked because of the Steam Punk. So most things are Steam Punk.

Figure 4.2: Postmodern Perspectives of Whitby Goth Weekend attendees

Conclusion

Studying the Gothic tourist from a postmodern point of view enabled rich and vivid descriptions that portray the characteristics of this subculture, which within itself is deeply fragmented. However it was possible to identify notions which can be used to demarcate the Gothic tourist, as the subculture is a common denominator amongst those that identify themselves as members of the genre. Even if 'Gothness' only depicts a small part of the individual, there are traits which help to define this segment. Denotations of indigenous cultures seemingly describe the Gothic culture well. There is the voluntary perception of cultural distinctiveness, an experience of subjugation, marginalisation and dispossession, self-identification and identification by others as being part of a distinct cultural group, and the display of desire to preserve that cultural identity; social, cultural, economic, and political traditions and institutions distinct from the dominant culture with many variations amongst the different sub genres; handicrafts that resemble economic systems oriented more toward traditional systems of production than mainstream systems; and unique ties and attractions to traditional habitats and ancestral territories evidenced through the passionate interest in history.

When making travelling decisions, the culture and history does play a role, aside from the wish to visit Transylvania. Goths are drawn to destinations that cater for their needs by acknowledging the many subgenres and offering entertainment and cultural attractions for them, which in many cases could be more sophisticated than a host might anticipate. Acceptance by the host and the host culture also plays a main role in this. Many Goths are seeking destinations where they can express themselves freely without being stigmatised. It is an incredibly diverse niche market which is bringing economic benefit to many destinations, as tourism products like the Gothic cruise by Carnival Cruises indicate, and as Brill (2006) states "They won't like me saying it, but their life-style...is a middle-class sub culture."

Discussion questions

1   Which characteristics of the Goth outlined within the chapter can be identified as postmodern?
2   What are the differences between a Goth and a mainstream tourist?
3   What attracts Goths to Whitby?
4   Is the Gothic subculture similar to indigenous cultures?
5   How important are niche markets such as the Gothic to the tourism industry?
6   How do the definitions for indigenous tourism (Overarching 4 Hs/ Identity) relate to the examples from the interviews?

References

BBC (2012). *Whitby's Goth visitors' £1m seaside bounty.* Available at http://www. bbc.co.uk/news/uk-england-york-north-yorkshire-20188996. Accessed on 29th June 2015.

Brill, D. (2006) in Winterman, D. (2006) *Upwardly Gothic.* Available at http:// news.bbc.co.uk/1/hi/magazine/4828230.stm. Accessed 29th June 2015.

Brill, D. (2007). *Fetisch-Lolitas oder junge Hexen? Mädchen und Frauen in der Gothic-Szene.* In: Gabriele Rohmann (Ed.), *Krasse Töchter. Mädchen in Jugendkulturen.* Berlin: Archiv der Jugendkulturen KG.

Brill, D. (2008). *Goth Culture: Gender, Sexuality and Style.* Oxford: Berg Publishers.

Butler, R. & Hinch, T. eds. (2007). *Tourism and Indigenous Peoples: Issues and Implications.* London: Routledge.

Eagleton, T. (1985). Capitalism, modernism and postmodernism. *New Left Review,* **152,** 60-73.

Eagleton, T. (2013). *The Idea of Culture.* New York: John Wiley & Sons.

Fey, J. (2000). Spirituality bites: Xers and the gothic culture. In R. Flory & D. Miller (Eds.) *GenX Religion,* London: Routledge, 31–56.

Firat, A. F., & Venkatesh, A. (1995). Liberatory postmodernism and the reenchantment of consumption. *Journal of Consumer Research,* **22** *(3),* 239-267.

Goffman, E. (1971). *The Presentation of Self in Everyday Life.* Harmondsworth: Penguin.

Goulding, C. (2003). Issues in representing the postmodern consumer. *Qualitative Market Research: An International Journal,* **6**(3), 152-159.

Guardian (2015). *Gothic weekend in Whitby – in pictures.* Available at http://www.theguardian.com/uk-news/gallery/2015/apr/27/gothic-weekend-in-whitby-in-pictures. Accessed on 29th June 2015

Habermas, J. (1987). *The Theory of Communicative Action, Volume Two: The Critique of Functionalist Reason.* Cambridge: Polity

Hodkinson, P. (2002). *Goth: Identity, Style and Subculture.* Oxford: Berg.

Hughes, W. (2003). An angel satyr walks these hills: 'Imperial Fantasies for a Post-Colonial World'. *Gothic Studies* **5**(1), 121-128.

Jarvis, R. (2015). The Whitby Witches. Available at http://www.robinjarvis.com/whitbyhome.html. Accessed on 30th June 2015

Kok, I. & Timmers, W., (Dirs.) (2011). *Framing the Other.* 25 minutes. English and Mursi with English and French subtitles. Netherlands and Ethiopia. I Camera You/ Ethiopian Film Initiative co-production.

Lee, A. (2012). Popular music (Goth Rock) as a popular culture. *Culture Scope,* **95**, 18-23.

Lee, Y. J., and Gretzel, U. (2013). Perceived host gaze in the context of short-term mission trips. In Moufakkir, O., & Reisinger, Y. (Eds.). (2013). *The Host Gaze in Global Tourism.* Wallingford: CABI.

McEvoy, E. (2010). West End Ghosts and Southwark Horrors: London's Gothic Tourism. In L. Phillips & A. Witchard (Eds.) *London Gothic: Place, Space and the Gothic Imagination,* Continuum Literary Studies, pp. 140-152.

Macdonald, K. A. (2011). This desolate and appalling landscape: The journey north in contemporary Scottish Gothic. *Gothic studies,* **13**(2), 37-48.

Miles, S. (1999). A pluralistic seduction? Post-modern consumer research at the crossroads. *Consumption, Markets and Culture,* **3**(2), 145-163.

Poon, A. (1993). *Tourism, Technology and Competitive Strategies.* CAB International: Wallingford

Rojek, C. (2000). *Leisure and Culture.* London: Sage.

Said, E. W. (1993). *Culture and Imperialism.* Vintage.

Smith, V. (1996). Indigenous tourism: the four Hs. In R. Butler, & T. Hinch (Eds.), *Tourism and Indigenous Peoples.* London: International Thomson Business Press, pp. 283-307.

Spracklen, K. (2009). *The Meaning and Purpose of Leisure.* Basingstoke: Palgrave Macmillan

Spracklen, K. & Spracklen, B. (2012). Pagans and Satan and Goths, Oh my: dark leisure as communicative agency and communal identity on the fringes of the modern Goth scene. *World Leisure Journal* **54**(4): 350-62.

Spracklen, K., & Spracklen, B. (2014). The strange and spooky battle over bats and black dresses: The commodification of Whitby Goth Weekend and the loss of a subculture. *Tourist Studies, 14(1), 86-102.*

Sugawa-Shimada, A. (2015, January). Rekijo, pilgrimage and 'pop-spiritualism': pop-culture-induced heritage tourism of/for young women. In *Japan Forum* **27** (1), 37-58.

Sugawa-Shimada, A. (2015). 'Rekijo'and heritage tourism: the Sengoku/ Bakumatsu boom, localities and networks. *The Theory and Practice of Contents Tourism=* コンテンツツーリズムの理論と実例, 21-26.

Timothy, D. J. (2011). *Cultural Heritage and Tourism*. Bristol: Channel View Publications.

Trower, S. (2012). On the cliff edge of England: tourism and imperial gothic in Cornwall. *Victorian Literature and Culture* **40** (1), 199-214.

United Nations (2006). *United Nations Development Programme.*

United Nations (2015). *United Nations Development Programme.*

Williams, D. (2009). Re-thinking deviant leisure. *Leisure Sciences,* **31**(2), 207-213.

Whitby Goth Weekend (2015). Whitby Goth Weekend News. Available at http://www.whitbygothweekend.co.uk/news.php?item=54, Accessed 2nd June 2015.

5 Deborah:

Having a personal connection to what has been variously described as dark tourism, thanatourism, death tourism and macabre tourism

Tim Heap

This chapter is about having a personal connection to dark tourism, but it is also an attempt to provide an alternative to the term 'dark tourism'. I have never been happy with the term, neither through academic snobbery, nor as an attempt to be critical of those who have used it, and by their use have confirmed it within mainstream tourism writing. I was, however, confronted with its 'power' as I read an article in a respected academic journal, where the authors had canvassed views of 'icons, memorials and cemeteries' and that 'dark tourism' was complicated by the religiosity of the 'visit' by the tourist. It was noted as being essentially about religion and pilgrimage, a review of cultural capital (or creation) and about turning memory into history or vice versa and it is 'where religion meets consumerism'. Wow! Now I know. In today's secular society I did wonder at religion being the focal point, especially as none of the primary research referred to questions on religion and belief.

The chapter contains many questions within the text (sometimes one after another) that can be taken as rhetorical or used to stimulate debate/discussion about views, opinions, and thoughts about your associations with dark/light tourism. The emphasis is upon you, and there is no need to validate them through referring to the academic texts, but only to validate them within your own sense of belonging to those moments.

The discussions and many other articles I read all seemed to provide circular arguments as they increasingly relied upon referring to each other whilst frequently admitting that there is little empirical research as to why people visit. Did the term 'become invented' and then an academic body arose from the 'darkness' to justify the term as was done years ago with the 'New Tourist' and more recently with 'Pro Poor Tourism'. I also now know from further reading that apparently war tourism and dark tourism sites are not really connected, and that we visit heritage sites such as war cemeteries because we feel morally obliged to do so. I wondered; obliged to whom or what? I also found out that commemorative events are intended to reinforce a sense of national pride. I am still trying to establish who decides what constitutes a dark tourism site and who decides which is in and which is out, before I can explore such complex notions as national pride.

I thought I had better join my own group of one on an individual journey, and individual experience, on my own journey towards 'Light Tourism' in the hope that others would follow and so arouse another academic body from the 'darkness'. My own experiences and reflections outlined in the chapter are an attempt to provide an alternative viewpoint as I introduce the term 'Light Tourism'. This, it could be argued, is simply my postmodernist position alongside those many academics alluded to above who have positioned dark tourism in their own ways; but I think that we may emerge out of darkness into light in the process of viewing, exploring and consuming those sites, and within the reflections that come from those sites. In my opinion, many historical dark tourism attractions include artefacts for remembrance, are 'of an age' thereby enabling us as individuals to make sense of that history and finding our own place within an historical context.

Is it about unravelling the past as evidenced by many people who, for example, are increasingly interested in investigating their family trees thereby confirming how 'brave', 'interesting', 'on the dark side' their ancestors were. This could be as simple as finding a name etched on a memorial that contains thousands of names with no known graves. How many of us look for our own surname on those memorials or in cemeteries, and when we find them wonder how, if and where we are related? So the question whether dark tourism is about contextualisation for the individual made me wonder about the darkness, of the experiences being more light than dark. Have I re-joined the dark tourism debate?

The discourse is about exploring the contrasting emotions that arose whilst in the process of creating a medium to view and consume, that 'dark/light side' within the physical context of a relic from the First World War. The chapter emerges from a personal relationship with a female First World War mark IV tank named (Deborah D51) that is to be the centre piece of a 21st century 'visitor attraction'. She appears as a metaphor of the First World War as she stands as a rusty memorial; on one side with two small shell holes and on the other side blown apart by those shells (Images 5.2 and 5.3).

Image 5.1: Deborah D51 1919, amid the destruction of war.

Image 5.2: Deborah D51 2015, reincarnated.

Image 5.3: The author, 2010, with the ghosts of 1917.

My association is through my grandfather (2nd Lieutenant Frank Gustav Heap) who commanded Deborah at the battle of Cambrai in November 1917 and was awarded the Military Cross for bravery during the action in which she was disabled. The relationship is mixed with the horror of her destructive powers, the actions my grandfather took, and the seconds in time that saved his life; meaning I am here to write this chapter. But also how that has been softened by her emergence from the grave where she was buried on the battlefield she died in, which could appear as a reincarnation.

My journey from darkness to light is therefore through pilgrimage, confirming my identity and placing myself within a series of stories that leave Deborah in 1917 and follow through two world wars to the present day. The medium for displaying Deborah is to be through a new visitor centre being built in Flesquieres in Northern France which aims to tell the 'stories' of the Battles of Cambrai in 1917 and 1918. From the beginning I was worried that we will perhaps simply create a 'hyper-reality of death' by positioning Deborah back in the battle and providing the sounds and lights of explosions, of death, smells and anything else that modern visitor attractions seem to think are necessary to interest the public. This is something I would not want, as in my mind it is the people that matter in the end, but is there really room for a personal view within a tourism industry that commodifies, constructs and then brands within a product portfolio for a set of 'demographics/consumers'; and then makes money? Is the actuality that it is necessary for the individual to construct their own dark tourism product to avoid consumption being controlled by an industry that sees the packaged heritage of war as an attraction for pilgrimage, entertainment, remembrance, education and controversially a celebration of death? Among the most visited sites of the First World War are: the largest monument to those with no known grave, the tragedy of the first day of the Somme, the grave of the youngest person to die in the war, the largest cemeteries, the biggest mine crater, etc. So many battlefield tours cover the same well-trodden tracks across Northern France; it is as if we are already 'packaged' and do not dare to be different

The chapter is, therefore, a narrative, a story, a series of reflections, but also an attempt to personalise, distance and lighten our associations with war, destruction and death. Deborah emerged from her 'bunker' on the Hindenburg line in 1988 and was re-introduced to my family in a bizarre set of circumstances/co-incidences, which in themselves are light not dark. My brother William was working at the proofing range in Bootle, Cumbria at the time she was brought 'back to light' and was talking to a major from the Tank Corps whilst on a break from proofing tank shells. The major was reading an article about a First World War tank that had been recovered from the battlefield of Cambrai in Northern France. William was shown the picture and he immediately realised it was 'grandfather's tank' or 'bus' as he had grown up with the picture of Deborah hanging on a wall in the house. He went home, returned with the picture (Image 5.1) and our association with her was born.

Thinking again about that picture makes me realise that grandfather's association was perhaps not a dark association, as why would he want to be reminded daily of the 'horrors' of war'? Did he have the picture framed as a celebration, a remembrance of the crew that died the day she was destroyed? Was this actually the epiphany for him as he had survived those few moments of her destruction? Had he actually enjoyed the memories of war as the horrors faded? We often attach the revulsion of horrors as reasons for silence in veterans, could it perhaps be the silence of guilt that they were happy to survive or actually 'enjoyed' those intense moments of war and killing? We shall never know in grandfather's case as he took his thoughts with him to his grave, meaning I can attach altruistic motives and not dark motives to his actions.

My own association again began with a chance meeting; in this case as we were passing through Cambrai for a few hours on the way to Switzerland. In a car park I noticed three people wearing poppies and could not resist asking them where they were visiting.

'We have been to visit the tank'.

I replied: 'You mean my grandfather's tank'.

This seems now like an obvious attempt on my part to be involved in their experiences, and probably to show off even though I had not even seen Deborah at that time. As we talked about the tank and my grandfather I began to feel very guilty as these people had found out about Deborah, made the trip across the channel to see her, to consume, to wonder and were obviously full of collective pride in my grandfather's achievements and began to laud me simply for being his grandson. There was nothing in their conversation, demeanours or expressions that were in any way dark; the event was more of a celebration. We went straight from the car park to find Philippe Goryzinski at Hotel Beatus and began a 13 year love affair with Deborah.

Since that meeting and her emergence from death, I have been increasingly involved with her reincarnation, through my first and most important friend from Deborah that I met that day: Philippe Gorcynski. A very special man who located and reincarnated Deborah, and whose passion for what is right has led to the building of the centre to house Deborah. The process and continued involvement with Deborah has made me think deeply about the relationships we must all have with death and destruction. We may not all have such direct links with death as I do, but we all seem to increasingly need to search for those links as we justify, or come to terms with the past. We cannot see ghosts; but I can see the ghosts within the body of Deborah as I was aware of the crew that were in the tank and the five men that died with her. That first time I viewed Deborah I was standing looking into her inner soul and imagining the horror created by the explosions and felt that strange personal sense of guilt that grandfather survived and I was here to experience those emotions. The family story is that he got out of the tank to orientate himself with the use of a map and compass, which was often affected whilst inside by the metal of the tank. The tank was then hit by a shell from a German gun concealed behind the wall of the house in the picture. I have always believed the story, but was it really embellished by my grandfather for the benefit of my father, an apocryphal tale that has survived the 80 years of telling? It had to be 'seconds' not 'minutes' as the time factor is crucial in the telling. But I have my evidence in front of me in Deborah because if grandfather had been sitting in the commander's seat when the shell exploded he would have undoubtedly died in 1917. My selfish thoughts are upon his miraculous escape and not on those crew members who died when he was in the act of commanding from the outside!

To come to terms with those hidden emotions it was necessary to find the relatives of the men who died in those few seconds, so as to suggest they still live in other people's hearts. If there were no relatives then any links in terms of letters, medals, photographs etc. must serve as those tangible links with the men. I suppose it was necessary for me to justify my presence by the presence of other relatives who had similar links to Deborah. The search for the crew was led by

Philippe and carried out by an incredible team of people (now further friends from Deborah) who were all drawn to Deborah not out of a wish to reconstruct horror or to create an aura of mystery, but to understand how she died, where she died, and what were the stories of the crew and their subsequent families. You only need to read John A. Taylor's book in press called; *Deborah and the War of The Tanks* to fully understand the detail that that team unearthed.

The following letter was discovered during this process and was written by my grandfather to the parents of George Foote four days after the tank was destroyed and George had died. The letter is full of clues about my grandfather and it confirms him in my mind as a hero, sincere, caring, brave, religious and driven to 'avenge' the crew. But that makes him even more of a real person and not simply a picture in a museum.

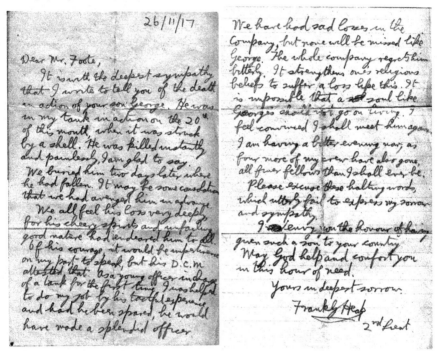

Image 5.4: Letter to Mr. Foote from Frank Heap, November 1917

He wrote (in pencil with many crossings out); '*It may be of some consolation that we had avenged him in advance*'. Grandfather is telling us that he killed Germans and that the tone seems to relate to it being not just a duty, but also a 'settling of a score' and 'justifiable vengeance'. He sounds as if they had enjoyed the process, maybe for the benefit of the parents where his friends needed to do so in his memory, but perhaps more realistically to justify his own actions. In my mind he must have been a hero as straight after the destruction of Deborah he was in action again and I glossed over any other images.

'*We buried him two days later where he had fallen*'. The significance is that he did not die in vain as they had battled to keep the ground upon which George had lost his life. These words were meant to relieve the darkness. '*He was killed instantly and painlessly. I am glad to say*'; words of sympathy and understanding for the parents that for all we know may have been lies, but I can justify those lies in my mind. '*Of his courage, it would be impertinence on my part to speak*'; this is my grandfather expressing how much braver George was than himself, and as he had won the Military Cross then George had committed actions of bravery far above Grandfather's actions. This is reinforced by '*he would have made a splendid officer*'. The language is of its day, but shows my grandfather to have been an educated man, but then I knew this as he had attended King's College in Cambridge before the war; as a successful sportsman if not a diligent scholar!

He continues to paint a picture of both his surroundings and his distress at losing the members of his crew in; '*I am having a bitter evening now, as four more of my crew have also gone, all finer fellows than I shall ever be*'. My picture is of this brave man sitting in his dugout on a cold November night with the sounds, smells and terrors of the battle around him as he tries to paint that picture for George's parents and '*I did not get out of this lightly and I cannot keep those dark images from my mind*'. It ends with a reinforcement of his religious beliefs and a statement that needs the emphasis upon 'envy'; '*I envy you the honour of having given such a son to your country.*'

Returning my gaze at Deborah, I realise that she needs to be shown to the world as she is unique; she has a story and is simply amazing to look at. Her guns have been taken away and in their place are simply holes where the destructive powers of the machine guns dealt death to untold German soldiers. Has her darkness become something that is suggested as opposed to being real, has she softened? The dilemma is how does that fit with the increasing demand for real accounts of destruction, I equated it with the us and them of my imagined battles against the Nazis played out by myself and friends on the mountainsides in the Lake District where I grew up in the 50s and 60s. In my mind I killed those Germans just as if I had been in Deborah in 1917, even though I had no notion of death, of war, of conflict, but subconsciously I still had to fight the battle and here was the proof that my family were involved in killing real Germans.

The association with Deborah very quickly became an association with my grandfather, as exampled above in his letter and pictures, and my thoughts about him emerged as a perfect being of the 1950/60s comic books; the superhero instead of a purveyor of death. The little I know or remember of grandfather is mainly anecdotal as he died when I was only 5 years old, so I relied upon my brothers, my father's brief anecdotes about grandfather and the pictures of a happy, smiling, larger than life individual – one of which hangs in my house. But how much of our dark and light impressions of dark tourism sites are based upon such hearsay and tentative evidence? In Auschwitz we have the tangible evidence and the darkness is obvious; on the battlefields of the Somme we have rising ground and our imagination. Do we need something or someone else to paint the picture, and what is the truth of that picture?

My grandmother had divorced him, but he still left money in trust for her when he died, he was still in love with a memory up until his death; he was very capable of love and loving. So he becomes a 'nice' vehicle from whose perspective I can view death. The survivors of D-Day recently on our screens were described by commentators and writers as 'lovely' individuals, not because they survived the death and destruction and killed people, but because they became old, and had forgiven. Do we view those butchers of Auschwitz any differently today as they appear as benign old men with old memories and apologies? Do I need to review my thoughts about Deborah simply because she 'survived' to tell the story, and that she is in fact 'nice'? Am I really playing games with my thoughts on the death of the crew, simply because it is right to do so? Do I need to construct death and destruction to remember, or simply take the benign view? How will others want to view Deborah, will they be interested in my association with death, and is this chapter really about 'Light Tourism' as opposed to 'Dark tourism'?

Image 5.5: Frank Heap, 1930s, climbing in the Lake District

I have pictures of my grandfather climbing on Pillar Rock in the Lake District with a rope tied around his waist, a nonchalant pose with no look of fear or concern as to the danger of the situation. It is a staged photograph (he climbed a lot, but was not really a natural climber), but does the staging actually tell the truth about the man? Does our presentation of Deborah needs to be staged within the context of the truth? This confirmation of a man who knew no fear is not a dark experience, but is one that lightens the association with a person who killed other men. Deborah was the vehicle for that destruction ,so does she take on the aura of a Jean d'Arc, burnt at the stake, but on the right side? The next image is of him standing beside a car in the '30s in a snow covered landscape (probably in the Lake District) that softens the picture of a man (grandfather), the ubiquitous pipe in his mouth benignly looking down on a boy (my father) who is dressed in shorts (in winter). Not the darkness of a man who takes his son walking in the Lake District in winter wearing shorts, but the father looking after this small boy. The pipe is crucial to the scene that is playing out as it is safe and suggests security. My thoughts are continually being reinforced with the notions of good guy, upstanding, adventurous and heroic who killed Germans in Deborah because it was obviously the right thing to do at the time, and probably can still be justified today. The Germans, however tried to destroy this man and Deborah – just look at the holes, the destruction, the melting of the aluminium block on the engine, imagine the heat, the confusion, the death.

Are all the crew similar paragons; are they all in memories of others as the great uncle, great grandfather who fought in the Great War? Must we develop a set of positive images and stereotypes because if they really enjoyed the death and destruction, then could I really accept them into granddad's tank? The brave commander of built upon, constructed images and second/third hand recollections would simply not allow this to happen. Can Deborah actually then remain dark in any sense of the word?

I was now putting the Germans into neat dark boxes called hatred, distrust, enemy and death. But how could that be as my mother was Austrian; my Austrian grandfather was on the German side in the same war, how can I accept that he was in that box and that in my dark tourist mind I had put those Germans in the compartment for the bad guys. Is it necessary to do so or is it simply that dark tourism is really an attempt to package death in a sort of 'gory way' without right and wrong and Deborah does that with her evidence of destruction and is divorced from the individuals?

'Did they find any bodies in the tank when they dug it up'?

'No'.

'Oh' is all I ever get back from the questioner and from the rest of the audience as I have, on occasions, stood in front of Deborah and explained how she died.

'Oh so there is no real association with death' seem to be the thoughts going through the minds of the audience.

Have we forgotten the Germans in the story of Deborah?

My Austrian grandfather (Josef Repetschnig) fought against the Italians in the Dolomites when 'grandfather England' was driving his tank around 'some foreign field'; was he another paragon? This was Alpine trench warfare where the battles were often two to three thousand metres up in the mountains, played out in ice and snow and among rocks that created 'amphitheatres of death'. You only have to stand by the ossuary at Verdun and look across the valley to understand that notion of 'amphitheatre'. There was fear of avalanches, blizzards and strong winds and rock falls alongside the machine guns and artillery shells. Movement was always difficult, but often impossible with evacuation of the injured and the supply of munitions, food, medical supplies and men requiring tortuous routes through the mountains. This was the 'Somme with attitude'; this was seriously dark. According to my mother (Josephine Heap, nee Repetschnig) he hated the Italians and never forgave them for 'taking' a small part of 'his' Austro-Hungarian Empire. His hatred would probably now be re-enforced by the 'celebrations', the 'commemorations' and the museums of these battles for the hundred years being in the Trentino Alto Adige region centred on the museum in Roverto. The interpretation boards are only written in Italian, and the Austrians have not been involved in the process or the outcomes of those reconstructions of the battles; to the winners go the 'spoils of war', a hundred years later. I am now taking sides against the Italians, but is this not what our personal exploration with dark or light tourism is all about? Otherwise we return to the interpretation of the academic, the historian ,whose views are naturally the 'right ones'.

My sister (Heidi Foster, nee Breulich or Repetshchnig) tells of how he ran away from the Italians and from certain death as he escaped over the Dolomites; was he a coward? My uncle Willie (a Luftwaffe pilot in the Second World War) took me to the area in which granddad had fought high up in the mountains (the rusty metal ladders still fastened to the rock up which the soldiers carried all their supplies), and he in turn had not forgiven the Italians for stealing a part of his history. My images are of bravery, strength and determination, and not of the hardship and the death and the suffering; my thoughts are light. These are then confused with the dark as he had died in the Lienz Krankenhaus in 1942, still a young man, but one who drank to forget and also smoked continually to calm his nerves frayed by his experiences in the mountains. This was Willie talking, he who flew in spotter planes in the Second World War whilst being based in Norway looking for allied convoys on the Russian run. Willie who was regaling me a 16 year old boy with stories of being back at base enjoying being a pilot, adored by Norwegian girls when the death and destruction was happening out in the North Atlantic away from his sight and mind. 'Wasn't he lucky', not 'he was creating the scene for killing allied sailors'; he was a funny uncle not a harbinger of death. 'Do we like the Russians or the Italians?' were the thoughts that played through my mind.

How funny was it when he told me how he was captured by American soldiers following the Normandy landings? He and a friend had walked towards the Allied lines rather than take their plane up to almost certain death. They had walked towards the Americans with a mind filled with propaganda about these evil people from the U.S. that would probably torture them before killing them. There was double fear as they had thrown their pistols away so if they had met other Germans they would be shot as deserters. This is real dark tourism; this is playing with death, but now without Deborah. As they walked down a deserted lane they were suddenly faced (no impact if it had been 'gradually faced') with Americans 'festooned with grenades, bandoliers of ammunition, chewing gum and unshaven' (straight from my picture books); his words, with an emphasis upon 'unshaven' as if a German soldier would be unshaven, or even a German pilot in the act of deserting! The first words of English were 'let's go'; he had no idea what they meant, but he put his hands up and hoped for the best. Not a hero, but a very scared and timid man. He was captured and spent nearly two years as a prisoner of war in England. 'We were building prefabricated houses in South London and could not believe how nice the English were; they gave us tea as we were clearing the rubble from bombed out houses, destruction that had been caused by our comrades in the Luftwaffe'. He explained that he had been taught English so when he returned to Austria he was able to start a business, as he could deal with the army of occupation who spoke English. He said this as I was sitting in his new Mercedes as we drove up to the Franz Josef House overlooking the Großglockner, the highest mountain in Austria. I thought him as brave as my grandfather and as 'light' as it was possible to be, he was forgiven by his enemies as they had recognised that he was a good man and therefore he could not continue on the side of the bad men of the comic book and my box.

I then thought of my sister Heidi born in Austria in 1943, her father a German soldier (Hans Breulich) from Leipzig who died at the siege of Stalingrad, knowing about his daughter, but never seeing her. Again the mixed emotions of the sadness of death contradicting my thoughts of if he had not died I would not be here to write this chapter. There were two versions of how my mother and Hans got together; the English version was about mother being 'raped' by a German soldier (no name as he did not merit a name), but the Austrian version was of two people obviously in love as they posed for a picture in Obervellach prior to Hans going to the Russian front. He looks confident in the picture like my English grandfather in his, as after all the German army were still pushing the enemy back as they retreated farther into Russia. After he died my mother had to hide in the mountains as Hans' mother and sister came to look for Heidi, to take her back to Leipzig; as their son was a hero of the Reich, the Austrians could not resist their claims. If they had found my mother and Heidi I would probably have never seen her as the images from Leipzig are amongst the most dark of the Second World War. But it turned out to be light as Heidi came to the UK in 1957 to live with us and married an Englishman and had four children in her new home.

My sister had told me of my uncle Johan Repetschnig (Hansel) who was called up into the Hitler Youth when he was 16 and sent to the Russian front in 1944. He returned alive, but not the happy carefree boy that had left, but an arrogant, cruel person that when he got married beat his wife and his children. That his oldest son committed suicide at 16 years of age by hanging himself is perhaps testament of the impacts of his cruelty. When I visited Austria I was never allowed to meet Hansel as he had 'had an accident' and was in a special hospital. My mother blamed Hitler, not the war, as she had loved her young brother and I think felt guilty that she could not protect him. She by then was in England.

Have I moved too far away from Deborah, are the links becoming tenuous to the concepts of Dark and Light tourism? How can these stories have any resonance to anyone but me and how do they show there is something called 'Light Tourism'? The answer probably lies with Deborah, where during early meetings to discuss how she was to be 'presented' to the consumer within the context of the wider picture of the Battle of Cambrai (and subsequently Battles of Cambrai to include the one in 1918), it soon became apparent that we (stake-holders) all wanted individual inputs into that construction and management. I felt that my personal involvement with Deborah was fading as the realization dawned that my position was perhaps a selfish one. I thought about the many battlefields I had visited and how the significance of the individual was lost within the descriptions of attack, counter attack, mistakes, bravery, and failures and vanity.

Within all these constructions, acts of individual bravery were highlighted, often presented by the medals and defined by self-sacrifice for the greater good. The written words were well presented and often poignant, but they were someone else's words. I thought "Deborah does not need words – she is the battle, she is the metaphor, and she is there for individuals to construct and then to consume their own dark or light experience of the moment." Or could it conversely be a 'light tourism experience' of not being the person who had to go into Deborah on 20th November 1917? It sounds rather Biblical when we talk about coming out of darkness into light, but is this really what all tourism experiences are about and most especially those dark reconstructions of war or death? I watched children building sandcastles on the beach at Arromanche on a sunny day on June 6th 2014, whilst memorial services were going on to commemorate the 70th anniversary of the D-Day battle. It made me think that it is really the 'light tourism' that we end up remembering as we come out of the dark experience of sad constructed memories. It was the sunshine, the smiles on the veteran's faces as they joked with an admiring public that were lasting memories, but also that they were nothing without the tears of remembrance from those individuals' just seconds before during those acts of remembrance.

This chapter has been about a series of encounters along a journey of my own Light Tourism experiences so creating my own selfish place in history. In education/academia I wonder if we are losing that personal link, that viewpoint as we standardise the way we teach and look for articles to publish in tourism. A colleague recently sent in an article that included a conceptual framework which had been tested, but was putting the model forward to encourage debate and discussion on the merits or otherwise of that model. Every journal editor came back with the criticism that they needed an article with an introduction, literature review, methodology, results and analysis. This was even though they all state on the websites that they encourage authors to put forward new concepts for debate. We seem scared to even contemplate anything that is not 'validated'!

The tenuous link to academe in this chapter is done on purpose, perhaps in support of a philosophy of learning that is disappearing in our clamor to standardise curriculum, to teach to learning outcomes and to produce a series of Power Point slides and YouTube clips that take those students on a journey to the promised land of where WE want them to be. We can then provide 'model answers' for them to follow to ensure we do not allow them to think for themselves. We say "please do not use the first person as you have to justify or validate your writing within the body knowledge and you need to confirm or refute those views, but only if you have the research to back these notions up". I do not know if my interpretations of my grandfather's writing are true to him or not, I do not know if my ideas about Uncle Willie are true, but they are true to me. In my opinion we need to view tourism sites of war, etc. (not call them dark or light) from a personal viewpoint and not through any claims that they justify, decry or prove points, but they simply 'are'.

The following was written by my son for a remembrance event in the Flesquires Cemetry and spoken by him on a cold dark night in November 92 years after Grandfather's letter to Mr Foote. It was spoken over the graves of four of the crew members whom had died in Deborah on the 20th November 1917. It is my confirmation that perhaps 'Light tourism' is individual and personal and can never be a perfectly constructed liturgy, but rather a moment or series of moments of pure emotion.

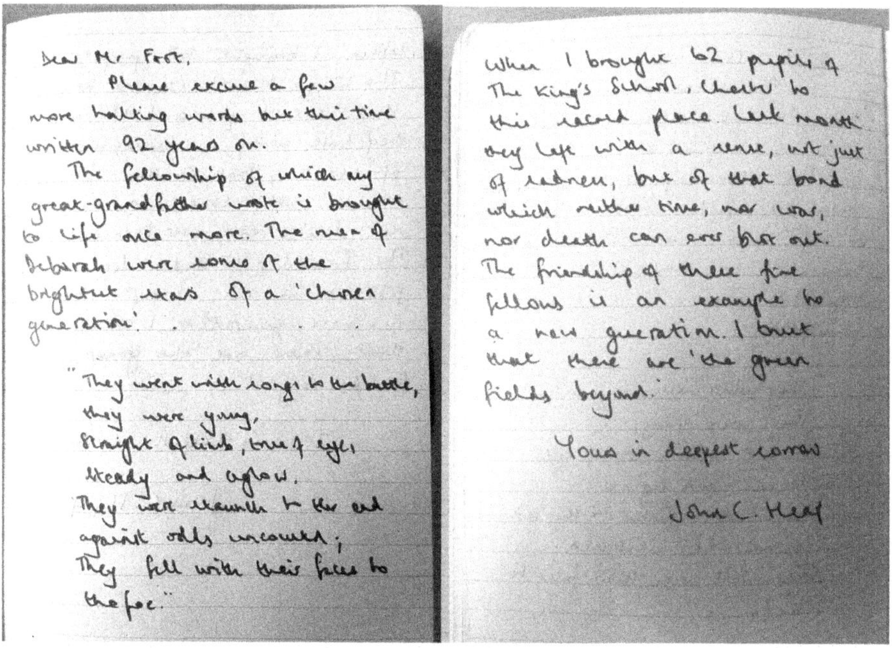

Dear Mr Foot,
Please excuse a few more halting words but this time written 92 years on.
The fellowship of which my great-grandfather wrote is brought to life once more. The men of Deborah were some of the brightest stars of a 'chosen generation'.

"They went with songs to the battle, they were young,
Straight of limb, true of eyes, steady and aglow.
They were staunch to the end against odds uncounted;
They fell with their faces to the foe."

When I brought 62 pupils of The King's School, Chester to this sacred place last month they left with a sense, not just of sadness, but of that bond which neither time, nor war, nor death can ever blot out. The friendship of these fine fellows is an example to a new generation. I trust that there are 'the green fields beyond'.

Yours in deepest sorrow

John C. Heap

Image 5.6: Letter to Mr Foote from John Heap, 2009

Notes

This chapter contains many questions within the text (sometimes one after another) that can be taken as rhetorical or used to stimulate debate/discussion about views, opinions, and thoughts about your associations with dark/light tourism. The emphasis is upon you, and there is no need to validate them through referring to the academic texts, but only to validate them within your own sense of belonging to those moments.

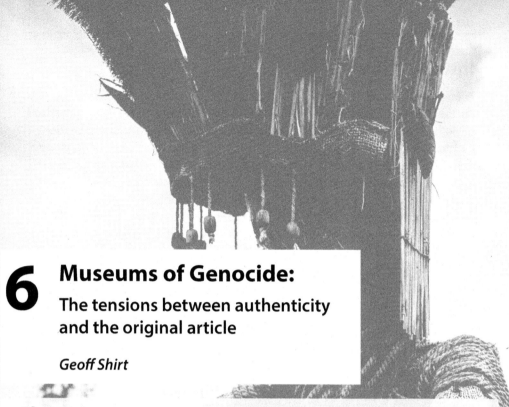

6 Museums of Genocide:
The tensions between authenticity and the original article

Geoff Shirt

Abstract

In recent years, sites associated with genocide have attracted 'dark tourists' with an apparent insatiable attitude for death and the inhumane treatment of social groups by others. The majority have taken on the role of a museum, and Auschwitz is no exception. Established as a concentration camp in 1942 and quickly developed as a 'Death Camp', this site has relatively quickly come to epitomise the worst horrors of *Holocaust*. The chapter investigates the several challenges, both ones particular to Auschwitz and those to be found elsewhere on the dark tourist's tick-list. Faced with a threefold increase in visitor numbers between 2006 and 2012, the management team of the Polish National Memorial has recently taken some controversial steps to protect their site. The strategy addresses significant concerns, whilst attempting to present an authentic experience. The potential challenges and solutions do not appear as stand-alone issues however, rather ones that are inextricably linked together. The reader is confronted with these issues and will be asked to make sense of the wider questions from beyond the immediate study area of tourism management.

Learning outcomes

1 To appreciate the context in which a site used during World War 2 has become a premier tourist attraction.

2 To understand the challenges facing such facilities 70 years after their original function was no longer required.

3 To critique the way in which the management has responded to the challenges.

4 To identity other sites where knowledge and experience may be effectively transferred.

Introduction

Almost by their very nature, sites historically associated with genocide take on the persona and role of a museum; a place where history is categorised, packaged and then sold to the 21st century visitor. There are many challenges and tensions that can be identified within such sites – perhaps the most obvious one being the contested morality of presenting a site where mass execution took place as that of a tourism attraction. This chapter investigates these issues and probes the options and choices available to managers in the light of the consumer becoming increasingly sophisticated. Some of these tourists of course are invariably seeking an experience that will provide a 'real' insight into what it would have been like when it was operational. The chapter will explore this theme by using the Auschwitz Birkenau death camp in Poland as a case study, whilst encouraging the reader to identify similar issues at other settings and scenes of genocide.

Until the 1960s, the vast majority of Western Europe's residents had neither heard the word 'Auschwitz' nor had any concept of what took place there. The outbreak of World War Two was caused by the invasion of Poland by the Nazis in September 1939, but it ended with Eastern Poland becoming a part of the Soviet Union and as such, remaining largely hidden behind the Iron Curtain, (Rees, 2005:15). For post-war UK, the concentration camp at Bergen Belsen in northern Germany became the focus of Nazi atrocities, perhaps due in part to the fact it had been the British Forces who liberated the camp in 1944, whereas for Auschwitz, the liberators were the Red Army. Following the activities of the Polish Solidarity movement in the 1980s and the subsequent collapse of the Berlin Wall and Soviet Communism in 1989, the death camp established close to the village of Oświęcim very quickly began to gain a much wider audience. By the early 1990s, the word *Auschwitz* (the German name by which the Nazis had replaced that of Oświęcim) had not only entered the Western vocabulary but had become virtually synonymous with the *Holocaust* and entered into our collective consciousness (Cole, 2000).

This chapter does not attempt to provide a comprehensive history of the evolution of Auschwitz nor to justify or rationalize the thinking behind using this site to 'honour' those that died in the way that it does. However, it is necessary to provide a thumb-sketch of what remains of the original site(s) and outline how the location is currently presented as one of Poland's *'must see'* tourist attractions.

Dark tourism

Dark tourism, the name now given to the mass visitation of sites where large numbers of men, women and children lost or had their lives taken from them,

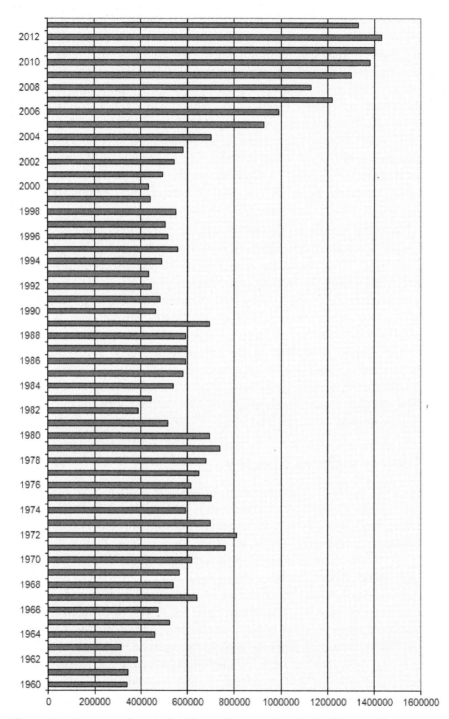

Figure 6.1: Visitor numbers to Auschwitz-Birkenau (Auschwitz Birkenau Memorial and Museum, 2015)

has become a high growth area. Interest in the phenomenon is not new; visitors have been attracted for many years to sites where the darkest secrets of various global communities can be brought into the open (Lennon & Foley, 2000). It has been argued that the growth of contemporary dark tourism began following September 11th 2001, when corporate grief by strangers who shared no direct link with the victims, became socially acceptable (Lisle, 2004). In the years that followed, *Ground Zero* has become a magnet for US citizens and international tourists alike, with an approximate total of seventeen million visitors filing past the former site of the World Trade centre since 2011 where 2819 workers lost their lives (911Memorial, 2014). But long before the attack on the Twin Towers, visitors were attracted in large numbers to concentration camps (Beech & Chadwick, 2000).

What cannot be disputed is that the Auschwitz camps have witnessed more than their fair share of visitor number growth over the past decade. Indeed, between 2006 and 2012, the authorities have witnessed a three-fold increase (Auschwitz, 2014). This has placed considerable pressure on those charged with the custodianship of the Auschwitz sites, both in terms of physical and psychological carrying capacities (Swarbrooke, 1999). Consideration of visitor numbers at the Auschwitz Concentration Camp World Heritage Site, can hardly be attempted without reference to the European low cost airline industry although it would be flattering to suggest Michael O'Leary of Ryanair or the EasyJet management team are anything other than supporting actors in the drama, indeed crisis, that has been unfolding close to the Polish city of Krakow for well over a decade.

Auschwitz: a short history

From May 1940, political prisoners began to arrive at a small converted army barracks, built near the town of Oświęcim in southern Poland. In keeping with Adolf Hitler's aspirations for his domination in Europe, the Nazi camp immediately assumed the German derivation of the town's name, that of *Auschwitz* (Lachendro, 2010:6). The buildings had been constructed some years earlier in red brick and positioned in lines with a central access road of loose stones. Auschwitz was not unique, rather one of several camps and shared the now familiar and cynical words 'ARBEIT MACHT FREI', (Work Brings Freedom) at its entrance. However, at what has now become retrospectively known as Auschwitz No. 1, the capital letter '*B*' was cast and placed upside-down within the phrase above the gateway; this a veiled attempt by the early prisoners to inform those that followed that all may not be as it seemed.

Those initially brought into the concentration/work camp were Polish dissidents, and soon to be joined by gypsies and dissidents from other parts of Europe. In 1942, Jews whom the SS physicians classified as fit for labour were also delivered to the camp. From among all the people deported to *Auschwitz 1*, approximately 400,000 people were registered and placed in the camp and its sub-camps (200,000 Jews, more than 140,000 Poles, approximately 20,000 Gypsies from various countries, more than 10,000 Soviet prisoners of war, and more than 10,000 prisoners of other nationalities). Between 1940 and liberation in 1945, Auschwitz functioned as a concentration camp, and over time became the largest such Nazi establishment (Auschwitz, 2014). Over 50% of the registered prisoners died as a result of starvation, labour that exceeded their physical capacity, terror that raged in the camp, executions, the inhuman living conditions, disease and epidemics, punishment, torture, or inhumane medical experiments.

It is within this original, compact site that the legacy of Father Maximilian Kolbe was established; a Catholic priest who chose to die in the place of a man who was due to be executed. Located between two blocks stands lies the (reconstructed) wall where some early prisoners were blindfolded and shot. In one corner of the complex, close by the Commandant's residence, was the group of buildings that housed the gas chamber and ovens.

The construction of an additional and adjacent installation began in October 1941, one that was to become known as Auschwitz Birkenau or more commonly and simply Birkenau. The village of Brzezinka, three kilometres from Oświęcim was the chosen location for what could only accurately be described as a 'death camp'. The incumbent Polish civilian population was evicted and their houses demolished. In sharp contrast to the existing and substantial buildings at *Auschwitz 1* and with time at a premium, over 250 wooden sheds were quickly constructed, each based on a design attributed to that of horse stabling. Here at Birkenau, the Nazis also built (and subsequently destroyed) the four gas chambers and ovens that had been designed to use industrial techniques for mass homicide. In so doing, the Nazis destined these buildings to become a magnet for dark tourists. A third site known as Auschwitz Monowitz was constructed seven kilometres from the original site for the production of chemicals for war effort but this has been razed to the ground and redeveloped in the 1950s as an industrial estate.

Both Auschwitz No 1 and Birkenau remained the III Reich's darkest secret until 1945, the latter providing a rapid, low cost solution for Hitler's ethnic cleansing programme for mainland Europe (Hart-Moxon, 2007), and where the vast majority of the victims were murdered. They became (jointly) listed in 1979 with UNESCO, controversially yet predictably as a museum (Lees, 2005).

Auschwitz in the 21ˢᵗ century

So what remains today? Attempts have been made by the Polish authorities (who are custodians of the site) to keep the buildings at Auschwitz 1 at least water-tight and indeed, they have successfully preserved most in how they would have appeared in the early 1940s. All the buildings remain intact and are used for property administration, storage or as a home for the numerous (and well documented) collections of genuine artefacts; spectacles, hair and suitcases taken from the arriving prisoners to name but three. Several buildings present static exhibitions of the countries from where prisoners were brought; this in an attempt to paint a larger canvas of the 'Final Solution'. The cell where Maximilian Kolbe spent his last hours is now a place of pilgrimage for countless Catholics, providing one of the many paradoxes found within this predominately Jewish site. Surviving also are buildings containing the ovens and chimney, so central to the narrative and dominant theme of death. This collection of artefacts will be revisited later in the chapter. Several authentic replicas have been erected at Auschwitz 1 to provide a snapshot of how the buildings would look and feel (Black, 2005). However as Auschwitz survivor Kitty Hart-Moxon remarked on returning as one of the first western visitors in 1978, the site now contains far too much grass. "You see green. I don't see green. I see mud. Just a sea of mud", (Hart-Moxon, 2007: 215).

Unlike the original barrack conversion, Birkenau contains far fewer original remains, and most of these in what can only be described as in generally poor condition, excepting the single substantial brick structure that is the gatehouse, under which runs the equally iconic railway line. The stairs that provide access to the same panoramic views the guards had over 60 years ago remain, only now the view is not of wooden sheds, rather of what remains; just primitive fire places and ghostly chimney stacks.

Auschwitz: the tourism site

Visitors arriving today at the town of Oświęcim generally do so by coach, private minibus, motor car or having used the public bus service from Krakow. Once inside the reception area, visitors are greeted by information boards in the many different languages that confirm the wide appeal the destination has; a list far longer than the languages spoken by the prisoners during the early 1940s. Those groups not bringing their own guide, meet the fully trained speakers provided by the site's custodians, at a reasonable cost per head. There is an optional, introductory presentation, lasting about ten minutes, given in the cinema, providing a brief background and context to the Auschwitz sites. It has been personally observed that many visitors take up neither the guide, nor cinema presentation option. Few visitors seem to be aware that they are queuing in the very spot where the prisoners waited to be assigned their destiny some 70 years earlier.

Until 2004, movement around the site was completely unregulated and visitors were free to visit the buildings and 'exhibits' at leisure and in any order.

However as numbers grew, progressive restrictions began to be enforced year on year. By 2010, only pre-booked parties with authorized guides are allowed onto the Auschwitz 1 site between 10.00am and 3.00pm during the summer peak months; these parties were taken along a pre-set route within a tight time schedule. This includes the several buildings given over to the much documented displays of hair, suitcases, artificial limbs and some containing maps and models of the gas chambers at Birkenau. There is no provision for heating or seating. Most exhibitions are located on both the ground and upper floors providing significant challenges for visitors with mobility limitations. Outside, the main 'attractions' are the wall where prisoners were shot and the buildings containing the gas chamber and ovens. Within yards of these artefacts, the commandant's house still stands but is out-of-bounds; this having subsequently been sold as a private dwelling.

Many visitors arrive initially at *Auschwitz 1* and are surprised to find *Birkenau* is not within walking distance. Facilities at the second site are even more basic, with a small toilet block, book shop and several information boards. In comparison with Auschwitz 1, Birkenau is a vast area of over 40 square hectares with little cover from the elements. To the right of the entry gatehouse, five wooden huts have been reconstructed to the original design to give visitors an insight into the cramped, cold conditions the male prisoners faced in 1942; these were 'refurbished' during 2010/2011 at a cost of a around £1M each, 85% of the cost being provided by the EU through their Economic Regional Development Fund. It is doubtful any of the original buildings remain and even the concrete bases have been replaced. To the left of the gate are the outlines of the women's quarters, beyond them, the brick buildings used by the captors and as kitchens. Ahead is the location of the four gas chambers and the monument erected by the Polish Government in 1967.

The original railway line runs through the gatehouse and down to the four concrete gas chambers. Parked midway between is a fully restored, weathered cattle truck similar to those originally used to bring prisoners onto the site. Undoubtedly the greatest attractions at *Birkenau* are the gas chambers, each built to a factory-scale design. Four had been built, but the departing Nazis had attempted to destroy them as they were likely to provide the most damning evidence of their atrocities. Although not completely destroyed, they were successful in reducing them to little more than rubble.

Facing tomorrow's challenges today

Challenge 1: Balancing increasing numbers with capacity

At first sight, the greatest challenge to the sustainability of the Auschwitz Birkenau sites is posed by the sheer number of visitors attracted to a museum site that began life as a small barracks for a provincial army. Many, indeed perhaps most, museum sites have seen an increase in numbers at some stage in their history, but few have seen such a vast increase within such short a time. So why is this? It is suggested one reason for this rise is an increase in the number of low cost air travellers.

Ryanair fly into Krakow from many airports in the UK: East Midlands, Birmingham, Edinburgh, Manchester, Leeds Bradford, Liverpool and London Stansted, Ryanair (2015), as well as airports in Ireland (Dublin and Shannon), Italy (Trapani, Cagliari, Milan Bergamo, Rome Ciampino, Pisa, Bologna), Spain (Malaga, Madrid, Palma, Alicante, Girona Barcelona) and six other European countries (France, the Netherlands, Germany, Belgium, Malta and Greece). When the other major low cost carrier EasyJet is added into the equation, we find the numbers visiting this single city are boosted by regular flights from Bristol, Liverpool, London (several airports) and Newcastle. An investigation as to the motivation is complex but is the result of at least three drivers:

1   Since the breakdown of the Soviet Union and subsequent absorption of Poland into the European Union, travellers from Western Europe have been keen to visit this part of Eastern Europe, tempted by a fine array of historical buildings, the low cost of living and unfamiliar culture. Krakow Old Town itself is listed on the UNESCO sites of significant importance, as is the Wieliczka Salt Mine located on the edge of the city limits.

2   The growth of interest in dentistry, medical and cosmetic surgery within Poland in general, and Krakow in particular has increased rapidly, due in part to the fact National Health Dentists themselves began to become as scarce as proverbial hens' teeth. As their availability reduced, so clientele that previously used the NHS looked elsewhere for their treatment. In Poland, demand has risen steadily over the past decade, where cost of treatment is perceived to be substantially less than the UK. Ryanair cited this growing trade as being the main motivator for the announcement of the service from East Midlands airport in October 2006 (Easier Travel, 2006). Clearly this arrangement proved to be symbiotic; interest fuelled by the low cost carrier and vice versa. Dental patients in particular but not exclusively, began making the journey from the UK and increasing numbers of British people are choosing Krakow for their medical procedures, including cosmetic surgery. Alongside patients seeking hip replacements and minor operations (collectively known as Medical Tourists), the

patient 'traditionally' stays on for a short period of recuperation, often taking advantage of the several heritage attractions offered locally, at rates below what might be expected for similar services in the UK. Auschwitz is less than an hour away from Krakow and has a surfeit of tour operators and guides plying their trade from the town.

3   In striving for recognition as a major receiver of tourists, Krakow has now successfully wrestled the 'cheapest Stags night out' crown from Prague and tempted the Hens to come scratching for a long weekend party. Following a night on the beer or wine, how better to rid yourself of a hang-over than with a trip to a well-known visitor attraction? How better to impress your work-mates and family when returning from a boozy weekend, than with a cultural, if hazy, recollection of a visit to Auschwitz?

Whilst the Krakow tourist administration team has done a remarkable job in terms of enabling visitors to be collected from the many hotels and hostels in the city, there are many other groups of tourists arriving with coach parties. These come from all over Europe, often the relatives of those that lost their lives at Auschwitz on a sort of pilgrimage. It is interesting that latterly, many hundreds of visitors from the USA and Israel come to Poland and visit one of the other death camps sites that is less busy and so provide for a time of quiet reflection.

One of the consequences of attempting to manage greater numbers is to maximise every minute the visitor is on site. At busy periods, there is no time to stand and reflect. The guides talk constantly as they lead their procession around the grounds and even through the gas chamber at *Auschwitz 1*; this in direct contravention of the '*Silence please*' notices placed on the wall.

Challenge 2: Maintenance

From their inception as a single UNESCO unit, the two remaining Auschwitz sites have fulfilled the same role and purpose whilst facing quite different challenges. As a preserved concentration camp, the challenge at *Auschwitz 1* has been to remain a time capsule, allowing visitors to recreate a mental image of a wartime concentration camp. Being allowed to stand in the same cell where prisoners stood some 70 years earlier, or where so many perished in the gas chamber are central to the 'enjoyment' of the visitor. One particular past challenge at *Auschwitz 1* was to prevent the *natural* desire of the sapling trees planted in the 1930s to keep growing beyond the roofs of the buildings and thereby dominate the *man-made* architecture. In 2006, the Authorities spent £60,000 on the task of stopping the trees growing any more. However this approach did not work and the plan was superseded by one that completely removed the original trees; this being done over a two year period between 2009 and 2011. The replacements were young saplings – the size of the ones planted in 1930s. Authenticity favoured over originality.

Internally, some of the original indoor exhibits are in danger of deterioration beyond repair; despite the best efforts of controlled environments. Regular testing of the samples of hair, for example, has recently revealed that the preservative used has caused the fibres to become brittle. This in turn has caused physical damage to individual strands supporting the top layers in the display cabinets. These research findings come some years after a project that identified the preservative had removed all traces of cyanide left from the donor's time in the gas chamber.

In contrast to the maintenance of the largely weather-proofed *Auschwitz 1* site, the maintenance challenges at the Birkenau death camp are how to preserve the 70 year old wood and concrete remains within the hostile natural, legislative and social environments. The concrete structures are deteriorating quickly now as the component parts of the concrete seek their individual identity once more. How long the Polish health and safety authorities can trust visitors to execute common sense and keep off the crumbling remains is unknown, but a barrier of any description, would doubtless detract from the atmosphere and is being resisted.

> The condition of the ruins is deteriorating from year to year, due to atmospheric conditions, the high level of ground water, the natural erosion of the building material, the pressure of the earth against the parts of the gas chamber walls that are still in existence, and, at times, the irresponsible behaviour of groups of visitors.
>
> Auschwitz (2014)

As noted earlier, many of the wooden structures quickly built at Birkenau have perished. Other wooden structures, such as the sentry towers, are in poor condition but it is unlikely many, if any, are original to the site.

Challenge 3: Contested ownership

In 1947, the Warsaw pact countries sought to erect a monument to the Martyrdom of the Polish and Other Nations, and the decision was taken for this to be done collectively for both the remaining Oświęcim sites. Auschwitz was but one of six sites of mass gassings of Jews in Poland but was chosen over the other camp near Majdanek, it being geographically more central. Facing the West, (collective), Auschwitz was to remain a poignant reminder of past fascist oppression and a warning of the potential threat still posed (to the Eastern bloc countries) by a capitalist (West) Germany.

Auschwitz celebrates the role of various eastern European groups rather than national representations of Jewish society (Cole, 1999:100). In 1974, visits to *Auschwitz 1* for Polish school children was made compulsory, with sovereignty and national pride the focus. Perhaps strangely it was at Birkenau where the physical and National memorial had been erected. However, by 2000, the

'Holocaust' had begun to be recognized as a distinctly Jewish phenomenon within the global psyche (Cole, 2000). The latter appears to be decreasingly seen as a site of the mass gassing of Jews, rather *the* focus of the collective Jewish memory of the Holocaust (Finkelstein, 2015:94).

The story of Maximillian Kolbe, already briefly introduced, has led to Auschwitz becoming a place of pilgrimage for Catholics to pay homage to a man who (literally) gave his life for another. This act of self-denial ironically became and remains one of a number of tensions between such pilgrims and the families of murdered Jews who died with no choice, feeling the status and fame of Kolbe grossly unwarranted. A much wider rift between the two religions being the reluctance of Catholics to even recognize the State of Israel; the (Catholic) Church itself assuming the mantle of a 'New Israel' or 'New Jerusalem'.

With the dedication at a site adjoining Birkenau of Father Kolbe, an inmate who had spent his entire captivity at Auschwitz 1, the almost 'mythical' Auschwitz had begun to take shape. Auschwitz was to become a singular attraction 'drawing inspiration' from the two remaining Oświęcim camps; a hybrid that borrowed elements from both and intermixed them almost at will. An imaginary Auschwitz has evolved, divorced from geographical realities (Cole, 1999:105). Auschwitz had become a place in the mind, rather built in the earth, a social construction rather than one of physical bricks and mortar. This single Auschwitz is an attempt to be a symbol that neither denies nor confirms exclusivity. It denies neither the Jewishness nor endorses the nationality of the victims sent there.

Challenge 4: Authenticity

> We weren't interested in Oświęcim, we were on our way to Auschwitz. We were tourists of guilt and righteousness: guilt at an almost pornographic sense of expectancy of the voyeurism ahead, righteousness that we had chosen to come and see this place.
>
> (Cole, 2000:97)

The task of ensuring *the authentic* is made all the more difficult by the trend, steadily gaining support over the years, that the two sites should be blended into one; to become an homogenized 'Auschwitz-land' or 'tourist Auschwitz'; a post-war Polish creation (Cole, 1999:110). From the moment one enters *Auschwitz 1*, the bombardment of images and statistics more associated with the *other* camp 3 kilometres away is instant. Moreover, in attempting to present an authentic experience, visitors are directed to a building without which any visit to Auschwitz could be complete; the gas chamber and ovens. But as Ryback observes:

> The crematorium chimney is a free standing structure, in no way connected to the ovens. One entrance to the gas chamber does not have

a door, or even any evidence of hinges. To one side, there are pipes where a bathroom once stood. In the centre of the room is a manhole with an iron cover.

Ryba ck (1993) in (Cole, 2000:109)

Cole explains that the building had a varied life because, in 1941 it was converted from a mortuary into an experimental gas chamber. For an initial period of 14 months, up to 10,000 prisoners may have been gassed here before the building was converted once again, on this occasion into an air raid shelter in 1943. At liberation, most of the building was demolished by the Red Army but quickly rebuilt by the Polish authorities in 1948 to represent a history of the incinerators – based on the ones at Birkenau, Cole (1999:109). The addition of a free-standing square chimney is reminiscent of the design used in the gas chambers at Birkenau. The ovens in the building next door appear in a hastily restored state; two restored out of the original three that had previously existed.

Auschwitz is a location with many paradoxes. At the original Auschwitz 1 site where visitors gather, is the first. It is here where visitors meet their guides and purchase memorabilia. This is done in a noisy, bustling single story build-ing with an entrance at the car park and at the other, the lecture theatre that welcomes visitors onto the site. Most visitors might believe this to be a modern addition to the complex; a practical means to an end. A rain-proof corridor from the car park to the 'Arbeit Macht Frei' gateway. In reality, it was constructed in 1942-1944 as a place where prisoners were registered, tattooed, robbed, disin-fected and shaved (Van Pelt and Dwork, 1996, in Cole, 2000:110). Today it could be said that the same building continues to promote robbery, albeit on a lower level. Down a flight of stairs, the visitor finds the toilets; accessed at a cost of 2 zloty (approximately 35p). This is not funding the museum, rather providing a handsome return on capital for the private contractor responsible for the toilet facilities, but more of this later.

The issue of authenticity is often of much more importance for the host community (Smith & Duffy, 2003:133), but as we saw in the previous chal-lenge, this is quite complex at Auschwitz. Bauer (1994:306) states that whether the 'Holocaust' is presented as an authentic experience or not, in accordance with the historical facts or in contradiction with them, with empathy and understanding or as a monumental kitsch, it has become a ruling symbol in our culture. Unsure whether this is good or bad, he simply states this appears to be a fact. Most traditional tourism brochures show empty beaches and empty hotel rooms. In contrast the 'official' Auschwitz website invariably shows images, not of deserted buildings, but of the residents that lived within them. Moreover, these images strive to show similar timelessness; that what they are seeing is unspoilt and original (Smith & Duffy, 2003:119).

Unlike almost every other significant museum in the world, the authorities at Auschwitz do not operate a system that provides for an IT-based, hand-held guide to aid understanding and enhance the presented learning opportunity (Black, 2005). Instead groups of 20-30 are led around the sites by a trained guide, only recently aided with a microphone that facilitates one-way communication through an ear piece worn by each member of the group.

Challenge 5: Finance

Polish law prohibits an entry fee being charged to anyone and so becomes extremely attractive to the low spending, low frills travellers identified earlier. Indeed, according to the official Auschwitz web-site:

> The Auschwitz-Birkenau State Museum is financed by the Polish government budget, which bore for over 40 years the entire financial burden for the upkeep and preservation of the camp.

> Auschwitz Birkenau Memorial and Museum (2015)

The situation changed slightly in 1990 when The International Auschwitz Council was formed, providing valuable expertise and links to other museums. In the same year, the Auschwitz-Birkenau Death Camp Victims Foundation was established with the following goals:

- Preserving, maintaining, and conserving the buildings, documents, and archives of the former Nazi camp,

- Promoting knowledge about the Nazi crime of genocide, in particular as it was committed on the grounds of the Auschwitz-Birkenau death camp,

- Carrying out research and publishing activity and supporting artistic expression on camp themes, as well as subjects associated with genocide and the camps,

- Raising funds and generating income for the above-mentioned aims,

- Cooperating with groups and institutions in Poland and abroad which are interested in honouring the memory of the victims of Auschwitz concentration camp.

> Auschwitz Birkenau Memorial and Museum 2012

It should be noted that although a UNESCO site since 1979, Auschwitz has received very little support since the last millennium, as funds have been diverted to other areas considered more in need of protection, principally countries in the Middle East. Indeed the Auschwitz-Birkenau State Museum relied on local government funding and its own income generating activities. In fact, these latter activities fall into just two or at times three categories: the short introductory film, paid guides and at certain times, additional exhibitions housed within the barracks. But the majority of visitors did not use either of the first two services, although invariably many used the cafeteria, the car park, the book shops and the toilets, all of which are contracted out with the rent being paid directly to the Polish government.

Some drastic action was required and this was taken in 2009. It took the name of the 'Perpetual Fund'. This was a brave and ambitious plan put forward by the Foundation that sought to release it from the restrictions of local authority funding by raising sufficient funds that would allow *their* site to be protected and preserved in perpetuity. The sum of €120 Million was considered adequate for this purpose; the donations readily accepted from individual benefactors and willing members of the International community. Germany almost immediately pledged €60 Million and Austria a further €6M. These have been followed by USA (€14M), United Kingdom (€1.6M) and Netherlands (€400,000). Poland has now pledged a further €10M to be released over the next four years taking the total nearer to its target. "Auschwitz is above all a worldwide symbol of the Holocaust. It is a place that says more about human nature than we want to hear. For us Poles, it is also our largest cemetery. In no other single place have so many Poles died," said Foundation President Dr. Piotr M.A. Cywiński, Auschwitz Birkenau Memorial and Museum (2011). Although not having reached the full target to date, it has raised enough funds to ensure that the long-term future of the Auschwitz museum is secure.

The fact there is no admission charge to either Auschwitz site is a grey area within the several glossy brochures of the dozen or so tour operators based in the city of Krakow. Most charge approximately £80 pp (group of four) for a guided day trip; one that infers the cost includes an admission charge. For an example see Escape2Poland (2014), and the chapter by Johnston, Tigre-Moura and Manderlartz in this book. At least one company operates a daily tour bus to Auschwitz that includes 'museum entrance tickets' (Auschwitztours, 2014); something that exists but is a souvenir rather than a paid pre-requisite.

Challenge 6: Sophistication

Observers have noted there are several readily identified character traits of the 21st century museum visitor. The first of these is that the sophisticated consumer is becoming more demanding in terms of presentation and amenities (Black, 2005; Negroni, 2015). Moreover, the museum visitor accessing the site is much more informed than previously; this is due in part to the plethora of educational programmes on cable, satellite and terrestrial television on the subject. An excellent example of a progressive, modern museum may be found in Amsterdam where four synagogues have been converted into one, to celebrate Jewish history and European culture, and incorporating interactive displays and original artefacts. In sharp contrast to Auschwitz, the visitor is informed within a warm and inviting environment. When compared to the state-of-the-art Holocaust museums in the United States and Israel, the facilities in Poland reinforce the post-communist austerity image the Polish authorities are trying so hard to consign to the last century elsewhere in their country and economy. Whilst museums around the world, including several on the Holocaust in Israel, New York and even at the Anne Frank house in Amsterdam, integrate interactive displays and thought provoking activities within their walls (Ashworth & Hartmann, 2005), Auschwitz struggles to make the experience one that is stimulating, inclusive and accessible to visitors of all ages and physical abilities.

Perhaps one of the most important factors when operating a high profile visitor attraction is the need for each visitor to be given an individualised opportunity to receive the correct level of background and factual information for him or her. Many facilities, such as the British Museum and indeed most stately homes, do this via individual headset that allow the visitor to select focused, detailed information with minimal audible disturbance. Another approach, used by the aforementioned Jewish Museum in Amsterdam is to provide interactive displays, activated by satellite touch pads. Reliance upon a trained guide can produce low satisfaction ratings as the listener is out-of-range or gets engaged in conversation with a member of the group.

What may however be on the side of the *Auschwitz* site custodians, is the fact that visitors experience may be impaired if the overall 'feel' of prisoners' deprivation was lost. But if the driving *raison d'être* for the camp is education, there are now much more effective teaching tools than piles of spectacles behind a sheet of glass. Whilst not having the same geographical location or hard resources as Auschwitz, Vad Yashem outside Jerusalem has adopted an inclusive, hands-on approach;

> It is now clear that this challenging job of preserving memory and passing it on to future generations cannot be accomplished through historiography alone. Other means are necessary to achieve this monumental task… We must not allow the Holocaust to remain in the realm of large numbers and generalized statements.

> Professor Aharon Appelfeld, author and Holocaust survivor, Yad Vashem,

> Holocaust Remembrance Day Eve, 1997

An alternative approach is taken in Anne Frank House, where an extension of the original house has been given over to an intranet of facts about the Holocaust, life in pre-war Holland and other related links from the World Wide Web. Their 'Right to Choose' exhibition currently provides an interactive arena that challenges mind-sets and prejudices in a warm, airy atmosphere.

As the rights and demands of our inclusive European society become more widespread, so the impact of disability discrimination law will become greater. Currently at the *Auschwitz 1* site, none of the exhibition buildings are accessible by wheelchair; most buildings direct one-way traffic along both floors of the building. Although this practice may be seen as unacceptable by amenity managers and governments across Europe, the issue of accessibility is significant and will become more so. At Auschwitz 1, it is not simply the steps that provide the barrier, but also the 30-40mm diameter stones that are the pathways between the barrack buildings. These make the forward movement of a traditional wheelchair quite a difficult task.

Challenge 7: The Holocaust Industry

'It seems to me that the Holocaust is being sold – it is not being taught'

Rabbi Arnold Wolf, Hillel Director at Yale University, Berenbaum
(1990)

1993 was deemed to be the 'Year of the Holocaust' when *Schindler's List*, directed by a third generation American Jew, Steven Spielberg, was released and the American Holocaust Memorial Museum was opened. Both had the effect of thrusting the Holocaust into our collective consciousness. Gentrification had been gradually taking place over two decades, including the concept of 'trivialisation' – a distortion of the reality of war, especially in computer games; making it commonplace, instead of awesome and frightening (Cole, 1999:15). Spielberg saw the Holocaust as being something not simply to imagine but to recreate. By the end of the 20th century, the Holocaust was being consumed; that is to say planned, visited and then ticked off a mental list. It is impossible to separate ethics from the question of development in general and tourism development in particular (Smith & Duffy, 2003:3).

But there is a much deeper, indeed darker, side to the Holocaust industry in which tourism has a part to play. A more accurate description would perhaps be 'the industry that has grown up around the Holocaust' and one of the most vocal commentators here has been Norman Finkelstein. As an American Jew, he finds it hard on the one hand to understand interest in the Holocaust, when compared to the American War of Independence or the Great War. He points to the fact that between 1891 and 1911, some 10 million Africans perished in the course of Europe's exploitation of Congolese ivory and rubber resources. Yet the first scholarly volume in English was not published until 1996 (Finkelstein, 2015:143). On the other, he has seen how relatively easy it has been for various, powerful (mainly American) Jewish lobbies to secure massive amounts of compensation for groups and some individuals from governments and institutions, especially the Swiss banking system.

One of his fiercest indictments to the Holocaust industry is in relation to the evolving definition of a Holocaust survivor. Initially the term was reserved for those liberated from the camps. Today however, the term has been expanded to include those who avoided capture, such as the 100,000 who fled from Poland to the Soviet Union (Finkelstein, 2015:83).

As will be noted in the following passage, one of the greatest assets any historical event has is the truth found within personal testimonies.

Challenge 8: Holocaust denial/revisionism

Holocaust denial is a propaganda movement, especially active in the United States, Canada and Western Europe, which seeks to deny the reality of the Nazi regime's systematic mass murder of six million Jews in Europe during World War II. Alternatively, it may be referred to as revisionist thinking. 'Holocaust deniers' deny the established facts about the Holocaust. They assert that the murder of approximately six million Jews during World War II never occurred and that the Germans are victims of a Zionist plot to extort vast sums of money from them on the basis of a hoax. Under a rallying cry created by Holocaust denier David Irving – 'Sink the Battleship Auschwitz!' – they deny the existence of the poison gas chambers in the Auschwitz-Birkenau death camp, as that camp lies at the symbolic core of the Holocaust and stands as the icon for Jewish suffering.

David Irving, one of the most well-known revisionists in the United Kingdom, was jailed in February 2006 for three years for challenging the extent of the Holocaust. His name came to the attention of the general public in 1989 when he proposed a view that Adolf Hitler knew nothing of the Holocaust and that the story of gas chambers as part of the Final Solution were a hoax (BBC News, 2006). At his trial, Irving said he had now seen the evidence and changed his mind, but the debate goes on. The libel case had been brought by Deborah Lipstadt although successful has not made the belief that the Holocaust has been exaggerated go away. Indeed, as she stated in 2006:

> I am not happy when censorship wins, and I don't believe in win-
> ning battles via censorship... The way of fighting Holocaust deniers
> is with history and with truth,

> BBC News (2006)

Lipstadt was able to prove Irving wrong, in effect by him needing to prove the historical actuality of the Holocaust, Gutterplan (2005). If history is being untruthfully presented, as may be argued is the case with the gas chamber and chimney at Auschwitz 1, then continued credibility will be given to such suggestions and distorted truth.

Bearing in mind the 70th anniversary of the release of Auschwitz is celebrated in 2015, it is not hard to appreciate that the vast majority of those living through the camp's operation have now died. It is accordingly of paramount importance that what hard evidence remains, provides a truthful, faithful and objective account of man's inhumanity against man.

Conclusions and observations

It will be noted that the challenges are many, varied and inter-relate to a considerable degree. One thing is certain, they are not simple.

Stated earlier, it could be suggested that the main issue facing '*Auschwitz*' is the rapid increase and sheer number of visitors. In reality it is perhaps more true to say it is the tensions that exist between visitor numbers, ownership and authenticity. It is asserted that every effort must be given to provide truth and integrity at this most sacred of WW2 sites. It is likely, for instance that the majority of visitors arriving at the original camp visit this 'shrine' and believe it to be presented in its original state. This undoubtedly presents the authorities with a dilemma. Should the authorities now promote the fact that one of the most visited areas of their 'attraction' is not an original structure, rather a badly restored replica? It would be politically incorrect to rebuild it, although the plans of the conversion into an experimental building do exist. To leave the collection of buildings and structures as they are, runs the risk of simply fuelling the revisionist theory that no-one could possibly have been gassed in this way, and thereby undermine the integrity of the whole site.

Discussion questions

1   Discuss the pros and cons of introducing hand-held, self-guiding devices as a way of easing a continuing increase in visitor numbers.

2   Discuss the feasibility of introducing a levy imposed upon low-cost airline carriers and any possible extension to local transport providers.

3   Discuss the ethical and practical implications of focusing all funding to Auschwitz at the expense of the five other Polish Death camps.

4   Consider the £2.15M donation given by the British Government to the Perpetual Fund, given that no British citizens lost their lives at Auschwitz.

5   In striving to stay true to the facts and keeping authenticity at the centre of all they do, should the Auschwitz Management team treat the two sites as discreet entities: one essentially a concentration camp, the other a camp of death rather than a hybrid of the two.

References

911Memorial.org (2014). 911 Memorial. Available at http://www.911Memorial. org. Accessed 10th October 2014.

Ashworth, G. and Hartmann, R. (2005). *Horror and Human Tragedy Revisited; the Management of Sites of Atrocities for Tourism,* Cognizant Communication Corporation.

Auschwitz Birkenau Memorial and Museum (2015). Attendance. Available http://www.auschwitz.org/en/visiting/attendance/. Accessed 27th May 2015.

Auschwitz Birkenau Memorial and Museum (2012). Annual Report. Available http://www.auschwitz.org/auschwitz.report.2011.pdf. Accessed 18th November 2014.

Auschwitz Birkenau Memorial and Museum (2011). Victims Foundation. Available http://www.auschwitz.org/deathcampvictimsfoundation. Accessed 27th May 2015.

Auschwitz Birkenau Memorial and Museum (2009). Annual Report. Available http://www.auschwitz.org/auschwitz.report.2008.pdf. Accessed 27th May 2015.

Auschwitztours (2015). Auschwitz-Birkenau tour from Krakow. Available http://auschwitztours.com/auschwitz.htm. Accessed 27th May 2015.

Bauer, Y. (1994). *The Significance of the Final Solution* in Cesarani, D (Ed) *The Final Solution: Origins and Implementation*, Routledge: London.

BBC News (2006). Holocaust denier Irving is jailed. Available http://news.bbc.co.uk/2/hi/europe/4733820.stm. Accessed 13th April 2015.

Beech, J. & Chadwick, S. (2005). *The Business of Tourism Management*, London: Prentice Hall

Berenbaum, M. (1990). *After Tragedy and Triumph,* Cambridge: Cambridge Press.

Black, G. (2005). *The Engaging Museum,* Oxon: Routldege.

Cole, T. (1999). *Selling the Holocaust: From Auschwitz to Schindler; How History is Bought, Packaged and Sold,* Oxon: Routledge.

Easier Travel (2006). Ryanair announces 10 new routes from Nottingham East Midlands. Available http://www.easier.com/45801-ryanair-announces-10-new-routes-from-nottingham-east-midlands.html. Accessed 13th April 2015.

Evans, R. (2002). *Telling Lies about Hitler: The Holocaust, History and the David Irving Trial,* Verso Books: Brooklyn NY.

Finkelstein, N. (2015, 2nd Ed.). *The Holocaust Industry: Reflections on the Exploitation of Jewish Suffering.* London: Verso.

Gutterplan, D. (2005). How many Jews does it take? in *Index on Censorship,* May 2005, accessed through EBSCO 10th October 2014.

Hart-Moxon, K. (2007). *Return to Auschwitz,* The Holocaust Centre: Notts.

Lachendro, J. (Ed.) (2010). *German Places of Extermination in Poland,* Parma Press: Katarzyna Sosnowska.

Lees, L (2005). Auschwitz: *The Nazis & The 'Final Solution',* BBC: London.

Lennon, J. & Foley, M. (2000). *Dark Tourism: The attraction of Death and Disaster,* Cengage.

Negroni, M. (2015). *Dark Museum (Salvo)*: Parma Press.

Ryanair (2015). Route Map, Available at http://www.ryanair.com/ie/cheap-flight-destinations/. Accessed 13th April 2015.

Smith, M. & Duffy, R. (2003). *The Ethics of Tourism Development* Oxon: Routledge.

Swarbrooke, J. (1999). *Sustainable Tourism Management,* London: CABI.

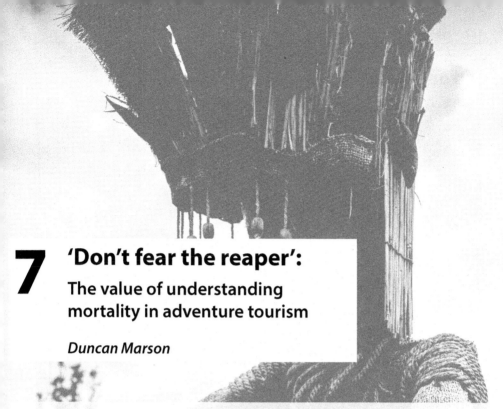

7 'Don't fear the reaper':
The value of understanding mortality in adventure tourism

Duncan Marson

Abstract

The chapter provides an overview of the theoretical relationship between death and adventure tourism, in terms of death as uncertainty, death in adventure as a component of contemporary dark tourism, and death as a motivating and inhibiting factor for adventure participation. The chapter argues that the nature of the commodification of adventure allows for death to be perceived, and contested, in different ways. The perception of death should therefore be thought of as a tool for education and awareness in adventure activities, rather than a phenomena from which we should shy away. Whilst a fundamental part of risk management, where participants should be protected from negligent forms of risk, equal care and attention should be given to understanding the role of how the 'death defying' nature of activities can help further provide answers for our own acceptable level of participation, and how we can successfully negotiate this in our own leisure careers. This theoretical basis has benefits for both understanding the role of adventure in contemporary society, as well as developing innovations in adventure tour operations and educational components in modern adventure tourism activity.

Learning outcomes

1 To broaden the debate surrounding dark tourism by incorporating niche tourism products such as adventure into the discussion.

2 To further understand the relationship between the 'dark' connotations of death and adventure participation.

3 To question the role of death as a variable within commercial adventure activities.

Introduction

Image 7.1: Martinelli, Giovanni Memento Mori (*Death Comes to the Dinner Table*), ca. 1635, Oil on canvas, 123.15 x 174 cm

We begin our journey into a discussion of death, a subject which is potentially deemed in society to be a rather morose topic in the field of recreation and tourism, by using the work of Giovanni Martinelli. Our purposes for looking closer at the painting *Death Comes to the Dinner Table* (1635) are to attempt to convey the juxtaposition of such a discussion between death and tourism, particularly adventure tourism, but furthermore consider the challenge associated with looking at death whilst in life – the more astute would comment here *"Well, when else are we going to consider it?"*. It is not something most human beings necessarily relish thinking about.

Indeed, current statistics from the UK government regarding intestacy and estates passing to the crown suggest that a significant number of people still 'pass away' without organising a will prior to death *("I don't want to think about my own demise in any form")*, suggesting that the matter is not one to anticipate as a topic of discussion over the morning coffee/evening meal with friends. Yet this is what inevitably occurs to the revelers in *Death Comes to the Dinner Table*. Giddens (2013:260) associates this with the perception that death is the association with old age and subsequent stereotypes of illness, infirmity, inability, subsequently becoming socially ingrained. This could be described as a core reason as to why we are reluctant as modern human beings to discuss our own mortality openly. Yet the proliferation of dark tourism shows the fascination the tourist has with death. A key debate here is whether this presents itself, rather ironically, as a learning opportunity for everyday life, or whether it is a fleeting encounter where we learn little but self preservation, or a 'don't do that again' mentality.

The main argument proposed in this chapter is that the proliferation of commercially guided tours for the wider novice adventure market, creates a situation where death is actively avoided in the discussion, and replaced with more socially appropriate, less fatalist terms such as *perceived* and *real risk*, and the implications for such an avoidance. The growth of the adventure sector in the future relies on progress of industry innovation and creativity in dealing with a wide variety of challenges such as risk management, effectively developing clients to become self-reliant participants. The question of mortality is not one therefore to recoil from when participating in adventure. Like dark tourism, it is one to develop as an opportunity to educate and understand wider issues in the self as well as in society.

Look again at the opening image at the start of the chapter. We see in the painting an affluent group, as suggested by their expensive attire and the nature of the food on the table, (bright clothing, fashions of the day, fruit, wine, baked goods) with shocked looks of surprise and despair at the arrival of the uninvited guest. Death, personified as in many renderings as a skeletal figure, is goading or reminding the party-goers of the inevitability of the meeting and future encounters. The hourglass in the hands of our protagonist alludes to the fact that we all have a limited time, and that death comes to everyone, regardless of whether we seek it or not. The shock and surprise is interesting here – the last thing on the minds of the dinner party was the arrival of death, and the potential significant change in circumstance for one of the partygoers. Even the swordsman, whether this weapon is symbolically for show or whether it has tasted blood, is surprised at the arrival. The semiotic comparisons are here to reveal: the party as a form of leisure as per modern adventure activity; the surprise that something like death could interrupt such a playful atmosphere, etc.

It would be easy for us to surmise that the swordsman out of all of the party should be relatively accustomed to the notion of death, possessing a tool of which its primary use is causing a hastier encounter with death than anything else on a dining table (fatty foods and alcohol aside). Death it seems can come at the most inconvenient of times. After all, it seems a shame to disrupt such a happy and frivolous setting. *Death Comes to the Dinner Table* is a reminder to us all, that death can manifest itself anywhere and at any time. This is a telling debate, not only for human existence (perhaps a rather grandiose thought, but pertinent nevertheless) but also for participation/consumption in adventurous recreation and tourism.

Within adventure participation, as per human existence, we may not want to dwell on death, and yet we should possibly not obstruct our view of understanding it completely. Adventure activities contain a real risk inherent in participation, no matter how much this is managed externally. Understanding death in adventure can help us to understand the importance of participation itself. This chapter therefore wishes to explore death from an unobtrusive setting of how contemporary society may see it, so as to understand how and why death has become a difficult topic for discussion and further why its understanding is so pertinent to our own experiences in tourism, leisure, adventure, and to those experiences which we sell to others. This is in no way meant to diminish the nature and significance of death, or the feeling of loss when those who we are close to are taken from us prematurely. It should also be noted further that this is not a rallying 'call to arms' against modern risk management and duty of care procedures.

The nature of adventure participation relies on flirting with the notion of death, and yet as adventure is transformed into another consumable (Varley, 2006), the gap between the nature of real and imaged relationship between adventure and death is widening. The implications for this will also be discussed further. Drawing the discussion back into the painting in Image 7.1 for a moment, the nature of art is one that, like in film, we can immerse ourselves in the pre, in-situ and post setting of the subject matter. We cannot physically view it, but we can imagine that prior to Death's arrival in this scene, this group reveled in the hedonic impulses surrounding hospitality such as this, drinking and laughing – the level of happiness and the subsequent indulgence of pleasure that it generates.

This is why Death's entrance is such a shock. The immersion in the consumption of pleasurable behavior makes the opposite of this happiness ever the more brutal for the consumer. When we have a negative experience or a near-death experience, there is old adage that springs to mind that your *"life flashes before your eyes"*. Rather a clichéd statement in contemporary society, but one which acts in part as evidence for this brutalism. It is brutal because it is the antithesis of the feelings of pleasure prior to the encounter.

Our life flashes before our eyes because we move from one section of a continuum of experience (hedonism and the pleasure principle) to the other (mortality, death and the implications for yourself and others). The split second 'flash before your eyes' refers in this sense to the lack of real time we have to think, but the significance of the event forcing us to (*"this could be the end, this is the only chance I am going to get"*). It is important to understand however that this is part of the learning experience. The participation in adventure activities, and the unfortunate and almost instantaneous shift from an enjoyable, pleasurable experience to one which creates anxiety, panic and shock is a fine line when 'things go wrong' (this could any number of scenarios in adventurous activities where loss of control, *force majeure* etc, are experienced).

Like our previous painting, hedonism (the search and consumption of pleasurable activity) in adventure can make way for panic instantaneously regardless of individual level of skill, although experience can help condition for such eventualities, and it is this which can become all the more shocking for the participant. Whilst the ability to do anything in these situations is limited, understanding them prior/post activity could be argued as important to help negotiate near-death experiences if they manifest. Dark tourism partly provides the consumer with the opportunity to experience death objectively in a detached manner, and this can help make sense and question personal mortality. Adventure participation can include both perceptions of near death in a detached manner, as well as being able to question mortality, based on the activities we participate in. It is here where modern adventure tourism can learn from the phenomena of dark tourism. What is important here is to distinguish between experienced individual participation and guided adventure participation, as the nature of how an individual engages in mortality may be uniquely different dependent on their level of personal commitment to the activity (self organised or guided).

Mortality, personal participation and guided experiences

Let us take this opportunity to probe into the distinction between different types of participation by looking at a modern recreational activity such as rock climbing. Research conducted by Sport England suggest that rock climbing has increased in participation over the past 20 years to become an significant part of tourism demand throughout the United Kingdom (BMC, 2010). Recreational climbers interestingly refer to the preparation for rock climbing both mentally as well as physically when questioning if *'your head is in the right place'* before attempting a climb. This refers to the appropriate level of mental preparation which will allow a climber to commit at the right time on a rock face when the level of technical difficulty and/or the level of real risk is at its highest. Being both physically as well as mentally prepared is of fundamental importance and can be a precondition for success.

Fear, risk and the relationship between failure and death in traditional climbing (or 'Trad', where you place your own protection as you climb in the event of a fall) is a reward which drives most recreational climbers to commit to developing their level of technical competency through the grading systems. The term 'to commit' is also used in unison to the above, referring to the exact time-space on a climb where the crux (the most technical move on the route) has to be negotiated physically together with the mental ability to remain calm and complete the climbing line without falling off. This negotiation between the above characteristics – this 'game' that climbers play (to coin a phrase from Ken Wilson's 1978 edited seminal collection of stories) – for competent climbers at least, is an important part of the process, negotiating the real and imagined risk that is involved with this form of adventure. This does not mean that experienced recreational climbers are not susceptible to fear, or even death, it is that they become accustomed to committing in the right moments where the ending of one's life could be a possible outcome.

Image 7.2: Climber James Mitchell on 'The Nose', El Capitan, Yosemite National Park, California, Nicola Taylor Collection.

'The rock is steeper. I talk to the butterflies in my stomach. Old aspirations. No possible protection. Higgins flicks the rope. It jerks me. I nearly dirty my pants. Tom (The belayer) leans his head against the rock, baking in the sun. I pick out holds.

'Taking plenty of time and making sure I don't fall.'

'Don't blame you. Take all the time you want.'

'If I can just reach that thing up there.'

'Looks like a good hold.'

I guess I have to sort of commit myself.'

Source: Adapted form Amment and Higgins, in Wilson (1996:109)

For recreational climbers, this negotiation of death is an occupational hazard, but for commercial (guided or instructed) adventure participants it is worth looking further as to whether this same contemplation takes place and who are the key stakeholders in reinforcing the process. Kevin Krein, in MacNamee (2007:84) suggests that there is a valid discussion worth considering when looking into the relationship between risk, reward and death within a variety of skill levels. For guided individuals, where the decision-making is left to the role of the experienced instructor/leader, is real risk still the point of such an activity or is perceived risk the acceptable form through early experiences of participation? In essence, 'death defying' situations for the climber who participates regularly are both a byproduct of participation which we need to negotiate effectively to complete successfully an activity, and is furthermore a core part of the subconscious reward which motivates to further seek out and complete risky experiences.

The example portrayed in Image 7.2 is a route called 'The Nose', the famous 3000ft sheer cliff face in California's Yosemite Valley. The route can be a mixture of free climbing (climbing using features in the rock) and aid climbing (climbing on retrievable equipment placed in-situ). Some parts of the climb the climber will find easy, whilst the 'crux sections' the climber will find the most difficult on the route. Part of this reward is successfully completing this crux section without succumbing to the desire to 'back off', 'down climb' or indeed, fall and test the equipment you have placed along the route. For a route like 'The Nose' the reward also encompasses the feeling of completing a significant test of both mental and physical stamina. The route typically takes 4 to 7 days to complete, although for the purposes of the current discussion it is worth noting that the record is an almost superhuman 2 hours 23 minutes 46 seconds. It is interesting here to also consider the feeling whilst climbing the route. Imagine yourself as the climber in this picture, looking up and considering the next 2000ft of implacable granite rock and thinking of what potentially lies in store – success or failure, risk, reward, complexity, challenge. An experienced climber would argue that due to the exposure on the route, the participant restrains these feelings whilst in the act, as not to do so would jepordise the mental preparation that has taken place prior to the route's commencement, and that such restraint is therefore a method of negotiating life-threatening experiences. It is also argued here that these feelings do need to be engaged, as complete avoidance would be to trivialise the severity of the experience. (Note here also that most humans are incapable of turning off emotion where mortality could be questioned). Again, prior experience helps in this negotiation of experience. The nature of exposure: that of the variables which influence the perceived feel of the rock climb, including, but not limited to, position, height, technicality, severity of the outcome in the event of failure, etc., will further enhance both positive and negative feelings whilst participating in this adventure. It is possible in these scenarios to see that negotiating the route as a whole, including the crux sections, could not just be understood as a physical act, but also as a mental game, where the 'death instinct' (Buda, 2015:42) or the tempting of death through the completion of risky situations is a psychological trait which in part influences some adventurists to participate. As with dark tourism, the nature of death is a complex and challenging variable, and one that is not always interacted with flippantly, although to the untrained eye it may sometimes appear so. In this sense is there such a thing as 'unnecessary risk'? If the fascination of death within a contemporary dark tourism product can be an important learning tool for the tourist, is not 'flirting with death' in adventure experience an opportunity to learn more about ourselves, our life and our place in the universe? A rather grandiose concept, but one which is argued here as pertinent for any adventure participant, guided or otherwise.

If 'flirting with death' for some could be considered to be a primary intrinsic motivational factor for the recreational (unguided) experienced climber, then what for the guided inexperienced paying participant? Whilst they may not want to experience this *'Dance of death'* as a novice, it is argued here that their future progression in the activity relies on current instruction and education in helping to gain an insight into these facets of risk, near death experience, etc. For the recreationalist who participates on a regular basis and for whom the activity forms a key part of their own identity, reliance on technical, physical and mental experience and the understanding and negotiation of death is an important facet to more extreme forms of activity. It is important to make a distinction here between the recreationalist participating regularly, and the commercial adventure tourist, or as is segmented for the purposes of this chapter, the dabbler or sampler.

VisitScotland's (2007) report into the future of adventure tourism made reference to a segmentation method discussed by Page (2003) referring to four distinct adventure typologies:

- **Samplers:** Those who are trying an adventure activity for the first time or undertake the activity on a very occasional basis. e.g. special occasion groups, hen & stag groups, corporate groups

- **Learners:** Those that are learning an adventure activity or seeking to improve their skills. e.g.. youth groups, training groups, individuals seeking proficiency.

- **Dabblers:** People who occasionally take part in an adventure activity when on holiday or as part of leisure time. They have learnt how to undertake their chosen activity and have some knowledge or skills but will not be regularly undertaking the activity. Holidays provide a primary opportunity to undertake the activity for this group. e.g. friendship groups or individuals who have some experience in an outdoor activity.

- ■ **Enthusiasts:** People who regularly take part in an adventure activity and are very keen on it. They are experts in the activity which requires knowledge and skill.

Source: adapted from VisitScotland (2007)

Segmentation methods such as this can help identify specific demographic, geographic and psychographic variables which may influence the target groups and subsequent promotional strategy of a tourism product, or destination in the case of VisitScotland. Scotland as an adventure destination attracts a variety of adventure skill types, from the novice participant trying out activities for the first time (*the sampler*), to the occasional holiday participant (*the dabbler*) through to the expert and knowledgeable participant (*the enthusiast*). If we consider risk exposure within these segmented typologies, we could initially argue that the *enthusiasts* expose themselves to more real risk, due to nature of unguided participation, whereas the *samplers* have the risk component of their adventure activity carefully managed and monitored.

If adventure therefore can help our understanding of mortality and the role that death plays in our lives, we could further surmise here that the risk managed groups of *sampler* and *dabbler* potentially have less opportunity to exercise and question mortality due to the emphasis on management of the experience. We could therefore subsequently argue that a core component of the traditional adventure experience is missing. Figure 7.1 attempts to visually present (albeit roughly) the difference in opportunity for a 'Death Debate'. Is it too radical to suggest that we as human beings can learn about the meaning of life through questioning the role of death, and could this be a focal point for appropriate discussions regarding the development of *samplers* into *dabblers,* and then into *learners,* subsequently evolving into *enthusiasts*?

The argument proposed here which warrants further discussion is that the adventure sector should not shy away from these discussions, as it is a prime opportunity to develop the adventure experience of all participants, and make well rounded and realistic adventure enthusiasts for participation in the future. As Buckley (2010:51) proposes, modern adventure tourism contains both the motivation to experience risk as well as, in commercial adventure operations, to measure, minimise and manage risk. One of the key challenges here of course is how a sector akin to commercial adventure tourism implements discussions regarding death and mortality without demotivating the samplers and dabblers. It is not the suggestion here to merely state '*You could die*' at the beginning of an adventure activity. However, like the subtlety of using perceived risk in adventure, the question of mortality and death could also be raised in such a way as to instill confidence and provoke thought on realistic participation in the future, rather than limit a market through fear.

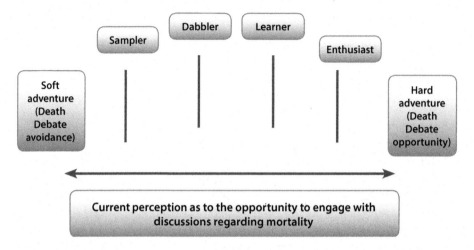

Figure 7.1: Current spectrum of opportunity to question mortality ('Death Debate')

The enthusiast may still be considered as an adventure tourist, but these are consumers who participate with increased regularity in their chosen adventure activity. The future of adventure tourism is based around the development of the increasingly growing, guided adventure tour market and the 'dabbler' / 'sampler' (insights, 2003, in VisitScotland, 2007) whose frequency of participation is sporadic and subsequent level of skill is lower. The emphasis is placed on the word 'tourist' here, as their nature of participation is one that craves the adventurous element of the activity, but does not have higher level of skill that is required to participate. For the modern commercial adventure tourist, the sampler and the dabbler, this relationship with mortality is paradoxical. From one perspective they crave the nature of fear and risk that is entailed within an adventurous experience, but do so with an increased sense of detachment due to the guided component or the sporadic nature of participation. It is argued here that this in turn creates a lack of opportunity of understanding mortality from an adventurous perspective.

Discussion topic

In a world of increasing consumerism, customer expectation and satisfaction, is it necessary to educate modern adventure 'samplers' and other commercially guided adventure tourists as to the nature of mortality in adventure participation? How do the terms 'consumerism', 'expectation' and 'satisfaction' impact upon this debate?

Further thoughts on commercial adventure tourism

Commercial adventure tourism has been alluded to previously as anything within the adventure tourism sector where a monetary transaction takes place for the purposes of guided and unguided recreational activity (Hudson, 2003, Buckley, 2007, 2011). The monetary transaction referred to here could be identified as being both varied and multiple, examples including payment to guide/instructor and/or contribution towards the local economy through the use of accommodation and other forms of hospitality. As what we deem as adventurous in society is largely subjective and individualistic, this can include a variety of different adventure experiences. The use of the term 'tourism' reinforces the financial nature of the relationship between participant and activity. Commercial, organised adventure tourism therefore is defined as a guided adventurous activity where the risk element is negotiated initially by the guide/leader through such conduits as leadership decision making, dynamic and static risk management, etc.

Dynamic risk assessment refers to a risk assessment undertaken in-situ at the specific time-space of the activity. Conversely, static risk assessment here refers to a pre-planned assessment of the expected risks associated with an activity, with the intention of managing the likelihood and severity prior to commencement.

Commercial adventure therefore includes participants from a wide variety of background, not necessarily novice, although as a participant continues within an adventure career, the need for a guide in certain situations (certainly not all) can become less of a primary facilitator for participation, because of the reliance on previous experience. That said, it is important to note the significance of the guide in providing an opportunity to develop skill and experience for all levels of participation. An experienced skier for example may pay for the use of a guide so as to benefit from local knowledge and understanding of an area when going 'off piste'. This kind of best practice is encouraged in ski resorts and acts as a way of minimising injury and off piste accidents due to lack of preparation.

Commercially guided adventure tourism therefore increases in demand due to the proliferation of tourists to consume adventurous experiences in a safely managed manner. In the contemporary paradox of the consumer/adventurist however, there arises a question as to whether there is a clear understanding by the participant of the real risks involved and therefore the role that misadventure plays in negotiating/developing the experience. This raises the distinction between what risk and what death are. Risk, its assessment and its management is quoted continuously throughout both academic and industry textbooks, reports, articles, etc. whilst death is a less used term.

Examples of the term 'misadventure' can be attributed to authors such as Colin Mortlock (2000:23), where the level of real risk being taken outweighs the level of personal experience or competency in the activity that is being participated in. The term has a strong association with death, as proposed by Mortlock:

> Like adventure, misadventure is a state of mind. Unlike adventure, the immediate reactions are essentially negative rather than positive. At one extreme the result is death or serious injury.
>
> Mortlock (2000:41)

Mortlock's model highlights the significance of balancing play with misadventure, through knowing one's boundaries and managing individual competency and risk effectively. On one hand, the understanding of the level of mortality associated with adventure is for all to see here. One of the tragic resulting factors associated with misadventure is serious injury and/or death. Participants find themselves in this situation due to a variety of foreseen and unforeseen circumstances.

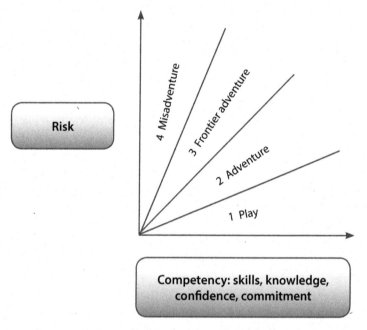

Figure 7.2: Mortlock's model. Adapted from Mortlock (1984, 2000), in Swarbrooke et al (2003:11)

The benefits of this early model were reinforcing the foundation that higher levels of risk coupled with low level of competency can lead to misadventure. Mortlock was inspired through his own experiences of working within the outdoor education sector in North Wales and further afield. The critical balance to address was the need to manage the adventure experience together with providing a conduit to understand risk and subsequently discuss and reflect on the nature of danger. Mortlocks omission of the word 'death' within some of this discussion is partly telling when considering society's aversion to dialogue regarding mortality and the use of the term as being inherently negative. What is also telling within Mortlock's narrative is his reference to the resistance that he himself found on occasions where his innovative ideas regarding adventure and discussions of danger/misadventure were met with resistance (2000:13).

For the commercial adventure sector, where the sampler and dabbler as market segments form potentially lucrative groups to target, discussions of death and mortality are considered in the same vein. This is perhaps due to mortality as an afterthought within the booking terms and conditions of *volenti non fit injuria (to one who volunteers, injury is not done)* or assumption of risk, in small type where the appearance is lessened so not as to put off would-be adventure tourists. The reflection on mortality can help us negotiate and understand the real and perceived dangers that are inherent in the adventure experience, allowing us to use commercial adventure as an educative tool. Just as dark tourism is a macro educator of how we can learn from dark, tragic periods in human history, so too can we learn by looking at both the positive and negative in adventure.

This could present itself in no more uncertain terms than in a critical investigation into perception and meaning of adventure activities in society. Key motivators for adventure participation in the 21st century include the need for prestige and status (Swarbrooke et al, 2003) and within an ever increasingly complex world, where we strive to understand and justify our own identity, coming as close to the edge as we can, through conduits such as a adventure, becomes an important tool to justify our role both within the chosen activity as well as in wider society. Much adaptation has been given to Hunter S Thompsons '60s ethnographic travel narrative *Hells Angels*, where he discusses the idea of 'the edge' and 'edgework' (1999).

Authors such as Allman et al (2009) have attributed these concepts to adventure activities such as BASE jumping – a rather extreme form of adventure where competency must outweigh risk and where experience is paramount for participation. Interestingly, the relationship between 'edgework' – the ability through adventure to understand the metaphorical line between success or survival, and failure or near-death/death – and BASE shows the significance of not only understanding the location of 'the edge', but also the fulfillment and satisfaction that is gained from negotiating this successfully. Commercial adventure with its push away from the appropriate discussions of mortality could be losing an opportunity to develop something more in the participant, regardless of whether they are a sampler or an enthusiast.

In edgework, the notions of play in the Mortlock context do not come into consideration due to the high real risk factor. 'Edgeworkers' are the voluntary risk takers who perplex most of society by actively seeking out high risk, life-threatening experiences (2009:230). Exploring one's own ability from this perspective can only be understood by having been to the edge and survived to tell the tale. The edge is therefore symbolic of life and death and this negotiation provides unique insights into those participants who dare to test the edge, and understand what it means to go over.

> ...The Edge... There is no way to explain it because the only people who know where it really is are the ones who have gone over. The others – the living – are those who pushed their control as far as they felt they could handle it, and then pulled back, or slowed down, or did whatever they had to when it came time to choose between Now and Later.

Hunter S. Thompson (1967:282)

All adventure participation features this component, regardless of the level of participation. The 'finite' edge is what the extreme high risk participants are looking for in adventure, but as models like Mortlocks' show, the adventure participant with limited knowledge of the activity and being guided, still wishes to test the edge of their own ability. It is here that reflection is needed into the nature of the edge for every participant, and what it is – and what therefore are the results of going over. Regardless of the level of participation, the edge is a location that is dictated by a participant's own level of skill and competency, and where death comes to visit, albeit possibly in a fleeting form, taunting each and every participant. In this sense, whilst the extreme BASE jumper in Allman et al's work is perhaps the true undiscovered finite boundary for everyone (equipment failure, gravity and the other relevant laws of physics largely dictate this 'edge'), we, as adventure participants regardless of level, all have an edge with which we play with in all activities, which can tragically sometimes result in devastation and death for the participant, sampler, dabbler, learner or enthusiasts, professional. Whilst it is the guide's or leader's responsibility to manage this in the early stages of participation, it is uniquely important for us all to learn this nature of a changing edge early on in our adventure careers, so as to understand the nature of participation, and the potential outcomes based on competency and real risk, regardless of who we are and how many times we have participated.

Balancing risk and competency in adventure tourism is made ever more challenging by the anticipated rewards attributed to adventure activities, coupled with the nature of perceived risk when undertaking a commercial organised adventure tourism product. These are two important facets that need to be considered when discussing the role of the 'death debate' in adventure.

Simon Priest's extension of Mortlock's (1984) model (in Miles and Priest, 1991) furthered the debate and the understanding of risk and competency through the increased focus on devastation and disaster, coupled with the ability of the participant to understand correct perceptions.

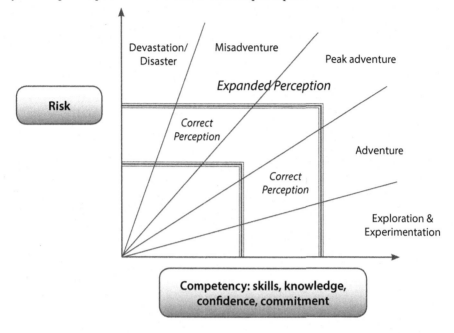

Figure 7.3: Mortlock's model with Priest's extension (1991), adapted from Nichols (2000:122)

As can be seen from the model in Figure 7.3, the boundary incorporating correct perception is when the level of risk and competency matches to help construct a realistic image of the nature of the activity being performed. As Nichols (2000) suggests, Priest is concerned with the role that perception takes when using adventure as an educative tool with individuals. What is interesting for the discussion regarding mortality and death is the distinction between correct perception and expanded perception. Correct perception is as suggested, a firm understanding of the risk involved coupled with the realistic appreciation of the level of technical competency.

Expanded perception is how increased participation in a given activity can be extended to further progress an individual's risk appreciation and competency levels. Understanding the outcomes of experience, including the relationship between adventure and death is argued here as being a further method of expanding the benefit of participation in a growing sector of adventure tourism, where the 'dark' nature of participation does not feature in a thanatological sightseeing tour of devastation and disaster, but features in an activity where physical participation is a requirement and a core motivational need. Of further interest in this model is the inclusion of more fatalistic terms related to questions of mortality – those of 'devastation' and 'disaster'. These are crucial components on the model as they allow (if implemented appropriately) for an adventure tourism provider to raise the resulting question of mortality with participants and therefore question:

- Why do people participate in adventure activities if there is a possibility of near death/death?

- What characteristics influence devastation and disaster? For example, lack of concentration, enjoyment, fun, preparation, competency, risk understanding and acceptance. And at what times when participating?

- How/when should participants retain this level of mindfulness when participating in the future.

Practically of course, when considering how and when to implement such discussion with an adventure tourist as part of the experience, it is unlikely that an appropriate method of implementing would initially be in the pre-activity phase, before participation is undertaken and safety briefings are given. This would suggest that the more appropriate time to develop such a discussion would be in the post experience, once the activity has been completed. Fundamentally, this could provide a reinforcement of correct and expanded competency and risk for dabblers who may turn into learners and/or enthusiasts in the future, therefore raise the question of lone participation, and the associated risks, and also the importance of further guiding/training for the adventure participant.

Discussion activity

According to statistics published by the Ogwen Mountain Rescue Service (www. ogwen-rescue.org.uk) incident rates in the Snowdonia National Park involving adventure participants and tourists have increased substantially over the past 50 years.

You work for a walking/trekking company based in the National Park which deals predominantly with domestic adventure tourists (samplers and dabblers). The activities your company offers range from single and multiple day walking holidays to scrambling experiences. You have been asked as part of a public relations exercise to develop a template to discuss mortality / accident rates with clients as a reflective exercise post activity, so as to help them understand safe lone participation. What methods and lines of discussion can be used to raise the questions proposed in this chapter effectively, so as to increase a tourist's personal responsibility when participating in future?

Concluding remarks: understanding the value of the 'death debate' in adventure tourism

Image 7.3 (Left): *Death and the Old Man* from Holbein's *The Dance of Death*, Knight, C. (1880), Bridgeman education, digitally cleared copy

Image 7.4 (Right): *The Abbot.* Woodcut from *The Dance of Death*, Kunstmuseum Basel. Wikimedia cleared copy in the public domain.

Images 7.3 and 7.4 are renderings from Hans Holbein the younger's *Dance of Death*, or *Danse Macabre* woodcuts (a late medieval artistic genre). Holbein was a 16ᵗʰ century artist who produced a variety of images that attempted to stimulate understanding as to the universality of death. Holbein in particular is interesting in this movement, due to the level of popularity that was achieved through printing of the woodcuts in the 16ᵗʰ century, as well as the symbolic impact they have in reinforcing the need for all, no matter age, social standing, vocation etc., to prepare for death appropriately. Death will punish those who concentrate too heavily on the earthly pleasure that life has to offer, regardless of who you are.

What is of further interest here is Holbein's inclusion, in the various renderings, of both the personification death as a mischievous, sometimes evil figure for some, toying with the human, for example the Abbot in Image 7.4, whilst simultaneously a friend and a helper for others (as seen befriending the old man in Image 7.3). It is this idea from the *Dance of Death* that is most striking, and one which associates well to both dark tourism, as well as adventure tourism's more thanatological elements. Dark tourism is a phenomenon that requires an association and application to a variety of different sectors and activities associated with more generic areas of tourism, be it events, sites, activities, behavior, etc.

It can be used as a further metaphor to reinforce the importance of discussing mortality with a variety of adventure tourism participants, regardless of skill level, experience, etc. We all have something to gain from questioning the relationship with death when participating in adventurous activities. The advent of dark tourism as a commercial product allows, as Stone (2011) suggests, for an ontological consideration of mortality and the opportunity to mediate between that of life and death, sometimes in a playful manner. It provides the tourist with a unique opportunity to not only gaze upon death, but to also gain personal meaning from this experience, in terms of the role of death in society, coupled with an opportunity of considering states of personal mortality.

Other key writing on this topic, such as that of Lennon and Foley (1996), and Sharply and Stone (2009) further raise the critical point that dark tourism as a phenomena in the wider tourism industry is multi-faceted and varied, incorporating many meanings, interpretation and subsequent attractions. These foundations have driven the discussion included within this chapter. The multifaceted nature of tourism means that dialogue in dark tourism cannot neglect other related sectors, such as adventure tourism. Previous authors on this subject have identified the important role that fatality plays in the modern adventure tourism sector (Bentley, Page and Laird, 2000; Williams and Soutar, 2005; Ball and Machin, 2006; Wilson et al, 2013,). However, like the studies of dark tourism that are proposed in this text, as well as others, what is important here is the consideration of death not as simply a byproduct of ineffective risk management or assessment procedures, or organisational or personal negligence. The 'Death Debate' is a learning experience, that due to such industry developments as the commodification of adventure (Varley, 2006) has been unnecessarily relegated to that of a villainous variable, to which the control of such a factor is fundamentally important for the sustainable future of a sector increasing in demand and supply.

By analysing death as human beings, social actors, adventurists, we do not mean to trivialise life. On the contrary, we embrace the relationship of life and death and the inextricable link between the two. We are entering life with our eyes wide open, embracing its diversity and its limits so we may test these through leisure and recreation as we see fit. As dark tourism teaches us, we should enter discussions of mortality in adventure with a level of impartiality that is seldom seen when all things contradictory to life are contemporarily discussed. This is one of the many learning experiences that can truly be gained from adventure participation, and one that all can learn from.

Discussion questions

1   Does the 'organised' nature of modern adventure tourism mean that tourists (one off participants in activities) are less educated as to the real risks involved in participation?

2   How and what can the commercial 'all-inclusive' nature of the soft adventure tourism sector learn from the hard adventure sector?

3   Do soft adventure participants 'shy away' from death, or is it the commercial adventure tourism industry that limits the potential to understand?

References

Allman, T., Mittelstaedt, R., Martin, B., & Goldenberg, M. (2009). Exploring the motivations of BASE jumpers: Extreme sport enthusiasts, *Journal of Sport & Tourism*, **14**(4), 229-247.

Ball, D., & Machin, N, (2006), Foreign travel and the risk of harm, *International Journal of Injury Control & Safety Promotion*, **13**(2), 107-115.

Beedie, P. & Hudson, S. (2003). Exploration of mountain-based adventure tourism. *Annals of Tourism Research*, **30**(3), 625–643.

Bentley, T., Page, S., & Laird, I.N.D. (2000). Safety in New Zealand's adventure tourism industry: The client accident experience of adventure tourism operators, *Journal of Travel Medicine*, **7**(5), 239-245.

British Mountaineering Council (2010). Climbing and mountaineering on the increase. Available at https://www.thebmc.co.uk/climbing-and-mountaineering-on-the-increase. Accessed 10th December 2014.

Buckley, R. (2010). *Adventure Tourism Management*. Amsterdam: Butterworth-Heinemann.

Buda, D.M. (2015). The death drive in tourism studies, *Annals of Tourism Research*, **50**, 39-51.

Giddens, A. & Birdsall, K. (2013). *Sociology*. (7th Edition) Cambridge, UK: Polity Press.

Knight, C. (1880). Death and the old man from Holbein's Dance of Death, Bridgeman education digitally cleared copy, Available at www.bridgemaneducation.com, Accessed 10th June 2015.

McNamee, M. (2007). *Philosophy, Risk and Adventure Sports*. London: Routledge.

Martinelli, G. (1635). *Memento Mori* (Death Comes to the Dinner Table), [Oil on canvas]. Galerie G. Sarti, Paris.

Miles, J. and Priest, S. (1990). *Adventure Education*. State College, PA: Venture Pub.

Mortlock, C. (2000). *The Adventure Alternative* (4th ed), Milnthorpe, Cicerone Press.

Nichols, G. (2000). Risk and adventure education. *Journal of Risk Research*, **3**(2), 121-134.

Stone, P.R. (2011). Dark tourism and the cadaveric carnival: mediating life and death narratives at Gunther von Hagens' Body Worlds. *Current Issues in Tourism*, **14**(7), 685-701.

Swarbrooke, J. Beard, C. Leckie, S. Pomfret, G. (2003). *Adventure Tourism: The New Frontier*. Oxford: Butterworth-Heinemann.

The Abbot. (nd). Woodcut from the series known as The Dance of Death, Kunstmuseum Basel. Available at http://commons.wikimedia.org/wiki/File:The_Abbot,_from_The_Dance_of_Death,_by_Hans_Holbein_the_Younger.jpg. Accessed 8th January 2015.

Thompson, H. (1967). *Hell's Angels*, London, Penguin Books Ltd.

Varley, P. (2006). Confecting adventure and playing with meaning: The adventure commodification continuum, *Journal of Sport & Tourism*, **11**(2), 173-194

VisitScotland (2007). *What will activity and adventure tourism look like in 2015*. Edinburgh. Available at www.visitscotland.org/pdf/adventure_tourism_forecast_march_07.pdf, Accessed on 27th September 2010.

Williams, P., & Soutar, G. (2005). Close to the 'Edge': Critical issues for adventure tourism operators, *Asia Pacific Journal of Tourism Research*, **10**(3), 247-261

Wilson, K. (1980). *The Games Climbers Play*. San Francisco: Sierra Club Books.

Wilson, I., McDermott, H., Munir, F., & Hogervorst, E. (2013). 'Injuries, Ill-health and fatalities in white water rafting and white water paddling', *Sports Medicine*, **43**(1), 65-75.

8

Life after the Black Death:

How dark tourism sheds light on history - a case study of Eyam's success in creating a future from the past

John Philips

Abstract

For centuries the village of Eyam has inspired poets, novelists and playwrights to tell and re-tell the story of its inhabitants' selfless bravery in isolating themselves to stop the Black Death spreading to surrounding communities. Different generations have used the villagers' decision in 1665 to make a stand against an unseen enemy as a metaphor for the issues of their own time. But the villagers, too, have built on the story. For the last 200 years, each generation has kept the story alive, added to it, re-interpreted it, until it became the basis for a highly successful tourist industry, by 2003 attracting 100,000 visitors a year to a village of just 1,000 (*The Guardian*, April 2, 2003). This chapter examines the parallel evolutions of the Eyam story and the tourism industry it supports, with a discussion of the nature of authenticity in relation to the tourism experience.

Learning outcomes

1 Understand how villagers in Eyam have nurtured the story of their ancestors and the plague.

2 How the story has been interpreted through the ages in the light of contemporary attitudes.

3 Why there is controversy over some aspects of the plague.

4 Be more aware of the meaning of 'authenticity' in relation to a tourist experience.

5 Understand how destinations need to re-invent themselves in the light of changing attitudes.

6 Be aware of how businesses can adapt a destination's story to encourage its economy.

Introduction

The Derbyshire village of Eyam where plague struck in 1665 is arguably one of the most potent dark tourism sites in Great Britain, described as 'the epicentre of Europe's plague heritage' (Wallis, 2006). Faced with an outbreak of the Black Death, brought to their community by an infected bolt of cloth from London where the disease had killed people in their hundreds, the villagers isolated themselves under the leadership of their vicar in an act of selfless quarantine intended to save neighbouring communities from the same fate.

The story prompted poet Ebenezer Rhodes in his 1824 book *Peak Scenery: Or, The Derbyshire Tourist,* (Rhodes, 1824: 31) to pen what might now be seen as a workable definition of dark tourism:

> Suffering has sanctified its claim to notice, and the curious and enquiring traveller feels a melancholy pleasure in tracing out the records of the ravages made in this little village by that depopulating scourge of nations.

By the Victorian era, this 'melancholy pleasure' attracted crowds in their tens of thousands to Eyam for the annual church service to commemorate the village's heroism. The story has also been used to show English superiority over the French; Protestantism's superiority over Catholicism; democracy over dictatorship; helped teach literature, drama and statistics as part of the National Curriculum and provided a musical metaphor for the Miners' Strike of 1984-5.

How much of the Eyam Plague story can be verified historically has been investigated comprehensively by Wallis in *A Dreadful Heritage: Interpreting Epidemic Disease at Eyam, 1666-2000* (2006), on which much of this chapter is based. The intention of this chapter, however, is to track how the heritage of the Eyam story relies as much on contemporary interpretation as it does on historical accuracy – and how that relates to tourism. It will show how the Eyam Plague story has been added to and re-told for centuries, sometimes to fit in with the perceptions of the day or even in a bid to influence them, on issues ranging from genetics, public health in Britain's own age of cholera, the AIDS epidemic and the even terrorist attacks of 9/11, as war correspondent Geraldine Brooks believes (Washington Post).

By tracing the story's influence – and influences in history which have shaped the story in turn – we can see how one example of dark tourism has been used to promote arguments and illustrate ideas which in turn have informed our responses to a wide range of important issues.

The chapter will also attempt to show how the success of the story in mutating in this way has been critical to the success of Eyam as a tourist destination, by keeping history not only alive, but also relevant. Eyam is also an exemplar of how tourism can be nurtured by the community which benefits from it, and this study in what authenticity means – not in historical terms, but in terms of an experience which provides an authentic link to the tourist's life and times.

The walking dead tour in Derbyshire

There are streets you can walk down where only time separates you from becoming one of the living dead, one of those touched by a silent, invisible killer called the Black Death.

> It's not a computer game about zombies; it's not a TV horror special, but a real place, with a history with an 'ongoing celebrity'... indebted to a combination of literary effort and contemporary events.
>
> (Wallis, 2006)

Eyam in the Derbyshire Peak District is a village worth a visit just for its picture postcard appearance. But most people go there because in 1665 no-one was allowed to: the villagers cut themselves off from the outside world in a selfless attempt to prevent the spread of the same plague, which according to contemporary official records had killed 68,596 people. The National Archives claim the true number was probably over 100,000. At its peak in September that year, 7,165 Londoners perished in just one week (National Archives, London).

Isolation – keeping infected Londoners effectively prisoners in their homes where they waited to die along with their relatives, infected or not – was used to prevent its spread, with houses sealed and guarded. No-one could bring food or any help, and diarist Samuel Pepys recorded hearing wails of woe from such houses, marked with red crosses and the words 'God Have Mercy': "We are become as cruel as dogs to one another," Pepys wrote in his diary.

But not in Eyam. When the plague reached Eyam in a delivery of cloth to the village tailor, it began a train of events which led to a perfect paradigm of the essence of selflessness and sacrifice which was to spawn a literary canon of its own, including plays, a television film, novels, a musical and a vibrant tourism industry. The lessons of the Eyam Plague have been used to teach everything from drama and statistics to genetics and immunology, and are now enshrined in the UK's National Curriculum.

Historical fiction or a very human truth?

'Eyam is an epicentre of Europe's plague heritage,' according to Wallis (2006: 1). Thousands of visitors come to the village each year to explore, on the streets where it happened, the story of how an heroic response to the plague by villagers prepared to sacrifice themselves to save their neighbours, inspired by the firm leadership of their Rector, the Reverend William Mompesson.

The story starts when old clothing, infested with plague-carrying fleas, arrives for the village tailor in 1665 from London, where the plague was beginning to die out. The disease struck soon after, but the number of deaths waned in the winter. Spring's promise of new life came with more deaths, however, and Mompesson is credited in nearly every version of the story with proposing that his parishioners put themselves in quarantine to stop the disease from spreading. With the support of the Earl of Devonshire, the major landowner in the area, it was arranged for supplies to be left at strategic spots, where villagers left payment in coins deposited in vinegar in holes drilled in a large rock.

The holes can still be seen today in the stone, standing like a sentinel in open pasture.

> Outdoor services replaced those in church to limit infection, and ordinary life came to an end as 259 people, including Mompesson's wife Catherine, died from a population of 350 had died.
>
> (Trueman, 2014)

Two centuries later, thousands of tourists would meet in Eyam for outdoor services to celebrate the story of the villagers' sacrifice. And yet at least one researcher has questioned just how much, in reality, there was to celebrate. Wallis (2006) claims the accepted Eyam narrative was "largely fiction; produced not by doctors, but by poets, writers and local historians".

> Eyam's ongoing celebrity is indebted to a combination of literary effort and contemporary events, particularly, but not exclusively involving the threat of disease, during the late eighteenth and nineteenth centuries.
>
> (Wallis, 2006)

> During this period a tradition was established, manipulated and reshaped to fit changing literary and historical fashions, while the fabric of the village itself was adapted to suit the tourist trade on which it increasingly became dependent.
>
> (Wallis, 2006)

Daniel Defoe's *History of the Plague Year* written in 1772 was published when plague was epidemic in Marseilles, and it seemed likely that the disease would reach England again. Defoe could draw on accounts from people who lived through London's plague, but Eyam did not find its amanuensis until the mid-eighteenth century when the almost forgotten story was brought back to life in different forms, ranging from poetry to tourist guidebooks.

> The construction of the Eyam plague story offers an unusually clear case study in the social and intellectual dynamics of the creation of heritage and history.
>
> (Wallis, 2006)

That the story of the plague of Eyam has not become widely dis-
seminated until so long after the event allowed it to develop without
the influence of a dominant 'authentic' interpretation from the time
of the epidemic itself.

(Wallis, 2006: 4)

This distance from the actual events frees the authors of its legend from the
responsibility towards those who lived through it, but more importantly allows
them to use it to explore themes of local and national identity, heroism and
leadership, says Wallis (2006). Three letters by Mompesson, the parish register
and the burial sites in and around the village are the only direct evidence of the
plague in Eyam, but it was only in the 1970s that historian Leslie Bradley noted
that 64 per cent of the village families escaped the plague, which killed no more
than half of the people living there.

Paul Slack also pointed out that controls on the movement of people around
Eyam was suggestive of similar rules imposed on a number of parishes and
towns in the same period. "Much of the coherency of the traditional account
dissolves when examined closely," claims Wallis (2006), who also points out
that the earliest oral stories credit the former Rector of Eyam, Thomas Stanley,
as the village's savour, while Mompesson, who sent his children away to safety
early on, might not have been so well supported in the village.

Removed from office for his Puritan sympathies on the restoration of the
monarchy, Stanley receives the first mention of self-sacrifice – although significantly only for his part, not of the village as a whole – when he is defended by
the Earl of Devonshire against those who wanted the clergyman to be dismissed
from his post because of his non-conformity. The Earl is alleged to have said:

The whole county should in more than words testifie their
Thankfulness to him (Stanley), who together with this Care of
the Town, had taken such Care as no one else did, to prevent the
Infection of the Towns adjacent.

(Wallis, 2006)

Wallis (2006) not only uses this as evidence that the Mompesson-inspired
self-sacrifice narrative might have no foundation in history, but also points out
that the author in this instance was writing in support of the commitment by
non-conformists to their parish. In other words, the first mention of self-sacrifice
is mentioned in a partisan way to make a point: a pattern which is repeated time
and again in the history of the story of the Eyam Plague.

But by the 19th Century, Mompesson was being compared to the two most
important figures in Christianity after Christ himself: "When we figure to ourselves this admirable man surrounded by his parishioners... preaching to them
as it were in a wilderness from a projecting rock... and inspiring them with for-

titude at a time of dread; is it possible to conceive a picture more truly sublime? Paul preaching at Athens, or John the Baptist in the wilderness, scarcely excites a more powerful and solemn interest than this minister of God" (Ebenezer Rhodes, Peak Scenery, 1824, 36).

On the same page, Rhodes invokes scripture directly to compare Mompesson to the Old Testament's Aaron, who intervened when God sent disease to punish the rebellious Israelites, representing the 17th century vicar as standing "between the dead and the living, and the plague was swayed" (Numbers, 16:48).

Compare that view of Mompesson to an Irish broadside printed in 1910. A broadside was a simple leaflet, whose content ranged from ballads, poems, political propaganda or simply advertisements. 'A Moral Ballad of the Eyam Plague' by Francis Macnamara is the story of a young girl who defies the self-imposed quarantine and runs away from the village, only to be stoned to death by the terrified people of Sheffield where she seeks shelter.

Macnamara, however, sees a darker motive in the quarantine, poetically comparing the freedom of wild animals to the fate of the poor in a hierarchical society which can control their lives with such 'wondrous power, the multitude to restrain':

> And the rich fled out of Eyam
> The rooks fled too, for they too are sure
> Of a lodging in every state
> But men have invented the poverty
> Which compels the poor to sit and wait.
> (Cuala Press, Broadside Number Six, Third Year, 1910)

Life after death

Eyam's Plague would make headline news if it happened today – but why did it make headlines in 1927? The *Singapore Free Press and Mercantile Advertiser* ran a story in June of that year under the headline 'Village that defied death – vivid memories of the plague.' Their reporter began: "In this little quiet Derbyshire village, men still talk about the Plague of London as though it happened last week. Eyam is the last place in England with a vivid memory of the terrible pestilence of 1665." (Unknown reporter, 1927)

Vivid memory? 238 years later? The story continues: 'I went into the church, where the elderly caretaker began to talk, as they all do in Eyam, of the Plague: – 'We used to leave our money in the well, where the water washed it clean,' she said. 'People from other villages would bring food for us and take the money out of the well. It was terrible. Everyone one frightened of catching the Plague.'

The reporter adds in parenthesis: "(She might as well have been talking about this year's influenza.)"

The use of the first person by the church caretaker implies immediacy, a personal involvement in events which it was impossible for her to have had any such knowledge of. *The Singapore Free Press* hints at an explanation:

> So many things have happened in London since the reign of Charles II that the Plague is not even a memory. But it was the last thing that happened to Eyam!
>
> (The Singapore Free Press)

That might be enough to impress people who visit the village, but in the late 1700s, why did the Eyam story have resonance nationally? Wallis (2006) believes that the Eyam story was part of a new concept of Englishness which emphasised its roots in a mythicised heroic past, continuing particularities of character and its distinctiveness from Catholicism and the European continent.

"Eyam's relationship to an idea of English character was most overt at the beginning of this process," he said. During The French Revolution, the *European Magazine* resurrected the deeds of dead aristocrats to contrast with the outrages of the blood-thirsty sans-culottes. The Bishop of Marseilles' leadership of his community during the plague of 1720 had been praised across the continent. Cometh the hour, cometh the man – or in Wallis' view, cometh the myth.

Mompesson was chosen by the *Magazine's* correspondent Curiosus as an example of English fortitude, self-sacrifice and civic duty. Letters from Eyam-born poet Anna Seward to the magazine following an account published in 1793 led to William Seward (no relation) in 'Anecdotes of Some Distinguished Persons' (1795-7), giving the Eyam story a momentum which has never stopped since.

Significantly for students of myth and history, Seward says: "Old and Modern England... for we trust that it is nearly the same as it has ever been, may congratulate herself in having cherished in her bosom a Parish priest who, without the splendour of character, and the extent of persons over whom (the Bishop of Marseilles) distributed the blessings of pastoral care, watched over a smaller flock...at no less risqué (sic) of life, and with no less fervour of piety and activity of benevolence."

Wallis (2006) points out that Mompesson's own modest status is a sign of character and therefore of the superiority of Englishness in contrast to the showy authoritarianism of Catholic France.

As an aside, it's interesting to note that this tension between Gallic and Anglo-Saxon attitudes towards moral responsibility remains today. The UK's policy of never paying ransoms to kidnappers, in contrast to that of France, is a modern echo of how Anglo-Saxon society stills sees sacrifice of the innocent individual as moral, if it is in the interest of the greater good:

> Last year there were more French nationals held hostage around
> the world than from any other country. This shows that doing deals
> does not necessarily make your citizens safer: one person is released,
> all French citizens in conflict zones become targets.

(John McTernan, *Daily Telegraph*, September 3, 2014)

By the 19th century, the Eyam story, unlike the plague which once raged in its boundaries, could not be contained. Writers, mainly local, produced epic poems, guidebooks for tourists and works which claimed to be histories. New elements were introduced, such as tales of rustic lovers separated by the quarantine, and gory descriptions of how the bodies were disposed of.

Having given us this lasting example of how an Englishman should behave in a crisis, Anna Seward widens the moral focus to Mompesson's wife Catherine and the dilemma of a mother torn between duty to her children and her husband.

Science also began to take up the story. While the Plague was not as much a threat in England, other communicable diseases were, and by the 1800s epidemics such as cholera among the poor in the cities were discussed with reference to Eyam. Mompesson's actions in galvanising the community "had the force and effect of a legislative enactment", Rhodes pointed out in *Peak Scenery* in 1824 – grist to the mill of those who wanted laws to enforce public health measures.

Eyam began to host memorial events in the mid-1800s which by the 1880s drew thousands of visitors as part of what Hobsbawm described as 'Mass-Producing Traditions' in his book of the same name. Traditions cement identity, and tourism has been put forward as a vehicle through which individuals can engage in the formation of identity (Desforges, 2000; Neumann, 1992; Noy, 2004).

In 1951, as local historian Clarence Daniel pointed out in *The Story of Eyam Plague with a Guide to the Village* (1985), the organisers of the biggest celebration of national achievement to date, the 1951 Festival of Britain, fixed tablets to buildings in Eyam to mark their part in the nation's story, although without "actual documentary or other evidence" to justify where they were positioned.

The 300th anniversary of the plague in 1966 even provoked a carefully-worded 'apology' from the Lord Mayor of London for sending the plague to Eyam. He would only go as far as to say 'history implies' that's how it got there.

Wallis (2006) makes an excellent case for questioning the Eyam story's authenticity, but solid evidence for some kind of quarantine remains in the fact that holes were drilled in stones on the boundaries of the parish where coins could be left in vinegar to disinfect them when villagers paid for goods from the outside world. The Earl of Devonshire, a contemporary witness, also credits the leadership of the village community with saving other villages.

Changing the characters

The 20th century brought more science and more scepticism to the story. Mompesson's actions were still seen as heroic, but with quarantine and isolation falling out of favour among medical experts, his actions had become 'unsound', according to the Annals of Medical History.

The flawed hero fitted the zeitgeist of modern writing better, too, and Don Taylor's celebrated play and TV film of 1973, *The Roses of Eyam* (the roses being the red marks on the skin of victims), Mompesson becomes "a youngster, full of arrogance and spleen."

In Margery Bowen's plague novel *God and the Wedding Dress* (1938) he is over-ambitious, and by 1995, *Eyam: A Musical* turned the plague into a pop opera with Eyam's lead miners mirroring the modern coal mining communities which were under threat, cynical about Mompesson's leadership.

But to understand the mind of a tourist, admittedly not an 'average' visitor, the most recent contribution to the Eyam literary canon is worth deeper analysis.

At the end of the last century, an award-winning war correspondent Geraldine Brooks from America was on a walking holiday in Derbyshire when she arrived in Eyam and became fascinated by the story. Recognising that there was little point in merely re-telling history, she re-interpreted the Eyam story in her novel *Year of Wonders*, but with slightly altered names – Mompesson becomes Mompellion; the Bradshaw family become the Bagshawes – to underline that fact. Brooks also added in a new twist – witch-hunting, which results in local healer Mem Gowdie and her daughter being lynched. And yet despite Brooks acknowledging that her story was not intended to be factual, one reviewer, Shaunagh O'Conner describes the novel as 'quirky, stranger-than-fiction tales from history.' To be 'stranger-than-fiction' you have to be seen as fact. In a Washington Post article after the 2001 9/11 attacks on America, Brooks (2001) said:

> Whether we also shall one day look back upon this year of flames,
> germs and war as a 'year of wonders' will depend, perhaps, on
> how many are able – like the passengers on United Flight 93 or the
> firefighters of New York City – to match the courageous self-sacrifice
> of the people of Eyam.

Expanding on this for a promotional interview for her UK publishers Penguin, she added:

> Eyam is a story of ordinary people willing to make an extraordinary
> sacrifice on behalf of others. September 11, 2001, revealed heroism
> in ordinary people who might have gone through their lives never
> called upon to demonstrate the extent of their courage.

Sadly, it also revealed a blind thirst for revenge that led to the murders of a Muslim, a Sikh, and an Egyptian Copt. I have imagined this same instinct to turn on and blame 'the other' in the lynching of the Gowdies. Love, hate, fear. The desire to live and to see your children live. Are these things different on a beautiful autumn morning in a twenty-first-century city than they were in an isolated seventeenth-century village? I don't think so. One thing I believe completely is that the human heart remains the human heart, no matter how our material circumstances change as we move together through time.

Brooks (2001)

In Brooks, we have the encapsulation of the evolution of a tourist myth: one who came knowing almost nothing about the story, but who re-interpreted it, re-invented it and gave back to future tourists a fresh and exciting vision of what they could experience at the destination. She also refers to American writer and political activist Susan Sontag's belief that fear of disease is a constant in the human experience:

Susan Sontag was so wise in talking about way we make disease into all kinds of metaphors. In some periods tuberculosis was the secret killer at the gate and then it was cancer, since we've kind of demystified cancer, now maybe it's Mad Cow Disease. The theme is this thing that comes to you through something you can't escape, like food, or your water, or your air. That even now that we do understand the mechanisms, we can still be totally superstitious as we saw with the reaction to AIDS.

Brooks (2001)

And Brooks points out another truth about the past: no period is homogenous in its experiences, levels of knowledge or belief systems:

I love that period [circa 1666] because so much was happening. The old medieval superstitious world was on the decline, but it was definitely still grabbing at the heels of modern scientific products. Isaac Newton was inventing calculus at the same time as the witch trials were going on.

Brooks (2001)

Inventing the authentic

So what was authentic in the days of the Plague? Not every tourist can be an award-winning novelist, but every tourism experience manager needs to have awareness that what they are selling is this spark of imagination, if he or she is to avoid mass tourism and give each visitor what they want: a very personal experience. Is this the lesson of Eyam, at least in tourism terms? This, then, is the background to the birth of the Eyam plague story. But how much of this matters? Is the value of a story just its effect? Is Mompesson a Robin Hood –a shadow of facts and wishful thinking?

A good myth, like the hero who is always central to it, comes to the rescue when it is most needed. And all the best myths ring true. There is nothing in Wallis' (2006) analysis to show that the story is untrue – not a very good starting point for an historian, but fertile ground for a story. Does authenticity matter? "Townspeople get the history wrong but the commerce right" – that was the rather cynical comment by David T Schaller in his *Re-inventing Skagway*, a feature on the eduweb website about the Alaskan town of Skagway town which relies on the tales of the Klondike Gold Rush of the mid-19th Century to attract its tourists.

One Skagway ice-cream parlour owner, Duff Ray, cut out a picture of an ice cream cone and hung it over the sidewalk near his shop, only to be challenged by his competitors on the grounds it violated to the City's Historic District Commission.

> Fighting for his historically accurate sign with historically accurate fervor, Ray dug up photographs from early Skagway of iconic silhouette signs – a teapot for a tea room, a shoe for a cobbler. He presented them to the Commission and won the right to display his cone.

> (Schaller, 2014)

And how about Balmoral? The Royal family's Scottish holiday home is part of an evolving tourism story has helped shape a nation. Kalyan Bhandari (2014) claims that Scotland is "a 'touristified' nation in the sense that its nationhood is highly exploited by tourism and vice versa."

'Literary medievalism' in the form the Ossian poems by James McPherson in 1760, are cited by Bhandari as one of the first forms of literary tourism to bring visitors to Scotland – even though they were "the most successful literary falsehood in modern history" rather than the distillation of ancient folklore the poet claimed.

They were soon followed by Sir Walter Scott's idealised view of Scotland which in turn led to the creation of 'Highlandism' as "...romanticism fuelled an antiquarianism and scholarly interest in Medievalism, viewing the landscape in terms of heroic figures involved in epic events and displaying flawless chivalry despite the barbarity of the times in which they lived" (Gold and Gold, 1995: 62).

For a modern analogy, just think of Mel Gibson in the 1995 film *Braveheart*. And when Prince Albert – a German prince – bought Balmoral for his English bride in 1848, he created an icon of Scottishness recognised worldwide today.

This was given more impetus when Queen Victoria published her journal of life in Balmoral.

The adoption of false Highland traditions is credited (Devine, 1994:86) with helping to form a new Scottish identity, with its images of tartan and bagpipes.

"This type of forgery is not new in tourism," argues Bhandari. "There is always a gap between the touristic images and the social reality of any destination, which happens as the result of 'staged authenticity' (MacCannell, 1973), which is crucial in the formation of tourists' impressions."

But with 13 per cent of employment in Scotland directly dependent on tourism, and heritage constituting the largest segment of all attractions, reality is going to trump authenticity.

Conclusion

In 1998, Eyam Museum won The Museum of the Year Shoestring Award, four years after it was created in a former chapel by a group of volunteers. In 2014, tourist website Tripadvisor gave the museum its Certificate of Excellence. Still staffed by volunteers, the museum has now expanded its exhibits to include the village's World War One story, called *Eyam: A Second Sacrifice*. In March 2013, after winning a £21,000 grant from the Heritage Lottery Fund, Ken Thompson (2013), Chairman of Eyam Museum said:

> We are excited to give visitors a unique opportunity to compare both these sacrifices made by the village. The local community in Eyam and the surrounding area has a long tradition of honouring the past and the sacrifices made by those connected to the region. The exhibition will continue this heritage at a time when the country as a whole is commemorating this landmark event.

The long tradition highlighted by Mr Thompson continues the work of the early poets and historians, the tourist guides and the church warden who still spoke in 1927 as if the Plague had arrived the day before, ensuring that Eyam has kept its heritage alive and commercially viable by moving with the times.

This is the point of the story: we decide what the point is. Each experience is as individual as the tourists themselves, and that is why tourist destinations need to constantly re-invent themselves.

Leicester, a city which did not even know it had King Richard III buried beneath a car park until he was discovered there in 2012, has capitalised on an era 500 years past to create a new heritage industry (King Richard in Leicester, 2015) including a visitor centre, a park-and-ride scheme and even a Richard III Flying Experience in a light aircraft – all in operation before the unfortunate man's remains were even re-interred.

Wallis (2006) titles one of the sections in his thesis 'Plague without a hero,' and at least Eyam didn't have to literally dig one up. A plague may have no hero, but a story must. Stories, to human beings, are more contagious than any plague, and their mutations as endless as those of deadly viruses.

And if a story of bravery inspires real bravery in others, it will, by its effects and in effect, come true. This is the power of the Eyam Plague, and so many other stories behind Dark Tourism which, by allowing the tourist to enjoy vicariously the extremes of human experience, shed light on how we ought to think and feel.

An authentic tourist experience may be based on history, but it is a past which must resonate with the present if it is to be seen as authentic to the modern visitor. This is something which the village of Eyam, by keeping its past alive today, has done to such great effect.

Paradoxically, a village famous for risking all to keep visitors away to prevent the spread of plague has proved hugely successful at spreading its message across the globe and attracting thousands of people to its streets.

Discussion questions

1   This chapter claims that 'melancholy pleasure' is a working definition of Dark Tourism. How can this be true, when 'melancholy' and 'pleasure' contradict each other?

2   What emotions are involved in the enjoyment of Dark Tourism but not in mainstream tourism?

3   Susan Sontag says disease is used by humans as a metaphor for our fears. What other Dark Tourism themes act in the same way?

4   Imagine you are the manager of Eyam Museum, and a tourist writes to complain that she believes the story of the plague is not true. How do you write back?

5   Make the case for and against the statement: "Meeting Mickey Mouse in Disneyworld is the most genuine tourism experience you can have."

6   You are the manager of a Robin Hood theme park, and need a new twist on the myth to attract more visitors. Write a brief for a novelist to follow in order to create a fresh version of the story for younger visitors.

References

Al Yafai, F (2003). Lottery Aids Plague Tourism, *The Guardian*. Available at http://www.theguardian.com/society/2003/apr/07/lottery.artsfunding. Accessed on 2nd April, 2003.

Bhandari, K. (2014). *Tourism and National Identity: Heritage and Nationhood in Scotland* (Vol. 39). Channel View Publications.

Bowen, M. (1938). *God and the Wedding Dress*. Hutchinson & Company.

Brooks, G. (2001). One Plague's Stoics. *Washington Post*. November 4, 2001.

Daniel, C. (1985). *The Story of Eyam Plague with a Guide to the Village*. Eyam.

Desforges, L. (2000). Traveling the world: Identity and travel biography. *Annals of Tourism Research*, **27**(4), 926-945.

Devine, T. M. (1994). *Clanship to Crofter's War: The Social Transformation of the Scottish Highlands*. Manchester University Press.

Gold, J. R., & Gold, M. M. (1995). *Imagining Scotland: Tradition, Representation and Promotion in Scottish Tourism since 1750*. Aldershot: Scolar Press.

Hobsbawm, E. (1983). Mass-producing traditions: Europe, 1870-1914. *The Invention of Tradition*, **263**, 279-80.

King Richard in Leicester (2015). King Richard in Leicester homepage. Available at http://www.kingrichardinleicester.com, Accessed on 24th June 2015.

MacCannell, D. (1973). Staged authenticity: Arrangements of social space in tourist settings. *American Journal of Sociology*, **79**(3), 589-603.

McNamara, F. (1910). *Broadside Number Six*. Cuala Press: Ohio.

Rhodes, E. (1824). *Peak Scenery; or, the Derbyshire Tourist*. Longman, Hurst, Rees, Orme, Brown and Green, and the author, Sheffield.

Trueman, (2014) Eyam and the Great Plague of 1665. Available at http://www.HistoryLearningSite.co.uk, Accessed 2nd June 2015.

Unknown reporter, (1927). Village that Defied Death, *The Singapore Free Press and Mercantile Advertiser*, 4 June, p.15.

McTernan, J. (2014). It might seem hard-hearted, but ransom payments only encourage more kidnappings. *Daily Telegraph*, 3.9.2014.

Schaller, D (1988). Re-inventing Skagway. Available at http://www.eduweb.com/Schaller/Skagway.html, Accessed on 24th June 2015.

Thompson, K, (2013). Eyam commemorates the First World War. Available at http://www.hlf.org.uk/about-us/media-centre/press-releases/eyam-commemorates-first-world-war. Accessed on 24th June 2015.

Wallis, P. (2006). A dreadful heritage: Interpreting epidemic disease at Eyam, 1666–2000. *History Workshop Journal*, **61**(1), 31-56.

9 'Welcome to the Home of Auschwitz Tours':

The online marketing of genocide tourism

Tony Johnston, Francisco Tigre-Moura, Pascal Mandelartz

Abstract

This chapter explores the online promotion by private tour operators of the Nazi extermination camp at Auschwitz-Birkenau in southern Poland. It contributes to understanding how genocide is commoditised by private enterprise, revealing some of the techniques used to transform 'atrocity' into 'attraction'. Data was obtained through content analysis of a sample of 25 commercial tour operators' websites. Results indicated that a hard sell approach, focused on price, comfort and convenience dominated the majority of the sample and that companies provide sparse information on the camp itself, with little attempt made to foster experience. Implications for management, which may arise from increased commodification, are outlined, as the chapter notes further potential threat to the memory of the camp. The chapter highlights the lack of ethical and moral considerations when promoting Auschwitz-Birkenau by private tour operators, resolving that ownership of the camp's memory may come under further threat without intervention.

Learning outcomes

1 To understand the methods used by private tour operators in commercialising the death camp at Auschwitz-Birkenau.

2 To understand the implications for management when dealing with private commodification of sensitive sites.

3 To critique the moral and ethical considerations when promoting sites associated with death and disaster.

4 To identity other sites where knowledge and experience may be effectively transferred.

Introduction

Between 1942 and 1945, more than one million people, primarily Jews, were murdered at the World War II Nazi extermination camp at Auschwitz-Birkenau in southern Poland. This complex of extermination camps, which were designed as part of the Nazi's systematic plan to eliminate the Jewish population from Europe, formed part of a wider network of camps which ultimately murdered approximately three million Jews in Poland (Auschwitz Birkenau State Museum, *hereon* ABSM, 2013).

Since the camp's liberation in 1945, it has been subjected to various 'ownership' claims and threats to the memory of the camp (Young, 2009). Today the camps exist as State museums, and the complex is listed by *Lonely Planet* as one of Poland's must-see tourist attractions (Biran, Poria & Oren, 2011). Auschwitz-Birkenau is visited en-masse by national and international tourists, who take part in regular guided tours, meet survivors and see original artefacts and interpretation material (ABSM, 2013).

The camp has featured prominently in tourism discourse throughout the last decade (for examples, see Lennon and Foley, 2000; Stone, 2006; Biran, Poria and Oren, 2011; Thurnell-Read, 2009), given the large numbers visiting the site and the complexity of the narrative on display. However, as the number of international visitors reaches almost 1.5 million annually, this chapter suggests that the prevalence of private businesses operating camp tours needs to be addressed carefully going forward. The companies, it would appear, compete on price, convenience and access, rather than one would hope, on interpretation, historical prowess or ethical and responsible standards.

Somewhat surprisingly the marketing of Auschwitz-Birkenau has not been researched in any great detail in recent years. Commodification of Auschwitz-Birkenau has of course been studied before, but it is worth returning to the debate at this juncture, given the increased interest in the site in recent years and the arrival of ever more tour companies offering packaged visits to the camp. While subjecting one of the most notorious sites of human suffering to an empirical marketing analysis is likely to raise discomfort with many, the prevalence of private industry tours to Birkenau is clearly a phenomena worth studying, and thus the focus of this chapter. Given that many private commercial companies offer tours to this most complex of sites, it would be a reasonable assumption that the camp would have featured more prominently in tourism marketing literature. The chapter helps address this gap and contribute to thanatourism literature by analysing and discussing the content of online tour operators' promotional material on the camp. Specific objectives of the chapter are to explore 1) how Auschwitz-Birkenau is promoted online by private tour operators, and 2) assess if the method and scale of promotion of the camp online is likely to threaten the memory of the camp.

Defining thanatourism

Thanatourism, the preferred term for this chapter, has been variously termed 'dark tourism' (Foley and Lennon, 1996), 'grief tourism' (Blom, 2000) and 'black spots' (Rojek, 1993), but all, in one form or another, describe tourism to sites associated with death and disaster. Although thanatourism is not a new practice (Casbeard & Booth, 2012, Johnston, 2013, Seaton, 1999, Seaton, 2009), it is an increasingly pervasive phenomenon in contemporary society (Stone, 2006). Many notorious global sites with complex and painful history have reported increased tourist numbers in recent years (Stone, 2009), most notably at Auschwitz-Birkenau (ABSM, 2013), which has more than trebled its visitor numbers in the past two decades. Such figures have appealed to the imagination of the tourism academy, and as a result, thanatourism has featured prominently in the literature since the mid-1990s. Travel to Auschwitz-Birkenau, has frequently been situated under the thanatourism umbrella; a significant proportion of the literature discusses the camp, which has even been termed 'the pinnacle of European dark tourism', Tarlow (2005: 58).

However, the terms 'thanatourism' and 'dark tourism' are contested and their usefulness is being increasingly questioned. Seaton (2009), for example, argues that 'dark tourism' has pejorative connotations and is loaded and subjective. Poria & Biran (2012) argue that thanatourism is not in fact a new form or appropriate classification of tourism, and is instead simply a form of heritage tourism, while others question if it really is a discourse worth furthering at all, specifically by questioning the appropriateness of the application of the label 'dark' to tourists. Biran et al (2011) and Bowman and Pezzullo (2010) further argue that although a site may be 'dark', the sought or actual experience of the tourist may be a socially 'bright' one, or at the very least one not motivated by a desire to contemplate mortality.

While the majority of early publications in the field tended to focus on the supply side characteristics of the phenomenon (Stone, 2009), recent research has discussed the motivations for visiting thanatourism sites and the impact thanatourism experiences have on tourists. Biran *et al* (2011: 836), for example, study tourist motivations to visit Auschwitz-Birkenau, resolving that "motives are varied, and include a desire to learn and understand the history presented, a sense of 'see it to believe it', and interest in having an emotional heritage experience". However, it could be argued that whether or not thanatourism is a supply or demand driven phenomenon is not yet resolved (Seaton, 2009), despite the recent publications. Further to this, Seaton (2009) laments the lack of empirical data in the thanatourism field more generally. He argues that the rush to theorise, model and categorise the tourism industry's reproduction of death, and subsequent tourist consumption of death, has been of detrimental value in how we understand the broad concepts of thanatourism. It would appear self-evident that analysis of promotional material can make a contribution to this debate.

As a result of its history and pervasive nature, thanatourism has attracted multi-disciplinary attention since it was coined as a term by Seaton (1996). Contributions have come from tourism scholars (Biran *et al*, 2011), legal scholars (Simic, 2009), geographers (Ashworth, 2004), sociologists (Stone, 2006, 2009) and many other social scientists, yet, as noted previously, are surprisingly absent from marketing, beyond appearing as a fleetingly example in conceptual marketing discourse by Brown, McDonagh and Schultz (2012), who theorise consumption of death within a 'dark marketing' framework. Brown *et al* propose that dark marketing "is the application or adaptation of marketing principles and practices to domains of death, destruction and the ostensibly reprehensible" (2012, p196).

However, beyond Brown *et al*, thanatourism appears to have been subjected to little empirical analysis in marketing discourse. This is surprising. It would seem that marketing should be an important area of consideration for the management of difficult sites, given the inherent dangers of the increased commodification of sites of suffering, and especially the danger of losing 'ownership' of the memory tragic events. Friedrich and Johnston (2013), for example, in relation to the Rwandan Genocide, warn that "negotiating complex history within the expectations of the demanding tourism industry creates many management and interpretation challenges. Thus, a great deal of thanatourism literature focuses on how genocide is (re)produced for tourist consumption" (p 304). Further to this, as a result of the cross disciplinary attention, labelling discontent and history of the phenomenon, tourism to sites of death has been theorised within a variety of frameworks, including Orientalism, (Seaton, 2009), secularisation (Stone, 2009), as being congruent with wider societal interest in death (Walter, 2009) and Romanticism (Seaton, 2009). Most controversially, the phenomenon is often situated within a postmodernist frame of reference, whether explicitly, as it is in Lennon and Foley's (2000) *Dark Tourism*, or more by implication, as it is in Rojek's (1993) chapter on *Fatal Attractions*.

While there is arguably some merit to drawing on postmodern theory to interrogate the late twentieth and early twenty-first century growth in thanatourism – such as, as suggested by Lennon & Foley, (2000), through consideration of society's discomfort with the project of modernity, society's misuse of rational planning, and the growing influence of the mass media – the notion of thanatourism being either temporally or phenomenologically postmodern has been challenged by several (see Casbeard and Booth, 2012, Johnston, 2013, Seaton, 2009). Seaton (2009), one of the strongest opponents notes that since travel to sites of death has existed throughout history, the postmodern frame of reference is rendered inaccurate, or, as Casbeard and Booth put it, 'incoherent and unhistorical', (Casbeard and Booth, 2012: 6).

Despite such challenges to usefulness of such an approach, Brown *et al* (2012) posit that thanatourism can be situated within a postmodern frame of reference for several reasons. Firstly, the compression of time and space is frequently investigated in the sub-discipline of thanatourism (for a recent example, see Stone's 2013 paper on Chernobyl as a heterotopia). This chapter further draws upon such a frame of reference, examining as it does, the relationship between internet marketing and genocide tourism, which allow immediate and virtual consumption of an 'attraction' from a distance. Second, given that "increasingly blurred boundaries between education and entertainment" often feature as a tenet of postmodernism (Brown *et al*, 2012: 197), tourism at a notorious site like Auschwitz-Birkenau – a place which should have deep educational value – is often categorised as postmodern. This notion gives rise to the overall aim of the chapter: to exploring the marketing of Auschwitz-Birkenau.

A large volume of the work on memorialisation, camp conservation and management examines the complex relationship between tourism and memory at Auschwitz-Birkenau, particularly in relation to who 'owns' the site (e.g. Charlesworth, 1994, Cole, 1999, Pollock, 2003). During the Cold War, for example, Polish communists used the camp to espouse nationalist beliefs (Young, 2009), a role which changed in the early 1990s with the end of the Cold War and the subsequent arrival of international visitors and particularly descendants and survivors. The camp has also been contested by the Catholic Church and various Jewish groups (Cole, 1999), with each laying claim on particular memories and narratives.

Since the end of the Cold War, the camp has received great numbers of visitors and has thus featured prominently in social science literature, incorporating work from geographers, sociologists, historians and many others. Studies related specifically to the management of Auschwitz-Birkenau have focused on a variety of themes, including morality (Charlesworth, 2004), ecology (Charlesworth & Addis, 2002), education (Charlesworth, 1996), interpretation (Miles, 2002), memorialisation (Keil, 2005), tourist motivations (Biran *et al*, 2011). While Auschwitz-Birkenau dominates thanatourism literature, studies at other Shoah sites related to tourism, include research in Buchenwald (Beech, 2000), Yad Vashem (Cohen, 2011) and Nuremberg (Macdonald, 2006), among others.

Despite the breadth of empirical material, little has been published related to site marketing. Observations from the authors on the methods and numbers of companies promoting tours to Auschwitz-Birkenau provoked questions relating to the marketing and promotion of the site by private enterprise. To date there is little existing literature containing empirical data on the scale or methods of companies who promote genocide as an attraction. Further exploratory analysis of this area gave rise to the first objective of the chapter; to examine how Auschwitz-Birkenau is promoted online by private tour operators.

The second objective for this chapter grew from consideration of the large volume of existing material on thanatourism and the management of Auschwitz-Birkenau. With reference to dark tourism, Stone (2012: 1573) posits that it "may engender personal meaningfulness and ontological security", or in other words, visits to sites of death can be exceptionally powerful experiences, which may have deep personal impacts on a tourist. Such impacts are particularly evident at Auschwitz-Birkenau. Charlesworth (1994) for example, notes the educational potential of a visit to the camp and the impact a visit had on some undergraduate students.

Based on this material, a second objective emerged concerning the threat to camp 'ownership', the dangers of commodification and (mis)interpretation and the ethics of cashing in on tragedy. This is an especially important and timely question, given the rapid and likely future increases in tourism to Auschwitz-Birkenau.

Thanatourism at the Auschwitz-Birkenau Extermination Camp

The Auschwitz-Birkenau Extermination Camp comprises three main sites; Auschwitz-1, Auschwitz-II Birkenau and Auschwitz-III Monowitz. Between 1942 and 1945, until the camp was liberated by Soviet troops, some 1.3 million people were killed at the site, the vast majority of whom were Jewish (Cole, 1999). Today the Auschwitz camps are preserved as memorials to the victims of the Holocaust. The sites are managed by the Auschwitz Birkenau Memorial State Museum (ABMSM), which employ 300 guides, working in 20 languages to meet the needs of the large numbers of visitors. In 2012, 1.43 million people visited Auschwitz; 446,000 from Poland where the camp features on the high school curriculum, followed by large numbers from Britain (149,200), the United States (96,900), Italy (84,500), Germany (74,500), Israel (68,000) and other countries (ABMSM, 2013). Biran *et al*, (2011: 837) term the camp 'the symbol of dark tourism'.

Figures from the Auschwitz Birkenau State Museum reveal that 72% of the 1.43 million visitors in 2012 were classified by the museum as 'young', meeting the desire of many for genocide education to 'penetrate the youthful fabric of society' (ABMSM, 2013: 7). Motivations to visit the camp have been recorded by the museum as seeking 'knowledge of the history of the camp' (33.2%), in 'remembrance of the victims' (19.6%), 'paying tribute to the victims of the camp' (13.7%) and 'curiosity' (12.6%), (ABMSM, 2013). While entry to Auschwitz is free of charge without a guide (ABMSM, 2013), and public transport to the museums is low cost and frequent (ABMSM), many private companies sell tours to Auschwitz. Departing from the nearby cities of Krakow or Katowice, but often from much further afield and even overseas, these tours include budget offerings of guided group tours and transport for less than €20 per person, to private tours with limousine transport and personalised itineraries. The investigation of the online promotion of Auschwitz by Polish tour companies represents the first main objective of this chapter.

Methods and materials

The use of the Internet as a marketing tool has been broadly accepted in tourism literature, while the assessment of website effectiveness has been supported by academic researchers for some time (Lepp & Lane, 2010). Thanatourism does not circumvent this movement, but it must be questioned if marketing scholars have dealt fairly with this 'hot topic', or has it been considered as simply just the marketing of yet another tourist attraction. As Brown *et al* (2012: 12) write, "all marketing, to put it in an admittedly contentious way, is dark marketing". Regardless of the experience fostered by websites, the Internet has increasingly become the most relevant communication channel for tourism attractions. It has allowed both suppliers and consumers to produce and disseminate information, conduct financial transactions and share tourist experiences to a global audience (Xiang & Gretzel, 2009).

Research design

In order to examine the online promotion of private company tours to Auschwitz Birkenau, a cross-sectional content analysis of websites was employed (Kassarjian, 1977). Content analysis represents a widely accepted and reliable method of investigating the depiction of websites' elements, and is validated across varied research contexts involving websites (Singh & Boughton, 2005; Tang, Choi, Morrison, & Lehto, 2009). With the purpose of enhancing the internal validity of the investigation, a triangulation process of investigation was conducted. The three judges were academics with postgraduate qualification and experts in the fields of online marketing and thanatourism.

The content analysis encompassed qualitative and quantitative approaches. The quantitative method of analysis to investigate web-content was conducted through a numerical coding scheme, where the depiction of thanatourism content was ranked on a five-point Likert scale ranging from 'Prominently depicted' to 'Not depicted at all' (Singh & Boughton, 2005). Through a systematic approach of evaluation, the written and visual web-content related to thanatourism and the promotion of Auschwitz tours were identified, evaluated and quantified, as the content analysis prerogative recommends (Kassarjian, 1977). This exact same approach has previously been validated, including, for example Murphy, Forrest, Wotring, and Brymer (1996) who applied it to evaluating hotel website features, producing a set of evaluation factors. Additional recent studies have also evaluated websites using only the numerical coding scheme, including Law and Leung (2002) who modified Liu and Arnett's (2000) model and Blum and Fallon (2002) who assessed 53 Welsh visitor attraction websites using a checklist that was originally produced by Dutta, Kwan, and Segev (1998). In the case of this present research, evaluation factors were modified by the researchers to fit the analysis of Auschwitz tour promoting websites, analysing websites under company profile, services offered and website features.

Complementary to the systematic quantification of web-content, images from the websites were also subjected to rigorous qualitative content analysis, using a method adapted from Rose (1996) to analyse image content, audience and production. Analysis focused on the analysis of signifiers of the information presented on the websites, including the type of image used by the website, e.g. barb wire fences, the 'Arbeit Macht Frei' gate, gas chambers, etc., image production methods and content, including use of colour, vantage point and components, etc. and finally, the audiences for the images, including circulation methods and storage. Each element was analysed

Thus, the unit of analysis of the investigation involved all webpages of the websites. This allowed a comprehensive and holistic investigation of online dark marketing practices, through the use of a mix-methods approach and represents a significant contribution of the chapter.

Pre-test and sample

Prior to the final data collection, a pre-test was conducted amongst three researchers with the objective of familiarizing them with the objects of investigation and to provide insights to possible modifications needed to the data collection instrument. A total of 15 dark-tourism related websites were analysed by each researcher, thus characterizing a triangulation procedure. Following this, results were cross-compared and inter-judge reliability results were over 80%, considered highly satisfactory (Kassarjian, 1977). Furthermore, whenever findings were inconsistent and when any discrepancies arose, consensus was achieved through group discussion. This allowed judges a much greater familiarity with the method used and provided the basis for a more rigorous final data collection.

The initial step of the final data collection consisted of the delimitation of the sample. A vast sample of enterprises promoting tours to the camp was first identified using multiple search engines, through the use of the following keywords: 'Auschwitz tour' and 'Auschwitz guided tour'.

After the initial list was created, the sites were screened in accordance with their suitability to the study, based on the availability of thanatourism content. The final sample of investigation comprised a total of twenty-five websites, from various countries, including Poland and the U.K. However, only the English versions of the sites were investigated. The final data collection was conducted from March to April 2013.

Results

A number of key themes emerged from the analysis of the websites, primarily related to company profiles, website design and website visual and textual content. In relation to the first objective of exploring the scale and methods used by private tour companies to Auschwitz-Birkenau, it was observed that a hard sell approach, focused on price, comfort and convenience dominated the majority of the 25 sampled companies. All 25 offered online booking facilities, of which 40% (*n*=10) highlighted that they were licensed companies, 56% (*n*=14) noted that Auschwitz was a UNESCO World Heritage Site and 64% (*n*=16) included customer reviews to boost company reputation and credibility.

The majority of tours included transport from Krakow to Oswiecim, where Auschwitz-Birkenau is located, with a guided tour of the camp. Several companies offered premium tours to the camp, such as offering limousine transportation, private guides, and in-transport documentaries for customers. Some tours included lunch, while others offered it as an additional extra, or the opportunity to stop for a break at the customer's request. 28% (*n*=7) of the companies offered tours to Auschwitz-Birkenau as part of a package deal, where tours to the camp could be purchased for a discount when purchased as part of a day trip to other local attractions, most commonly the Wieliczka Salt Mine. 44% (*n*=11) additionally sold accommodation, while 96% (*n*=24) offered other tours beyond Auschwitz, including organising stag parties, shopping excursions, pub crawls, shooting, go-karting and airport transfers.

In relation to the second objective of the chapter, concerning the threat to site ownership, ethics and interpretation, it was observed that the websites offered little information on Auschwitz-Birkenau itself and interpretation of the Holocaust was limited or non-existent for many. Additionally, any information which was offered by websites was frequently contradictory or vague. Figures related to the number killed at Auschwitz Birkenau, for example, varied from 1.1million to 'millions'. Although it is acknowledged that numbers do indeed remain contested, many of the websites offered no contextualisation of the figures. Further to this, 52% (*n*=13) made no mention of the origin of victims. Only one website advertised its tours primarily based on guides' expertise and only two through offering customers greater levels of privacy or intimacy. Reflection on the 'appropriateness' of touring Auschwitz as an attraction was very limited, with only one website negotiating the paradox of consuming death as an attraction.

Conclusions and implications

> Should one visit Auschwitz? It is a difficult question, and a deeply personal one.... And certainly, having seen the camps (regardless of how many other groups are also filing through) few will regret the experience. The camps and their legacy are an indelible part of today's world, and visiting them is both sobering and edifying.
>
> (Krakow Tours, 2013)

While the commodification of death for the tourism industry has long been recognised (Seaton, 2009) and the trivialisation of difficult heritage is an equally established discourse in geographies of tourism literature (Ashworth, 2004), it is nonetheless likely the pervasiveness and marketing methods of Holocaust tour companies may surprise many. The scale and methods revealed by the analysis present very little concern or empathy with memory, interpretation and the ethics of commodifying genocide. One company, for example, goes as far as categorising Auschwitz-Birkenau under 'theme parks' in its website structure; in what is arguably one of the least subtle exemplifications of Disneyfication a social science researcher will encounter.

Although trivialisation of Auschwitz has been discussed before (see Cole, 1999, for example) the majority of work related to site guardianship and management has focused on contestations related to governance, funding and memory, site ownership, political collaboration and religious tensions. Continuation of such approaches in future – at the expense of exploring the highly prominent online role of private enterprise – could be to the detriment of understanding some of the new economies and contestations emerging at the camp. This chapter does not suggest that the rapidly increasing demand to visit to the camp (ABSMM, 2013) is solely a result of the increased number tour companies, but there is a clear argument that such companies are assuming increased responsibility in delivering the camp to international audiences.

It has further been argued that great educational potential exists at Holocaust sites (Charlesworth, 1996). While Cohen (2011) suggests that 'dark' tourists who find their experience challenging are those who are most likely to find it fulfilling, this chapter suggests that private companies running Auschwitz-Birkenau tours do not attempt to foster challenging experiences and instead compete on pricing, convenience and comfort variables. The role played by such companies in relation to Auschwitz-Birkenau raises many ethical questions: for example, should one visit one of the most notorious sites in the world, hosted by a company which specialises in stag parties?

Managerial implications

It is an established notion that tourism turns culture into a commodity, and even though in the case of this research it is a thanatourism product under investigation, death is packaged and sold to tourists in the same way other products have been commodified for tourism. Research to date on tourism at Auschwitz-Birkenau has been relatively diverse, encompassing many moral debates. Yet questions remain surrounding managerial responsibility at genocide sites. Is there a responsibility on the supply side that should encourage an understanding of the moral and ethical values attached to a place in order to allow it to shape the minds of the tourist rather than the tourist shaping the identity of a place? One way of thinking in tourism studies is that the commodification of culture for consumption renders the resulting practices inauthentic. By comparison, other schools of thought have asserted that such transactions between tourists and the place generate new cultural configurations which are both meaningful and authentic to their participants. As post war generations will be the visitors of Auschwitz-Birkenau in the future, the camp will doubtless further evolve and be re-interpreted. This means that the *raison d'etre* of Auschwitz-Birkenau as a monument and remainder of a dark past might be under threat in the future.

In other words, responsibility is implicitly placed on tour operators to create awareness of the background and historic importance of the place to maintain it as the symbol that it is for future generations. As mentioned previously, Brown *et al.* (2012: 12) state that, "all marketing, to put it in an admittedly contentious way, is dark marketing", but it might be added that certain norms have to be fulfilled when handling sites that are irreversibly connected to death, grief and mourning and that have been established in a historic context.

In many ways the museum deals with the incoming visitors relatively well – group tourists take part in a compulsory standard site tour on arrival (Young, 2009). However the museum has equally been criticized by Young for failing to present the full site, glossing over certain periods of the camp's history and managing opening hours and large numbers of visitors poorly. Young also notes that distorted emphasis on certain artefacts, such as the *Arbeit Macht Frei* gate, which has been moved from its original location and now can configure the tourist's visit. Management is likely to become significantly more complex in future if visitor expectations are configured by online promotion material, such as in the websites identified in this article.

One could argue that the representation of these websites might simply follow the rule of the market, which is demand and supply, which might explain the perceived simplicity of the websites. Tour operators might, for example, have acknowledged the fact that people are looking for increased value when booking their trips, which led to the offering of lunch packages, etc. Considering the number of interested parties at Auschwitz-Birkenau, how can a tour operator sell this place of historical significance without ambivalence? The interpretation of an image is highly dependent on the audience, so people will attach various meanings and interpretations to the website, which makes including certain moral and ethical guidelines quite difficult, as again their interpretation is down to the individual. Only a shift in demand or guidelines provided by the majority of stakeholders could thereby lead to a reconfiguring of these websites.

Future research directions

In view of findings and the novelty of the topic, the results provide the basis for a wide spectrum of future research streams. Future studies should focus on broadening the samples to encompass the promotion of other extermination and concentration camps and identify generalizable practices and also case specific practices. Furthermore, studies should compare thanatourism attractions which have happened in different times in history, with the intent of identifying whether time influences the perception and promotional of dark related attractions. Also, the results yield the need be complemented by an investigation of the point of sale, in order to contrast the congruity between the online practices with the offline service and the role of employees on the delivery of the thanatourism experiences. Finally, there is timely gap which must be addressed in relation to the visitors' perceptions of the online promotional practices of such attractions. Cross-cultural studies may suggest the need of a cultural customization to minimize risk perceptions, moderated by culture, religion and personal connection with the attraction.

Discussion questions

1 Discuss the pros and cons of promoting Auschwitz-Birkenau online as a destination for those interested in the history of the Holocaust.

2 Discuss the feasibility of closing Auschwitz-Birkenau entirely to tourists. What implications would this have for regional tour operators?

3 Suggest methods by which museum management could reduce the influence of private tour operators in interpretation of the site.

4 How can tourism to Auschwitz-Birkenau be promoted ethically and responsibly?

References

Ashworth, G. (2004). Tourism and the heritage of atrocity: Managing the heritage of South African Apartheid for entertainment, in *New Horizons in Tourism, Strange Experiences and Stranger Practices*, by Singh, T. (ed.), London: Cabi Publishing, 95-108.

Auschwitz-Birkenau Memorial and Museum (2013). Report Auschwitz Birkenau Memorial 2012, Oswiecim, Auschwitz-Birkenau Memorial and Museum.

Beech, J. (2000). The enigma of holocaust sites as tourist attractions: The Ccase of Buchenwald, *Managing Leisure*, **5**, 29-41.

Biran, A., Poria, Y. & Oren, G. (2011). Sought experiences at (dark) heritage sites. *Annals of Tourism Research*, **38** (3), 820-841.

Blom, T. (2000). Morbid tourism - a postmodern market niche with an example from Althorp. *Norsk Geografisk Tidsskrift - Norwegian Journal of Geography*, **54**, 29-36.

Blum, V., & Fallon, J. (2002). Welsh visitor attraction websites: multipurpose tools or technological token-ism? *Information Technology & Tourism*, **4**(3/4), 191–201.

Brown, S., McDonagh, P. & Shultz, C. (2012). Dark marketing: ghost in the machine or skeleton in the cupboard? *European Business Review*, **24** (3), 196 – 215.

Casbeard, R. and Booth, C. (2012). Post-modernity and the exceptionalism of the present in dark tourism, *Journal of Unconventional Parks, Tourism & Recreation Research*, **4**(1), 2-8.

Charlesworth, A. (1994). Contesting places of memory: the case of Auschwitz, *Environment and Planning D: Society and Space*, **12**(5) 579 – 593.

Charlesworth, A. (1996). Teaching the Holocaust through landscape study, in R.L. Millen (Ed.) *New Perspectives on the Holocaust, A Guide for Teachers and Scholars*, New York, New York University Press.

Charlesworth, A. (2004). A corner of a foreign field that is forever Spielberg's: Understanding the moral landscapes of the site of the former Kl Plaszów, Krakow, Poland. *Cultural Geographies*, **11**, 291-312.

Charlesworth, A. & Addis, M. (2002). Memorialisation and the ecological landscapes of Holocaust sites: The case of Plaszów and Auschwitz Birkenau. *Landscape Research*, **27** (3), 229-251.

Cohen, E. (2011). Educational dark tourism at in populo site: The Holocaust Museum in Jerusalem. *Annals of Tourism Research*, **38**, 193-209.

Cole, T. (1999). *Selling the Holocaust*, New York: Routledge.

Dutta, S., Kwan, S., & Segev, A. (1998). Business transformation in electronic commerce: a study of sectoral and regional trends. *European Management Journal*, **16**(5), 540–551.

Foley, M. & Lennon, J. (1996). J.F.K. and dark tourism: A fascination with assassination. *International Journal of Heritage Studies*, **2**, 198-211.

Friedrich, M. & Johnston, T. (2013). The memorialisation and commodification of the Rwandan Genocide, *Journal of Tourism & Cultural Change*, **11**(4), 302 – 320.

Johnston, T. (2013). Mark Twain and The Innocents Abroad: illuminating the tourist gaze on death. *International Journal of Culture, Tourism and Hospitality Research*, **7**(3), 199-213.

Kassarjian, H. H. (1977). Content Analysis in Consumer Research. *Journal of Consumer Research*, **4**, 8-18.

Keil, C., (2005). Sightseeing in the mansions of the dead. *Social and Cultural Geography*, **6**, 479-494.

Krakow Tours (2013). Auschwitz Tour Krakow. Available at http://www.krakow-tours.com/tour/Auschwitz-Krakow, Accessed 13th March 2013.

Law, R., & Leung, K. (2002). Online airfare reservation services: a study of Asian based and North American-based travel websites. *Information Technology & Tourism*, **5**(1), 25–33.

Lennon, J. and Foley, M. (2000). *Dark Tourism: The Attraction of Death and Disaster*. London and New York: Continuum.

Lepp, A., Gibson, H., & Lane, C. (2010). Image and perceived risk: A study of Uganda and its official tourism website. *Tourism Management*, **32**(3), 675-684.

Liu, C., & Arnett, K. P. (2000). Exploring the factors associated with website success in the context of electronic commerce. *Information & Management*, **38**(1), 23–33.

Macdonald, S. (2006). Mediating heritage: Tour guides at the former Nazi Party rally grounds, Nuremberg, *Tourist Studies*, **6**(2), 119-141.

Miles, W.F.S. (2002). Auschwitz: Museum interpretation and darker tourism. *Annals of Tourism Research*, **29**(4), 1175-1178.

Murphy, J., Forrest, E. J., Wotring, C. E., & Brymer, R. A. (1996). Hotel management and marketing on the Internet. *Cornell Hotel & Restaurant Administration Quarterly*, **37**(3), 70–82.

Pollock, G. (2003). 'Holocaust tourism: Being there, looking back and the ethics of spatial memory' in D. Crouch and N. Lübbren (eds) *Visual Culture and Tourism*. Oxford: Berg Publishers, pp. 175–90.

Poria, Y. & Biran, A. (2012). Re-conceptualizing Dark Tourism, in *Contemporary Tourist Experience: Concepts and Consequences*, by Sharpley, R. & Stone, P. (eds.), Oxon: Routledge

Rojek, C. (1993). *Ways of Escape: Modern Transformations in Leisure and Travel*, London: Macmillan.

Rose, G. (1996). Teaching visualised geographies: Towards a methodology for the interpretation of visual materials, *Journal of Geography in Higher Education*, **20**(3), 281-194.

Seaton, A. (1999). War and Thanatourism: Waterloo 1815-1914. *Annals of Tourism Research,* **26**, 234-244.

Seaton, A. (2009). Thanatourism and its discontents: An appraisal of a decade's work with some future issues and directions, in *The Handbook of Tourism Studies,* by T. Jamal and M. Robinson (eds.), London: Sage, 521-542.

Simic, O. (2009). Dark tourism: Remembering, visiting and placing the dead: law, authority and genocide in Srebrenica, *Law, Text, Culture,* **13**(1), 273-310

Singh, N., & Boughton, P. D. (2005). Measuring website globalization: A cross-sectional country and industry level analysis. *Journal of Website Promotion,* **1**, 3-20.

Stone, P.R. (2006). A dark tourism spectrum: Towards a typology of death and macabre related tourist sites, attractions and exhibitions. *Tourism: An Interdisciplinary International Journal,* **52**, 145-160.

Stone, P.R. (2009). Dark tourism: Morality and new moral spaces, in *The Darker Side of Travel: The Theory and Practice of Dark Tourism,* by R. Sharpley & P. R. Stone, (eds.), Bristol: Channel View Publications, 56-74.

Stone, P.R. (2012). Dark tourism and significant other death: Towards a model of mortality mediation. *Annals of Tourism Research,* **39** (3), 1565–1587.

Stone, P.R. (2013). Dark tourism, heterotopias and post-apocalyptic places: The case of Chernobyl, in L. White & E. Frew (eds).*Dark Tourism and Place Identity* (pp 79 -94), Melbourne: Routledge.

Tang, L., Choi, S., Morrison, A. M., & Lehto, X. Y. (2009). The many faces of Macau: A correspondence analysis of the images communicated by online tourism information sources in English and Chinese. *Journal of Vacation Marketing,* **15**(1), 79-94.

Tarlow, P. (2005). Dark tourism: The appealing dark side of tourism and more, in *Niche Tourism: Contemporary Issues, Trends and Cases, Contemporary Issues, Trends and Cases,* by M. Novelli (ed.), London: Butterworth-Heinemann, 47-59.

Thurnell-Read, T.P. (2009). Engaging Auschwitz: an analysis of young travellers' experiences of Holocaust Tourism. *Journal of Tourism Consumption and Practice,* **1**(1), 26-52.

Walter, T. (2009), Dark tourism: Mediating between the dead and the living, in R Sharpley and P.R. Stone (eds.), *The Darker Side Of Travel, The Theory And Practice Of Dark Tourism,* Channel View Publications, Bristol, 39-55.

Xiang, Z., & Gretzel, U. (2010). Role of social media in online travel information search. *Tourism Management,* **31**(2), 179-188.

10 'Which part of this is on the exam?'

Journeys into darkness with school groups

John Heap

So Nature flourishes amid decay,
Defiant of the fate that laid her low;
So Man in triumph scorning Death below
Visions the springtide of a purer day:

Dreams of the day when rampant there will rise
The flowers of Truth and Freedom from the blood
Of noble youth who died: when there will bud
The flower of Love from human sacrifice.

There by the fallen youth, where heroes lie,
Close by each simple cross the flowers will spring,
The *bonnes enfants* will wander in Spring,
And lovers dream those dreams that never die.

Matthew Copse by Sergeant John William Streets

Introduction

I've started with a poem because that is what you expect to read because I'm writing about the First World War. I found the work of John William Streets when preparing to take a group of friends from Derbyshire to the battlefield at Serre, the horrific 'hinge' of the Somme attack, where the Pals Batallions were chewed up in the densest German defenses. Streets was a coalminer from Worksop, he was a dedicated auto-didact and heavily involved in the Methodist Church. Like so many others he met his fate on 1st July, 1916 without surviving witnesses to his death. Why did I choose Streets? Because he had a local link for my friends, initially. Because I felt that they probably shared some of the sentiments of his religious faith. Because he makes a good hero too. I'm always teaching, I suppose, which is probably quite an irritating trait. Or perhaps I'm just perennially didactic, which is worse. But in many ways I chose Streets because he envisions a day after his death and expects to be buried under a simple cross. In spring the flowers bloom in Matthew Copse but the scorning of death is much harder to achieve in a more profane era. I see leading trips to dark sites as part of my professional obligation, a duty to be performed for an uncertain greater good. But battlefield tours are also fun. Perhaps that sounds strange but I hope that many of my colleagues would agree. This chapter is inspired by twelve years of experience in leading and accompanying school tours to some of the darkest sites in European history.

I want to examine three phases of the dark experience in school travel with especial regard to the Western Front experience but also consider sites of genocide and imprisonment. The first will be termed the 'plan of attack' phase, when trips are marketed and their intentions examined. I will argue that this phase currently contains only a limited degree of thought; to have to justify visiting a 'dark' site would be anathema to most teachers. As a former colleague was fond of saying: "it ticks the 'Citizenship box". The sites are there, so we visit them. To question the importance of such a visit would be to find oneself on the wrong side of a moral certainty. I know because I've written the indignant response to a refusal to allow my pupils a day out of lessons to make such a trip feasible. The second is the 'operational' phase when the trip confronts the dark site and the good intentions of the planning phase are challenged. Here we can see good teaching practice highlighted and, at others, completely discarded. It will be demonstrated here how each individual, in attempting to create meaning in a confusing landscape of destruction and commemoration, will have a unique and largely unquantifiable dark experience. The third and final phase is the 'debrief'; the return to normality. Here we can see how schools routinely commemorate the act of commemoration itself.

In any attempt to examine the dark experience and, more specifically, the Western Front experience, a note of caution has to be sounded. There are no objective visitors to dark sites. There is nothing 'spiritual' about what I do, despite the apparent importance of this nebulous concept in school inspection regimes. But I behind that there is a sense of the civilising influence of History. I don't believe in the old adage that we must teach people about the past so that they will not repeat its mistakes, because that is lazy thinking. Genocides still happen precisely because nobody has ever taken an entirely fresh view of geopolitics which is unencumbered by historical resentments. However, I do want my students to confront difficult truths and I do want them to walk away from a dark site thinking that it doesn't have to be like that anymore. In other words, I have an agenda and would not wish to discard that agenda in a misguided attempt at objectivity. It would be like holding a clinical trial in which the patients received only placebos.

Sharp-eyed readers will also notice my relationship with the author of another chapter in this book and, therefore, my attachment to a tank called Deborah. Above my desk is a montage of photographs of the identified crew members, mounted in a frame which also contains a rivet unearthed in the initial phases of the excavation by my friend Philippe Gorczynski. I have visited sites where the dead were all victims of something over which they had no control. Without absolving governments or politicians or kings from blame I have never believed the teacher-myth that the Great War was completely unjustified and the men who died were all victims of wider forces. Of course, I say this as the sort of pacifist who abhors killing right up to the point where someone commits an unspeakable act and my atavistic side takes control and I want them wiped off the face of the earth. To see the war only as tragedy is to fundamentally mis-understand the nature of the dark sites of the Western Front and to see the war dead as simply having been herded to Belgium to die. Wilfred Owen's (1918) cattle. Everyone the innocent Isaac in his retelling of the Bible story in which the son is sacrificed not spared. But even Owen was awarded his Military Cross for capturing an enemy machine gun and using it to inflict numerous casualties on the enemy. He is buried alongside two soldiers awarded the Victoria Cross. Many men went to kill. If this were not true then it makes it hard to account for the 1,064,000 Germans dead on French and Belgian soil. Some of them are my heroes too: the plucky VC Private Dancox for example, prolific killer of the enemy, who is commemorated on the beautiful Louverval Memorial near Cambrai.

My relationship with the men of Deborah will always make me see their actions as those of fighters for a cause and not simply as victims. Again, there are no objective trip leaders in this field. Analysis of the political justification for the decisions these men made might now highlight significant discrepancies between what their governments were asking them to do and the reality of their trench experience. However, as volunteers for a unit which would guarantee their exposure to intense and immediate danger, armed with the machinery of death in the form of machine guns, which might fire six hundred rounds a minute, they must have known what they were doing. Of course, this revisionist description could be attacked as being as simplistic as the traditional view of the war as tragedy but it does at least provide much needed balance in the increasingly narrow teaching of the First World War in Britain. And, for good measure, telling students that it wasn't just 'Mad Jack' Siegfried Sassoon who killed the enemy is going to ruin a lot of lessons. This chapter will demonstrate how caricatures of Tommy Atkins have taken hold in the pity industry of First World War travel, throughout all the phases of travel.

The plan of attack

'Good-morning; good-morning!' the General said.
When we met him last week on our way to the line.
Now the soldiers he smiled at are most of 'em dead,
And we're cursing his staff for incompetent swine.
'He's a cheery old card,' grunted Harry to Jack
As they slogged up to Arras with rifle and pack

But he did for them both by his plan of attack.

(Siegfried Sassoon, *The General* from *Counter Attack and other poems*,
1917)

Sassoon's memorable poem was composed in a hospital bed where he was recovering from a bullet wound to his right shoulder which could easily have proved fatal. It is based on the cheerful demeanour of his Corps Commander greeting his comrades in the Royal Welsh Fusiliers on their way to the battle at which he would be wounded (Wilson, 1998) 'The Plan of Attack' is now a phrase loaded with irony because the plans all seem so futile. It is as if the war was planned by Geoffrey Palmer's Field Marshall Sir Douglas Haig in *Blackadder*, sweeping toy soldiers off his desk. There is a view that leaders ignored the very real conditions and dangers their men would face in any offensive. Pushing on regardless when confronted by the mud at Passchendaele or the surprisingly alert German machine gunners at Beaumont-Hamel or Serre this view does seem to have some merit. But much has been done in recent years to restore some reputations and certainly a powerful, if sometimes overstated case, has recently been made by Antony Seldon and David Walsh in trying to at least promote the subalterns from George in *Blackadder* to Stanhope, Osborne or Raleigh in *Journey's End*(Seldon and Walsh, 2013). Perhaps the greatest irony of all is that the planning phase of much battlefield tourism also ignores the conditions. Not in these cases, of course, compromising the safety of the pupils concerned but by not giving them any real sense of what the ground will be like and what they should do when they get there.

Websites

As Head of History in an independent school I transfer four or five travel company flyers to my waste paper basket every week. They come from a range of companies. Some are niche specialists in battlefield tourism and some are sub-divisions of larger corporations. What they have in common is a language, not just of memory and commemoration, but of competitive pricing, subject expertise and simplified paperwork. At least one regular leaflet contains a photograph which I took on one of their trips. Flyers generated by travel companies seem to be from another age. Some of the larger enterprises pay for immense glossy fold-out magazines as if a large picture of a graveyard will entice an otherwise hesitant teacher to plan to spend many hours away from home in a wet Belgian field with a group of teenagers, one of whom will inevitably eat too much chocolate and be sick on the coach. There is no more lazily poignant photo than one of the 'silent cities', after all. These leaflets must generate some enquiries but the vast majority sit in a folder in the departmental office waiting for a newly-qualified colleague to bring much needed vigour to the department's travel plans. Of course, marketing is often a vain and mysterious industry whereas reputation and consistency are the only criteria any sensible teacher will use when deciding which company to use.

Relationships between companies and their schools are precious commodities. More precious still can be established relationships with guides who know and understand the foibles of pupils and staff from their favoured schools. The very best guides can pick and choose their tours so if your kids have a bad reputation then you're likely to be stuck with the guides who are working their way up. Better still is to do your own guiding as it really requires no more preparation than for the average lesson.

Analysis of a range of companies reveals some interesting commonalities. The giant NST reassures us that "Since 1967 we've been creating expertly planned school tours – helping groups get more from their time away..." and describes its Western Front tours as 'established' (nstgroup.co.uk, 2015). Their slogan 'the experience shows' makes the likelihood of administrative error appear to be remote and gives a sense that the guides will have been there before. This company claims to take 100,000 pupils on tours around the world every year so they are obviously doing something right and they even own their own chateau. Smaller operators and newer entrants to the marketplace like Galina Tours have to be content with 'established since 1989.'

Those with a focus on the adult as well as school markets are more likely to illustrate their pages with pictures of their guides: all middle-aged men and the final preserve outside the month of Movember for the military moustache. I have only ever seen one female guide working on the Western Front. It is as if one is only likely to book a guide if they look, and sound, like the late and distinguished Richard Holmes of *War Walks* fame. So, a teacher who is new to the market will have to decide on a perception of experience and success. However, these are criteria which are hard to establish. An act of commemoration, as pilgrimage to a site of death, an instructive lesson in the weakness of humanity cannot apparently be handled by the young and lively enthusiast. The dead don't take kindly to being woken up. So, naturally in the cycle of memory that is teaching about the Great War, a trustworthy figure will be chosen and these are most likely to be found by recommendation. You might be happy for your students to go climbing, canoeing or hurtling down a ski slope with a fresh-faced gap year student but you won't ask them for a tour of a battlefield. The darkness of the Western Front demands someone with experience. Sometimes these are men with a military background, sometimes not. The retired officers can generally be identified by the pink trousers which they habitually seem to wear.

The language of war

Pupils embarking on a trip to the Western Front are unlikely to know why they're going there in specific terms. Given the tyranny of the intellect-crushing 'learning objective' agenda in education this is somewhat surprising. After all, even when studying the Holocaust, pupils will expect to be told what they are going to learn at the start of every lesson, yet when I have visited Auschwitz the experience simply cannot be reduced to a series of sentences starting with 'You will learn to..' Having said that I'm reminded of an anecdote related to me by a student about a headmistress who once accompanied their trip to Auschwitz. During the climax of the visit, in this case a silent candle-lighting ceremony near the gas chambers at Birkenau, she loudly asked one of the History staff: 'So, which part of this is in the exam?'

So, is it possible to give pupils some sense of what they are likely to expect? My early experiences of accompanying trips to the Western Front were with my first Head of Department. He was (and still is) a dynamic, energetic and caring teacher. However, he took a GCSE coursework group to Belgium and France with a single objective: to answer their coursework question. In this case they had to find out "Why was the First World War the first and last to be characterised by trench warfare?" This purposeful, educational approach gives at once a common sense of purpose but also a sense of discovery. This is what-the-hell-happened-here-and-why history of the very best kind. There is a 'hook', an enquiry, an open question. The fact that the 'enquiry-based' approach, by which students are given a question to investigate, is probably the only aspect of history teaching which has endured since I trained perhaps shows its merits. The question above is both academic and accessible and of the variety which could equally well be investigated by a school aged pupil on the Western Front, an undergraduate in a library or a television presenter striding across the fields of blood accompanied only by disconcertingly loud birdsong.

However, this necessary sense of direction can also be given by another approach. For seven years I was privileged to work with a colleague who was passionate about the commemorative approach and who brought to that approach an academic rigour which gave it a strong sense of direction. He even used to take his own children to visit graves when they were on holiday, something about which we used to wind him up mercilessly. Working in an independent school which had lost 52 old scholars on the Western Front, with five alone named on the Memorial to the Missing of the Somme at Thiepval, we had the opportunity to consult records and archives. By enlisting help from staff, pupils and the local regimental museum he was able to provide a stronger sense of the personality and background of those men. And this took us to places far beyond the Western Front: to the Second World War battlefields of Italy, the bridge at Arnhem and RAF burials in Berlin. Had the recession not intervened it might have taken us to Gallipoli too. Combined with a long-standing guide who valued our bespoke approach, these trips were open to pupils of all ages from years 8 to 13. By being able to plan our itinerary around defined acts of commemoration it meant that all pupils could find something to identify with. I'm not sure they read every page of our extensive guidebooks which, in the case of the 'Bridge too Far' trip to Arnhem, tipped the scales at over 12,000 words. And this isn't just an option open to independent schools with ancient foundations. Every school in the country is within a short distance of a war memorial and every school can access the Commonwealth War Graves Commission website to find men from their locality.

Before this appears to be an idealistic reverie, the most important feature of these trips wasn't just the commemorative and academic. Every coffee break was planned, every site visited in advance, *Campaniles* in hidden corners of Reims found by car months before we would have to find the same place by bus. After all, a coach of 50 pupils and staff will, at a conservative estimate, require 100,000 calories per day and produce 60 litres of urine. One of my groups once spent €1000 in a chocolate shop in Ypres. You can find the one because if you look like a teacher they'll give you some free chocolate and ask when you're bringing your students. It can take 15 minutes to debus and embus. Purpose and direction: essential in any lesson and essential in any trip. Because it is only when there is purpose and direction that spontaneity can take place too. This is the banal aspect of any visit to a dark site. But it makes a difference. Once my colleague discovered that one of our 'old boys', Pte Ronald Hill at Gorre British and Indian Cemetery, had been found to have a note in his pocket on his death which read: 'Do not let your faith be shaken. I do not fear death, rather am I proud to be able to lay down my life for my country.' We didn't visit his grave because the coach wouldn't have been able to turn round. Such is the relationship between reality and the commemoration of death.

The rise of the pre-packaged trip gives rise to very predictable trips with indifferent outcomes. Teachers who will happily decry textbooks as not being designed for their particular school will still accept a generic tour. I once met another group leader when carrying out an inspection who had carried out the identical tour, every year, for twenty-two years. At no point had they thought about changing or improving it.

Giving pupils a sense of enquiry and engagement will not simply happen spontaneously. There must be some sense of discovery. In a trip booklet from 2009 I find myself writing: 'Some of you will want to take copious notes whilst others will want to listen quietly and reflectively. Some of you might be fascinated by the minutiae of military history, others by the architecture of memory. If you can be truly fascinated in one moment then this trip has been more than worthwhile.' It sounds a little vague and idealistic but I suppose it at least models something of the emotional engagement with the dark sites which I would like my pupils to feel. It is perhaps no coincidence that this was the first time I had led a trip which took in a visit to see Deborah. But the next section in that booklet is a guide to military terminology. It might not be possible, or even desirable, to teach someone what they are expected feel at a site of memory, but it might be possible to teach them the difference between a battalion and a company. You may not clear the wire but you can at least provide some cutters. My most recent trip to the Western Front was run by my current Headmaster who runs everything with the lightest of touches. Unencumbered by intense discussions of military tactics but instead armed with a clear understanding of the principal mechanisms of trench warfare and the chance to explore and feel the ground the boys on the trip experienced that 'awe and wonder' which so many teachers aspire to achieve.

Taking casualties

The Western Front is an incredibly safe place to take students. Many hostels are set up with pin-code locks, all have fire escapes and appropriate levels of electrical safety. My research suggests that no pupil has died on a battlefields tour since a 15 year old girl from Kent died in her bed following an asthma attack in Caen, Normandy in 2003. Battlefield sites have some particular hazards, of course, but these are minimal. I once allowed a guide to conduct a 'debris sweep' in a field near Thiepval because he had a risk assessment in place. I suppose the thickness of the document might have been protection against detonation. However, despite clear instructions to the contrary we were twenty yards into the ploughed field when a pupil kicked a grenade-shaped lump in my direction: 'Sir, I've found something!' My career flashed before my eyes and the grenade-shaped lump did, indeed, turn out to be a British grenade. We also found bullets, shrapnel, a cap badge and various other metal remnants which might have been bits of tanks or just tractors. Although I don't think I would get that activity past an eagle-eyed Educational Visits Coordinator these days it did have the effect of getting pupils to feel something more pertinent. There are countless statistics about the 'iron harvest' but none of these have the same impact as finding some of it. Even better still if you can convince M. Gorcyznski to set fire to a small quantity of 90 year old cordite which burns brightly but safely in the right quantities.

So, if there is such a slim risk of accident then why bother to carry out such extensive safety checks? Of course, the lack of incidents is probably *because* health and safety is taken so seriously. But equally, there is so much talk of death and mishap on a battlefields tour that it is likely to infiltrate the mind of a worried teacher. Sometimes, though, the excessive control of risk seems ridiculous in such a damaged environment. I once carried out a risk assessment after closing time at Fort Douamont in Verdun. When I realised that I was completely alone, underground, in the middle of the place at which General Falkenhayn claimed he would 'bleed the French nation white' I just ticked the boxes and left. Of course, I wouldn't let pupils run into the woods at Verdun where the unexploded ordnance has never been properly cleared and nor would I allow them to stand helplessly in front of a train at the level crossing by Larch Wood Cemetery near Ypres where Alan Bennett wrote so movingly about his Uncle Clarence. I was once reassured by a guide that 'I know the way to the hospital' as pupils jumped around the 'trenches' at Sanctuary Wood. Being surrounded by death heightens the sense of danger. I've written guidance which has been lovingly ripped off as good practice so I'm no slouch with the paperwork. I wouldn't run my own trips until I had qualified as a first-aider. You can tell I'm worried about one of m'learned friends saying "Mr Heap, you wrote of your disdain for health and safety practices in 2015..." Of course, that isn't true but it is almost as if we become the donkeys if we don't play our part. I was once called in to make sure that I was going to use the pedestrian crossings on a theatre trip to Manchester. A generic risk assessment I was provided with by a travel company once identified 'abduction' as a risk at the Last Post Ceremony in Ypres. The risk to the pupil was not assault or death but 'reputational risk' to the travel company. Donkeys, indeed.

Have you decided why you're going? It doesn't matter why but there has to be a coherent plan and a coherent reason because there has to be a certain seemless dignity on a journey to a dark site. There can't be temper tantrums and the coach toilet won't cope with 60 litres of anything. And the DVD player never works. I saw one set on fire once proving that the 'luxury coach supplement' had been misspent.

The operational phase

There is a café at Auschwitz selling simple snacks and hot drinks. There is a family having a snowball fight a few feet away from the spot where the Commandant, Rudolf Höss, was brought back after his post-war trial to be hanged. We are there the week after racists stole the 'Arbeit Mach Frei' sign but it has been restored for the obligatory photographs. It is a confusion of symbols and meanings. The problem is that the views are all too familiar and all I manage to do is to take my versions of the same photographs. Some years ago, when 'praise postcards' to give pupils for good work became fashionable one mail order company sent round a mailshot of possible images. It was possible for some time to but a card bearing a picture of the converging railway lines at Birkenau and the words 'Well done in History.' I think it even appeared in *Private Eye*. So, maybe even this darkness doesn't shock anymore. Railway lines and guard towers fade into snow and fog giving a sense of unimaginable magnitude. Headsets are worn which allow the guides, who can only work there for a few months on account of the darkness of the site, to move around quietly and which also allow the visitor to linger at areas which they feel compelled to stare at. 'The Material Proof of Crimes' exhibit holds my attention – shoes, hair, suitcases. I knew it would, and it does. The disembodied voice gives another level of strangeness to the dark experience, much like the disorientating of the much misunderstood and maligned memorial to the Holocaust in Berlin. My late friend Eric, another Cambrai connection, had served as a young tank commander in the Second World War. In conversation he once described his visit to Auschwitz as the moment when the sacrifices of his young comrades suddenly made sense.

There is an essential problem with visits to famous dark sites. There is a script already established and I follow every line. Some of the words of memory sound like cliché. I want to say something original but it isn't popular. I try to give a bit of historiography to the group but I'm not sure how it goes down. 'Structuralists' and 'intentionalists' aren't of especial interest in the face of mass slaughter. The pupils are all intelligent and interested but they're just over-whelmed. The same is true in war sites. Although they don't have the same dark feeling I will still habitually look to established words and phrases in writing dedications or leading an act of commemoration. At dark sites, this is inevitable when taking young people there for the first time. They are being inducted into the world of memory where there is 'greater love', where men 'grow not old' and from where 'we gave our tomorrows for your todays.' I can't find any originality and, if I did, it wouldn't seem right somehow. Visits to dark sites are a connection with the past and for that connection to seem strong we read established poems, boys and girls lay wreaths and we hold silences.

The debrief

I never allow students to fill in the evaluation forms at the end of a trip. These are routinely provided by travel companies and we're asked to return them so that they can do whatever it is they wish to do. If you give someone a form and ask them to comment then they're likely to criticise. That's why most choices about hotel bookings now depend on what the stroppiest 1% of the population have said online and they're not people I would ask about anything. 'I enjoyed my holiday; now to evaluate it online' said nobody interesting, ever. Teaching contains enough bureaucracy without adding another level of it to my personal life. I know what's not quite right on a trip and change it for next time. The fact that there is a next time is sufficient evidence to show that the last time was fine. When given a form, the average student is likely to complain about the food because they generally don't like anything that isn't a sweet. I've often waited until after a meal is finished before telling the students that a Belgian hotelier has passed off horse meat as beef, much to their disgust. The codification of everything in education into forms to fill and self-evaluation sheets has always run the risk of killing dialogue. Talking to students will tell you everything you need to know about how much they've enjoyed a visit.

Of course, an evaluation form is a method by which anodyne quotes can be collected to show how wonderful the company has been and for display on their website. When asked, I've never known a student say 'the Menin Gate was boring' although they might grumble about having to fit their own sheets in a hostel; an experience which definitively proves that this generation would be ill-equipped for total war. So, the technical aspects of the debrief are overrated. Far more interesting are the last night dinners. It has always been a peculiar joy of trips to the Western Front and other places of death that there is so much laughter outside of the times when acts of commemoration are taking place.

It is as if the confrontation with death sharpens the sense of life. That seems to me like a valid aim for any trip. If you're all smiling on the last night then everything has gone well. And there is nothing mysterious about that.

I have always taken especial pride in photographic displays of a trip. It is as if it isn't enough to visit and commemorate without making some kind of visual record. And the usual signs are all there: bowed heads, readers reciting poems, shadows cast across the graves. And what do schools leave behind? There is artificial turf to match the artificial understanding of war at Essex Farm cemetery because so many school visit the grave of tragic Valentine Strudwick, killed at the age of 15. The grave of celebrated medic and 'Double-VC' Noel Chavasse is a mess of rain-sodden wreaths and rotting wooden crosses.

On the school website there will be photos and reports and maybe a little bit of video. There will be the usual assembly which is always more about teaching someone to speak in public than it is about communicating the truth about war.

Questions

1   How far can students be said to experience the horrors of war in visiting the battlefields of the Western Front?

2   "Teachers have more influence over the dark experience than the sites themselves." To what extent does this reflect the reality of battlefield tourism?

3   Is battlefield tourism more concerned with the sacred or the profane?

References

NST (2015) World War One Battlefield Tours, Available at www.nstgroup.co.uk/tour/history-in-the-wwi-battlefields-region-france/ Accessed on 17th June 2015.

Seldon, A. and Walsh, D. (2013). *Public Schools and the Great War: The generation lost*. Pen & Sword Military.

Streets, J.W. (1916). Matthew Copse [poem]. Available at www.greatwar.co.uk/poems/john-william-streets-matthew-copse.htm, Accessed on 17th June 2015.

Wilson, J.M. (1998). *Siegfried Sassoon: The Making of a War Poet*. Gerald Duckworth: London.

Conclusion

Pascal Mandelartz & Tony Johnston

Recently, the concept of thanatourism has been subject to a number of criticisms (Biran et al, 2011, Bowman & Pezzullo, 2010, Poria & Biran, 2012) who argue that it is not so much a form of 'dark tourism', as a subset of heritage tourism. This notion is disputed by Stone (2006), who points to theme park death attractions as exhibiting little by way of heritage characteristic, arguing that thanatourism exists on a light-dark spectrum, and is a multifaceted phenomenon, "complicated in design and purpose and diverse in nature" (Stone, 2006: 150). While general concern about the inauthenticity of extremely commercialised and steadily growing 'theme park history' condemns tourism as an inappropriate or immoral medium to present human suffering and disconcerting events (Strange and Kempa, 2003), "it is difficult to attach an all-embracing label to the enormous diversity of dark sites, attractions and experiences" (Stone and Sharpley, 2008: 578).

The debates about definitions of thanatourism are ongoing but rather than demarcating the term, the intention in this text was to broaden its boundaries whilst providing a sample of case studies to stimulate in-class discussion. Within the introduction chapter we suggested to view this book as a cadaver, where we would connect the single pieces to form a skeleton of knowledge, it seems that we have created a Frankenstein, by challenging the boundaries of what is perceived to be thanatourism. As we are dwelling on the complexities and possible subcategories we need not forget the common denominator inherent in all thanatourism study – namely heritage. Thanatourism is deeply rooted in heritage tourism, but not confined to it, and is hence itself a meta-narrative. The creation and nourishment of new debate is therefore the next step in that process.

Early scholars in the field like Seaton (1996) have provided room for extending the definitions by proposing various degrees of thanatourism, ranging from travel to watch death as it happens to travel to synthetic sites at which evidence of the dead has been assembled (museums). Building on these notions, authors within this book have discussed the travel to sites *before* death has occurred as well as the thrill and excitement that a closeness or risk of death might possess (Chapter 7) but also the management of death at destinations (Chapters 3). Heap (Chapter 10) reflects on travel to sites after death has occurred and travel to internment sites and memorials, vividly outlining the pedagogies of taking school groups to such sites.

Whether Gothic Tourism or Urban Exploration can be seen as part of the thanatourism narrative might be questioned by some, but examples like that of the undertaker who re-enacts the nature of the death-cult in Victorian England at the Whitby Goth Weekend are seemingly within the boundaries of the term

(Chapter 4). Urban explorers as well as Goths have told us about their experience of history and heritage when visiting monuments and the dark aesthetic of the activities cannot be denied. These subcultures also play a role in the creation of memorials and the establishment of synthetic sites (Chapter 2).

As wounds evolve from scars into memorials they may feature on the thanatourism spectrum. In Chapter 1, Johnston discusses the consumption of conflict in Sarajevo, illustrating the process by which death becomes commodified. Thanatourism may ultimately pave the way for the presentation and commodification of the heritage of death, but Heap (Chapter 5) reminds us about the importance of personal relationships to the sites, particularly to our personal interpretation of places, and that often positive notions can emerge from what initially was perceived as dark.

The development process is a fate that has placed a rather small village such as Eyam on the tourism landscape, where history and heritage are not only displayed and commodified, but where myths are created that turn its past inhabitants who suffered from the bubonic plague into heroes (Chapter 8). Shirt, as well as Johnston, Tigre-Moura and Mandelartz (Chapter 6 and 9) shed further light on Auschwitz as the notorious example of humanity's dark past and the tourism development in terms of interpretation, management and marketing of the death camp. The development and commodification of thanatourism sites over time, from their (re-)discovery to the creation of an infrastructure, is an issue that requires further research and investigation and the development of time vs. development of frameworks.

In the spirit of the first touristic explorers and discoverers of Thanatourism sites, we would like to encourage the reader to go on your own journey of shedding light onto what is dark in tourism. There is a lot out there that remains dead, decaying, waiting to be unearthed, to be experienced, to be documented, to be rearranged and reinvented or sustained and maintained. When studying Thanatourism one can expect a wide spectrum of emotions and feelings. Thrill, anger, sadness, curiosity, joy, the ordinary as well as the extraordinary.

The discussion questions provided within the chapters offer first steps into entering the arena of death, atrocities and the macabre. We were prompted to include these to stimulate discussion on thanatourism from several sources. Initially we observed from several social media sites related to dark tourism which we frequent that a narrow range of topics are considered by undergraduate students who research this area. These mainly relate to 'visitor motivations' to dark tourism attractions, draw on online research and rely on input from dark tourism social networks and special interest contributors. Secondly, a cursory review of recent papers published in the field highlight that there remains an absence of empirical research. To challenge horizons here we would like to conclude by offering a proposed list of thanatourism topics for future research, that may inspire dissertation topics, coursework, and other scholarly activity. This list is by no means meant to be exhaustive or indeed indicative of the most 'important' research areas, but it intends to stimulate new ideas and fresh perspectives in the field.

A non-exhaustive list of potential thanatourism dissertation topics

1   The ecology, topography and spatial organisation of thanatourism sites.

2   Methodological concerns in thanatourism research.

3   Alternative data sources in thanatourism research.

4   Thanatourism and development; the impact of commodified death on host populations.

5   The media and representations of commodified death.

6   The authenticity of sites in the tourism development process.

7   Heterotopia as visitor attractions (e.g. zombie walks, 'post-apocalyptic' attractions).

8   Propaganda and the political economy of thanatourism.

9   Signage and the portrayal of information at thanatourism sites.

10   Engagement and visitor flow at thanatourism attractions.

11   Subcultural interests in thanatourism.

12   Thanatourism and popular culture.

13   The cult of celebrity death.

14   Film, television and literature inspired thanatourism.

15   The impact of the social environment on the decision-making factor to visit dark places.

16   Racial, gender, demographic and societal differences and similarities in thanatourism.

17   The pedagogical value of thanatourism; what are we learning.

18   The longevity of thanatourism attractions.

19   How far will tourists go? Are there boundaries we won't cross?

20   Non-Western understandings of commodified death.

21   Analysis of thanatourism history and patterns in consuming death.

22   Consumption of places of non-human death (e.g. of places, animals or cultures).

23 Issues surrounding the blurring of death and non-death related attractions (e.g. Auschwitz combined with shopping trips).

24 Forgotten sites – why has society commodified some death, but neglected others.

25 The emotional and psychological impacts of consuming death (e.g. trauma, fear, sorrow).

26 The sensory and physical impacts of consuming death (e.g. touch, smells, sights, audio).

27 Euthanasia tourism– the ultimate form of 'consuming' death.

28 Issues concerning souvenirs, photography and the tourist gaze at thanatourism attractions.

29 The economic impact of dark attractions on the host population.

30 Moral and ethical issues in the marketing and promotion of thanatourism sites

References

Biran, A., Poria, Y., & Oren, G. (2011). Sought experiences at (dark) heritage sites. *Annals of Tourism Research*, 38, 820–841.

Bowman, M. S., & Pezzullo, P. C. (2009). What's so 'dark' about 'dark tourism'?: Death, tours, and performance. *Tourist Studies*, 9(3), 187–202.

Poria, Y. & Biran, A. (2012). Re-conceptualizing Dark Tourism, in *Contemporary Tourist Experience: Concepts and Consequences*, by Sharpley, R. & Stone, P. (eds.), Oxon: Routledge, Pp. 57-70.

Seaton, A. (1996). From Thanatopsis to Thanatourism: Guided by the Dark. *International Journal of Heritage Studies*, 2, 234-244.

Strange, C. & Kempa, M. (2003). Shades of Dark Tourism- Alcatraz and Robben Island. *Annals of Tourism Research*, 30, 286-403.

Stone, P. R. (2006). A dark tourism spectrum: Towards a typology of death and macabre related tourist sites, attractions and exhibitions. Tourism: An Interdisciplinary International Journal, 54(2), 145–160.

Stone, P. R. and Sharpley, R. (2008). Consuming Dark Tourism: A Thanatological Perspective. *Annals of Tourism Research*, 35, 574-595.

Index

Printed in the United States
By Bookmasters